University of London
Institute of Commonwealth Studies

COMMONWEALTH PAPERS

General Editor
Professor W. H. Morris-Jones

18
Expulsion of a Minority

D1609905

COMMONWEALTH PAPERS

Expulsion of a Minority
Essays on Ugandan Asians

edited by
MICHAEL TWADDLE
Institute of Commonwealth Studies
University of London

UNIVERSITY OF LONDON
Published for the
Institute of Commonwealth Studies
THE ATHLONE PRESS
1975

Published by
THE ATHLONE PRESS
UNIVERSITY OF LONDON
at 4 Gower Street, London WC1

Distributed by Tiptree Book Services Ltd
Tiptree, Essex

U.S.A. and Canada
Humanities Press Inc
New York

© *University of London* 1975

ISBN 0 485 17618 1

Printed in Great Britain by
WESTERN PRINTING SERVICES LTD
BRISTOL

PREFACE

Immediately Ugandan Asians were expelled *en bloc* from their country of residence in 1972 it became apparent that information about them outside East Africa and India was in very short supply. Apart from a handful of general studies at the East African level, there was only one book-length discussion of the Ugandan situation (*The Indians in Uganda* by H. S. Morris, London 1968) and this only took the story up to the mid-1950s. Besides data on subsequent developments, participants at the conference on Ugandan Asians held at the Institute of Commonwealth Studies, London University, on 23 March 1973 felt the need for much more intensive analyses of Ugandan politics in general and of inputs into them from India in particular than had hitherto been available, as well as their joint study in comparative perspective. This volume of essays is the result. Most of the essays have been specially written for the volume by conference participants since March 1973. The essays by Hugh Tinker and Dent Ocaya Lakidi were, however, originally composed for discussion at the conference, Anirudha Gupta has revised his paper for it beyond recognition (and published the original in *African Affairs*, lxxiii (1974), pp. 312–24), while two further contributions have been solicited by the editor from scholars not associated with the conference (Jessica Kuper and Nizar Motani) in order to present a more rounded treatment of particular aspects of the tragic expulsion of Asians from Uganda dealt with in this symposium.

W. H. Morris-Jones must be thanked for his constant encouragement and editorial advice. Michael Davies, Yash Ghai, Freda Hawkins, Kenneth King, Praful Patel, Bala Pillay, Judith Priceman, Alistair Ross, and Yash Tandon rendered valuable assistance at the planning stage. Other acknowledgements are noted in footnotes to individual essays.

M.T.

CONTENTS

WAS THE EXPULSION INEVITABLE?

Michael Twaddle

In 1972 Idi Amin ordered the Asian community out of Uganda. The expulsion caused an immense outcry over its implications for Britain and the Commonwealth but there has been little discussion of the social and economic characteristics of the unfortunate people expelled and even less debate about the political reasons for their rude disengagement from Uganda. When Amin's alleged lunacy has not itself been considered sufficient explanation of the expulsion, his charges against the Asians of economic exploitation and social exclusiveness have been accepted or rejected on their own terms rather than seen to be themselves as much the stereotyped products of recent Ugandan history as seriously debatable interpretations of it. The result has been a widespread set of assumptions about the Asians in Uganda in the pamphlet literature upon the subject (it really cannot be called much more) which seem economically unjust, sociologically illiterate, and historically unsound.

The assumptions may be summarized as follows. The crisis that caused the expulsion was a long time in the historical melting pot. The pot started to brew once Uganda and several neighbouring countries became British protectorates at the close of the nineteenth century and Asians started to take up trading opportunities in the East African interior which the British preferred not to fill themselves and for which local Africans appeared unqualified. As a consequence East Africa became the 'America of the Hindu', a place where hard work brought rewards and Africans were inevitably irritated by Asian trading activities. The resultant plural society was institutionalized by British colonial policy. As a recent (and not unfair) summary puts it,

The stratification of colonial society made the white settlers or administrators the upper classes, the Asians the middle class, with the Africans at the bottom. The inevitable consequence of this was a kind of ghetto-ization—white housing areas, brown bungalow quarters and black hutments in the fields. The Asians, fundamentally a shy and submissive people, have a tendency to withdraw and live within their religious groups, a hangover from the caste society of India. Finding themselves in the centre of class divisions in East Africa their propensity for social exclusiveness was nourished.

The result was sadly predictable. By the time East African countries became independent of British colonial control in the early 1960s, 'prejudice between the races was already deep-seated. It had its origins very largely in the class structure.' The expulsion of Asians from Uganda was therefore inevitable. 'The revelations which came to Idi Amin in his dreams or traffic-jam anger, therefore, were merely the catalyst for the reaction and made it more violent than it need have been for the Asians of Uganda.'[1]

Was this really the case? The participants in the conference on Ugandan Asians at the Institute of Commonwealth Studies, University of London, were not wholly free from stereotyped thinking, nor can it truthfully be said that the resultant essays have all freed themselves from Amin's mental sway. But in this book is to be found correction upon correction of conventional wisdom about the Asians in Uganda, sometimes stated quite explicitly in its chapters, at other times merely latent in particular passages. This introductory chapter can claim to be no more than a preliminary attempt at a general critique. Yet, by underlining the various points in the prevailing consensus on the subject where contributors to the present volume suggest that further thought is necessary, it can at least suggest where future attention should perhaps be concentrated.

To start with, East Africa was never really an 'America of the Hindu' in any substantive sense. If the old myth that the original Asian immigrants were merely coolies brought in to build the Uganda Railway in the 1890s has rightly been discarded, its place appears to have been taken by the new myth that they were all *dukawallahs* or small traders. Certainly a substantial number of early immigrants were shopkeepers, and one cannot deny the prominence that the *dukawallah* was subsequently to acquire in anti-Asian rhetoric among Africans. But, as the essays by Jessica Kuper and Nizar Motani demonstrate, many early Asian immigrants were clerks brought in to run the Zanzibar Sultanate and the infant administrations of the British protectorates on the East African mainland, and others were artisans. Comparative numbers are difficult to establish at this stage of scholarly ignorance,[2] but at least we can distinguish between established prominence in racial rhetoric and supposed position in (largely absent) occupational statistics.

East Africa was also never an 'America of the Hindu' in the sense of being a destination of large-scale Asian immigration. Again numbers are hazardous but neither by percentage (around 1 per cent of total population) nor by numbers (around 75,000 at the time of expulsion) can the Asian population of Uganda be considered to have been really substantial, and while the Asian population of neighbouring Kenya was always larger it was never more than double that of Uganda. To be sure, Asian immigration into British East Africa was deemed sufficiently large to require restriction under protectorate ordinance immediately after the Second World War but, as the contribution by Hugh Tinker makes clear, the area was at no time the subject of Asian immigration of the massive proportions occurring elsewhere in the colonial empire. Granted that Asian numbers in East Africa were thus comparatively small, the political support that Kenyan Asians in particular achieved in India during the 1920s appears somewhat paradoxical. Tinker considers that this support was forthcoming because the Kenyan Asians contained 'a sizable urban, middle-class element able to articulate their grievances and aspirations' rather than a mainly rural manual labour force. That may be so, but then it becomes doubly paradoxical that (as Anirudha Gupta points out in his chapter) one reason why India was to behave so coolly towards Asians in Kenya during the 1960s was the absence of a substantial stratum of poor Asians among them—an absence that predisposed India now to agree that this particular category of overseas Indians was indeed an economically exploitative one.

This particular stereotype is a difficult one with which to come to terms. At the conference participants tended either to ignore it (because it seemed at best simplistic, at worst immoral) or to treat it as a universal phenomenon (because Asian roles as economic middlemen were assumed to make them inevitably unpopular with their African customers). From the essays published in this symposium it seems clear that both reactions need to be questioned. On the one hand they take insufficient account of the role such stereotypes play in political rhetoric and the extent to which accusations of corruption among Africans as well as against Asians in East Africa tend to be made at times of social and political tension. On the other hand they pay insufficient attention to the people who invent such stereotypes in East Africa, not to mention those who subsequently manipulate them.

In Kenya, because of European settlement and the system of African 'squatting' that such settlement generated, the stereotype of the Asian as economic exploiter 'has its roots in the relationship of the African [squatter] to the Indian petty traders—a group that made up only a third of the Asian community of Nakuru district', remarks Frank Furedi in a timely article. 'Since it was with this group that Africans had the most contact, the general opinion towards Asians as a whole was based on that experience.' Furedi goes on to point out that the particular Africans who cultivated the stereotype for political purposes in Kenya belonged to the new class of African traders which emerged immediately after the Second World War:

By identifying their own particular interests with those of the African squatters, the new indigenous group of entrepreneurs were able to hit back at the Asian traders. Their own goal was to replace the Asian trader, an aim that was easily integrated within the mosaic of interests that formed the basis of African nationalism in Kenya.[3]

Such traders were not entirely absent in Uganda. Indeed, it would be difficult to account for the boycott of Asian shops that took place in Buganda during 1959–60 without at least some reference to this particular constituency.[4] But, as really serious rivals to Asian *dukawallahs*, African traders emerged somewhat later in Uganda and they were never as numerous as their counterparts in Kenya. Moreover, whereas in Kenya the new class of African traders seems to have developed largely endogamously from local economic structures, in Uganda Africanization of trade was a more exogamous affair, with British colonial policy in this sphere arguably provoking African grievances as much as reacting to them.[5] Just before the Second World War Asian traders had been withdrawn from the Ugandan countryside and concentrated in the towns in order to protect African traders from Asian competition in the rural areas, and after the war Africanization from above seems to have caused as much political trouble on the African trading front as actual demands for Africanization from African traders. Perhaps it was principally for this reason that African traders in Uganda had less political muscle in relation to their numbers than their counterparts in Kenya. But, whatever the cause of that, what cannot be controverted is the fact that in Uganda it was intellectuals rather than traders who first propagated the stereotype of the Asian as economic exploiter with real vigour.

Schooling as a source of grievance is mentioned only briefly in this symposium but the separate and (after 1945) more generous funding of Asian schools does seem to have had crucial implications for the socialization process of African intellectuals in Uganda. The essay by Dent Ocaya-Lakidi surely makes that clear. Furthermore, it was African intellectuals who competed for jobs in the colonial bureaucracy with Asian expatriates from Goa and Bombay, as well as confronting some of them in contrasting situations in shops and in licensing positions. Nizar Motani stresses the importance of job competition in the protectorate civil service as a province of racial tension between Asians and Africans before the Second World War, and in this connection it is perhaps not insignificant that for his principal statements of African opposition to Asian involvement in trade in Uganda Ocaya-Lakidi should go to statements made by African intellectuals in vernacular newspapers in Buganda during the 1920s.

Yet here one must be most careful. It was from African intellectuals that the most open opposition to the expulsion of Asians emanated in Uganda during 1972, and it was from Ugandan bureaucrats that mur-

murings were also heard at that time suggesting that the expulsion might imperil their salaries. This surely suggests that it is wrong to treat anti-Asian feeling among Ugandan bureaucrats as a phenomenon that grows cumulatively, and that once the starting-point has been established the analyst's work is done. In terms of historical time-scale, anti-Asian agitation in Uganda among all sections of the African population displays a markedly episodic character, erupting during some periods of crisis yet lying quiescent throughout others. Not surprisingly (as Gardner Thompson remarks in his contribution) Asian traders in Uganda learnt to live with the outbursts, treating them almost as if they were yet further aspects of the constantly fluctuating cost of living in Uganda. It is also not surprising that the scholars most startled by the expulsion of Asians from Uganda in 1972 were the historians.

Historically, the stereotype of the Asian as economic exploiter must be seen as the product of particular interest groups in East Africa before any serious attempt can be made to test its validity as an interpretation of recent Ugandan history. When that happens two related assumptions must also be called into question. One (which also figures prominently in the pamphlet literature) is that plural societies in East Africa during the colonial period forced Asians into economic roles that necessarily accentuated racial tension. The other assumption, which usually remains unstated, is that the 'colonial structure' of Uganda remained basically unchanged throughout the colonial period. Our discussion thus far has implicitly questioned both assumptions. It is now time to point out explicitly that the supposedly economic roots of anti-Asian feeling in East Africa are more frequently assumed than substantiated, while the myth of a basically unchanging colonial structure in Uganda is patently wrong.

In 1945 there were riots in Uganda, and there were further ones four years later. While in the first ones there were only the barest hints of anti-Asian animosity, in 1949 Asian *dukawallahs* in Buganda felt sufficiently disturbed for Apa Pant, the recently accredited representative in East Africa of the newly independent government of India, to feel obliged to visit them. Pant had already been told by Asian shopkeepers in Kenya of 'their fear and insecurity' following threats from African politicians 'of dire consequences if they would not hand over their shops to the Africans',[6] and doubtless Pant assumed that the same thing might be happening in Uganda. In the event, as Sir Amar Maini relates in his chapter, Pant told the *dukawallahs* that their future safety lay in 'identifying with African interests'. Maini was himself an important Asian political figure in Uganda, and he was as concerned at the plight of impoverished Asians in the bigger towns as about the anxieties of their less impoverished counterparts in the smaller towns. To deal with this problem and others, Maini and his friends had already revived the Kampala Indian Association and the Central Council of Indian Associations and now they were also cooperating with the protectorate authorities in restricting further Asian immigration into Uganda. Individual Asian communities also did what they could to alleviate the plight of their poorest members; of those featured in this symposium, Ismailis acted as pacemakers through their self-help schemes under the ultimate guidance of the Aga Khan, Goans seem to have made the most of post-war opportunities in Catholic education, while the Hindus of Bakuli appear to have done what they could with the advantages of geographical proximity to the now expanding government Asian schools in Kampala. Such was the success of these various 'solutions' that by the time Jessica Kuper and Rohit Barot visited the Goans of Kampala and the Hindus of Bakuli respectively immediately before the expulsion, the appearance of really dire poverty among them was mostly a thing of the past. To some extent the boom in the post-war colonial economy must have also helped (though we lack an adequate economic history of late colonial Uganda to be sure of the details). For not only does the post-war boom seem to have lifted most Asian families in Uganda above the poverty line, but it enabled their richer brethren (and benefactors) to weather the progressive restrictions imposed on Asian activity by the Africanization policies of the protectorate authorities during the 1950s. Yet, as the chapter by Maini also reveals, instead of reducing racial tension these developments had precisely the opposite effect.

Part of the explanation for this may lie, as a reading of Nizar Motani's essay may suggest, in an area of grievance other than trade: the colonial bureaucracy. Certainly there was still racial competition here between Asians and Africans after the Second World War, and many of the men prominent in the Kabaka's government at this time had experienced earlier brushes with Asians while protectorate clerks. Yet more important than any 'area of grievance', bureaucratic or otherwise, were crucial changes in power relations that took place in Uganda during the 1950s. For these years were ones in which vitally important powers were devolved to the kingdom of Buganda by the central administration of the Uganda Protectorate, powers that when combined with the policy of pre-emptive Africanization from above inaugurated by Sir Andrew Cohen took the ground away from beneath the feet of trade and cotton agitators such as Ignatius Musazi and brought to power in Buganda men like Mikaeri Kintu who courted cultural confrontation almost for its own sake. There is room for debate about the effective causes of this sea-change in British–Buganda relations during the late colonial period,[7] but two assumptions that look extremely tatty after any consideration of it are the twin notions that the 'colonial structure' in Uganda remained basically unchanged throughout the colonial period, and that anti-Asian feeling there was basically economic in origin. The pattern of anti-Asian agitation in East Africa during the colonial period suggests that grievances at the grassroots (economic or otherwise) were much less important in causing trouble (or creating opportunities for betterment) for Asians than structural changes in power relations at the centre.[8]

This point is nowhere illustrated better than in the process of decolonization in Uganda. For, as Gardner Thompson makes clear in his account of the response of the Ismaili community to it, decolonization did not necessarily harm the country's Asian minority. Rather the reverse. If the political sea-change in Buganda during the 1950s turned Asians into cultural scapegoats, the advent of general elections turned them into if not everybody's favourites at least favourites with the politicians. There are several suggestive footnotes in Thompson's chapter on marginal urban constituencies in the elections of 1961 and 1962, showing how dependent were both of the main African contenders for power at this time (the Democratic Party led by Benedicto Kiwanuka and the Uganda Peoples Congress under Milton Obote) on Asian electoral support. As regards its implications for Asians, much more serious than the shift from European to African hegemony in Uganda were changes in the pattern of Asian politics in the country. For, as Thompson also points out, decolonization also involved for the Asians of Uganda 'a change from communal to national politics, from nomination to direct election, and it implied an end to the conducting of Indian politics at an informal personal level between representatives of pressure groups and officials of governments'.

The result, as is well known,[9] was the formation of the Uganda Action Group which campaigned on the basis that the security of Asians in Uganda was best achieved by Asians identifying themselves wholly with 'the African cause'. UAG did not last very long, since once DP and UPC really got under way its members left to join one or other of those parties, but its impact on Asian politics in Uganda was considerable. Unlike the earlier generation of Asian leaders who had been concerned to unite the Asian community in Uganda in associations such as the Central Council of Indian Associations in order to enable them to tackle current problems more effectively, UAG members seemed more determined to divide it. Indeed, the principal strategy of UAG appeared to consist mainly of vilifying earlier Asian leaders for exploiting Africans unduly, keeping themselves socially aloof, and hindering rather than advancing 'the African cause'. With the advantage of hindsight, this strategy can be seen to have been self-defeating, providing gratuitous support for racialist rhetoric about supposed Asian economic exploitation and resistance to 'integration'. But in the shorter term, as the contribution by Sir Amar Maini points out, the result was simply confusion: 'There were a multitude of responses within the Asian community in Uganda to African independence, most of them designed to keep open as many options as possible. These resulted in certain inconsistencies of behaviour by Asians, which led in turn to inevitable charges of hypocrisy when private actions did not (and could not) match up to publicly stated aspirations.'

This confusion lasted right up to the ultimate demise of the Asian community of Uganda at the hands of Idi Amin. While the confusion certainly had roots in the plural society created during the period of British protectorate rule, we should beware of simply passing the buck yet again to 'British imperialism'. It is all too easy to assume too much about the supposed economic and political simplicities of the colonial period of Ugandan history, while paying insufficient attention to the perplexing ambiguities of the post-colonial situation. There is always a considerable historical jump between grievance and agitation. Anti-Asian agitation in Uganda tended to take place at times of tension in African society during both the colonial and the post-colonial periods. The early years of the Second Republic of Uganda were one such time, the Kabaka crisis of 1953–5 another. We have already referred to the xenophobia released by the Kabaka crisis. It is to the crisis of the Second Republic that we must now turn.

Idi Amin toppled the post-colonial regime of Milton Obote on 25 January 1972 with the assistance of a comparatively small section of the Ugandan armed forces.[10] Asians as a whole welcomed this particular transfer of power because of the way in which Obote had copied the earlier example of Kenya (in 1967) and harassed them through his Immigration and Trade Licensing Acts (in 1969), not to mention his earlier record of progressively whittling away their right to become Ugandan citizens. But in January 1971 Asians constituted only one of several support groups welcoming Idi Amin as the saviour of Uganda, and by no means the most important one.

That trophy must go to Buganda from where, as Michael Tribe points out in his contribution, 'a large proportion of the more successful [African] businessmen and public servants with substantial business interests came, who were most likely to have [had] their economic interests challenged' by Obote's final experiments in African socialism. Not that these experiments attracted much left-wing support for him in Uganda. 'Obote's handling of the "Move to the Left", including the lack of any form of leadership code (largely owing to the diversity of *his* support groups), mishandling of the negotiations of the partial nationalization of the banks and oil companies, the interminable delay in working out the details of the national service scheme, together with the lack of any grassroot base for the Uganda Peoples Congress, had alienated any "left wing" support.' Tribe also points out that in the last years of Obote the Ugandan economy was already in dire straits. 'Food prices, particularly for low income groups, had tended to fluctuate quite considerably, depending on variable weather conditions, but started to rise from 1968 without showing any signs of falling back to their former level.' This Tribe attributes to 'the rapid increase in the urban population, structural problems on the supply side, and a "ratchet effect" through irreversible price increases in times of shortage'. The situation did not improve under Idi Amin. 'The structure of government finance showed signs of being almost out of control, the balance of payments was extremely delicate so that additional capital outflow could not be accommodated, the uncertainties to which the Asian community in particular but also the economy as a whole were subjected made the investment climate rather unclear, and there was a substantial and continuing increase in the cost of living.' It is against the background of this seemingly inexorable rise in the cost of living that we must understand the growing importance of urban Africans as a support group for the Amin regime as enthusiasm for it waned in rural Buganda.

Especially important now were the Nubians. These, as Denis Pain points out, 'fit neither the facile racial analysis of African/Asian/European, so popular in African newspapers and to some extent here, nor that based on ethnic allegiance, so popular in the Western press and skilfully used by Amin himself'. Here was an urban-related category of Africans, descending from the families of Sudanese mercenaries hired by Captain Lugard during the 1890s for military service in Uganda, but now embracing a much wider constituency of Africans speaking Nubi and practising Islam. 'They are concentrated in the urban periphery and trading centres throughout the country and, with low education, find employment as petty traders, labourers, and soldiers.' When Amin seized power from Obote their importance in Ugandan politics increased, and when Amin lost most of his support in Buganda they appear to have become one of his principal support groups. But before Amin came to power their influence had been tenuous, and their existence ignored by political analysts outside Uganda.[11] 'Somewhat restricted in the army and excluded from leadership in an education-oriented society, they became poor images of the Asian trader, who at the same time was seen as a bar to their future advance.' This resentment was shared by other poor Africans living in the towns. 'It is such persons', remarks Pain, 'especially if led by a more cohesive community

with similar aspirations and qualifications who will support a move
such as Amin's expulsion of all Asians.'

Economically, the months immediately preceding the expulsion were
ones of crisis in Uganda. So too had been the last years in power of
Milton Obote, but then twin windfalls of a good cotton crop and
favourable world prices for it acted as economic cushions. Amin had
no such luck. As Michael Tribe points out, by mid-1971 it was clear
that a serious balance of payments crisis had arisen which was not
caused principally by excessive military expenditure. Food shortages
were frequent in the towns, and the prolonged dry season of 1970–1
now started to take its toll in price rises for what food urban dwellers
could get. Considerable dissatisfaction built up among urban dwellers
of all income groups. In the Ugandan army, as is well known, there
was also increasing disaffection throughout the year immediately preceding the expulsion.

The expulsion of Asians from Uganda in the second half of 1972
can therefore be said to have achieved several objectives at one stroke.
It diverted attention from other economic problems. It provided
rewards for army supporters ('much of the auctioning of Asian assets
was biased in favour of particular groups within the army'). It removed
one source of capital outflow. It also appeased the anti-Asian sentiments
of one crucial support group. But whether the expulsion was therefore
inevitable remains a moot point. It was certainly not rendered inevitable by the colonial legacy of a plural society in which class neatly
coincided with race, or by a 'colonial structure' whereby Asians
inevitably became vulnerable and unpopular because of their enforced
economic roles. Both colonial racial categories (Nubians resenting
Asians because of their earlier experiences on the urban periphery) and
economic imperatives (the parlous state of the Ugandan economy
after mid-1971, with food prices for poor Africans in the towns going
through the roof) prepared the way for the expulsion. Their conjunc-
tion in time certainly made another bout of anti-Asian agitation in
Uganda likely, but not necessarily a wholesale expulsion. After all,
Nubians constituted only one principal support group for Idi Amin,
and economically it was in Amin's interest to speed up the departure
of the Asians from Uganda only to the extent that replacement of key
personnel was not unduly disrupted. There are indications (considered
in several of the ensuing essays) that Amin planned initially to confine
his expulsion order to *dukawallahs*, but this was not to be. The nature
of the initial British reaction to the first expulsion orders was also not
without importance in shaping the course of subsequent events. But
of two things at least we can be sure. Historically, the operative
mechanisms behind the expulsion on the Uganda side will only become

apparent when structural changes in politics are carefully distinguished from the political stereotypes whereby subsequent actions are justified and, sociologically, the operative categories were ones internal to 'the Africans' rather than ones which simply coincided with race.

It was the same with the Asians. Another analytical flaw in the stereotype of the Asian as economic exploiter (and to some extent that of his social exclusiveness too) is that it diverts attention away from economic differentiation among Ugandan Asians, as well as distorting understanding of the economic importance of communalism. For, while it is true that communalism was to some extent a hangover from India and certainly not inconsistent with British colonial rule in East Africa, the important economic point about it is that locally established Asian communities provided a framework for the expansion of Asian trading enterprise in East Africa after the break-up of the great Asian trading empires of the early colonial period. The economic history of Asians in East Africa during the nineteenth and early twentieth centuries remains to be written, as A. M. H. Sheriff has recently reminded us, but one lesson that became deeply embedded in the consciousness of the inter-war generation of Asian traders in Uganda was the danger of depending excessively (as the great Allidina Visram enterprise was then commonly believed to have depended) on agents belonging to Asian communities other than one's own.[12]

To be sure, there were also other reasons for the flowering of Asian communalism throughout East Africa during the inter-war period, such as population growth among East African Asians and Hindu-Muslim animosity in India, as the chapter by Sir Amar Maini implies, and 'communal crystallization' whereby Ismailis acted as communal pacemakers for other Asian communal groups in such things as special legal and burial rights, as H. S. Morris has pointed out in his pioneering sociological study of Asians in Uganda.[13] But, as Peter Marris also argues,[14] there were also relatively uncomplicated economic reasons: the Asian family firm provided information as well as credit in an increasingly tight and competitive trading situation.

Caste, as opposed to community, was similarly not merely a hangover from life in undivided India. Certainly Asian immigrants into East Africa brought many of their customs with them and, as Anirudha Gupta remarks in his chapter, their cultural conservatism was sustained by continuing visits to and from the sub-continent. But, as the anthropological studies in this book among others demonstrate, over time there was a gradual erosion in its importance for younger Asians benefiting from the post-war boom in secondary education. It was among the poorest Asians remaining in Uganda, as Rohit Barot demonstrates in his essay, that caste ties seem to have remained strongest:

'Although Bakuli is often regarded as an African area, social contact between Indians and Africans, apart from their brief encounters in shops, is non-existent. During my stay there was not a single instance of an Indian knowing an African as an equal or a friend. Separation and distance between the two sides is a marked feature.' With hindsight it seems not insignificant that it was with such caste-conscious Asians that the poorer Africans in the towns came into contact (or rather, non-contact) most frequently.

At the conference which he summoned to deal with problems relating to the Asians living in Uganda (one of a number of conferences called to consider current issues in Uganda), Idi Amin castigated Asians for their supposed reluctance 'to integrate'. 'About seventy years have elapsed since the first Asians came to Uganda, but, despite that length of time the Asian community has continued to live in a world of its own to the extent that the Africans in this country have, for example, hardly been able to marry Asian girls.'[15] It is significant that the charge was not put the other way round for, as Dennis Pain remarks, 'Where politics are concentrated in the hands of men, statements concerning other groups permitting or prohibiting the men of one's group marrying girls from the other may be interpreted as political statements of superiority and inferiority.' Asians were not being asked to integrate but to annihilate themselves and it was hardly surprising that their leaders (now heading a reunited Ugandan Asian community) should have retorted that marriage is a voluntary matter and 'opposition to inter-caste, inter-tribal, inter-communal and inter-racial marriages is a familiar phenomenon to be encountered in any society in any country of the world'.[16] What is surprising in retrospect is the extent to which 'integration' had become the watchword of Asians wishing to support unreservedly the African cause in the post-colonial world.

Some of the reasons for this development have already been indicated. Partly it was a generational thing that the Uganda Action Group should have emerged when it did among Ugandan Asians. Partly it was a structural matter that 'integration' should have become the principal slogan of younger Asians, symbolizing the arrival of a mass electorate in Uganda in which a majority following very different customs predominated. But partly also, as several essays in this book make clear, it was the product of advice from local representatives of the government of independent India with its own rather different interests and a circle of social contacts in East Africa which rarely included lower-class Indians such as the Hindus of Bakuli.

The resulting problem with 'integration' was not really its vagueness ('its very vagueness is the source of its most explosive potential in verbal dialectics'[17]), nor yet its supposed bases in a colonial economic structure in which class neatly coincided with race. British colonial urban policy certainly did not help matters, as Dharam Ghai (quoted by Dent Ocaya-Lakidi) makes clear: 'concentration of the Asians in the urban areas, for which they themselves were not responsible, aggravated matters; it prevented racial integration, pushed up prices of property in urban centres making it difficult for Africans to start enterprises there, and made the Asians appear as a privileged group of town-dwellers where all the facilities were located'. But appearances can be deceptive and a slogan such as 'integration', advocating objectives which were as unattainable as they were ambiguous, hardly helped Ugandan Asians to work out a sensible plan for coexistence with the post-colonial order.

It was not even of much use with the Government of India when the real crunch came. After the Kenyan restrictions of 1967 and the British ones of the following year, India adopted the line that Asians holding British passports in East Africa were the responsibility of Britain. Clearly there were both domestic legal reasons for this stance—dual nationality for Indians had been abolished by the Indian Nationality Act of 1955[18]—and also political ones relating to the failure of the Bhagat mission to Jomo Kenyatta in 1967 (a failure that curiously foreshadows the visit by Geoffrey Rippon to Idi Amin in 1972) as Bali Ram Bhagat was then, as Prem Bhatia remarks, a rising politician and 'by no means indifferent to the importance he received by being chosen for the role of trouble shooter'.[19] But the situation really would only have been otherwise if, as Anirudha Gupta suggests, one of two conditions could have been fulfilled: that Indians in East Africa had constituted a poor stratum of society sufficiently large to arouse sympathy for their plight on a massive scale in India, or been mostly Indian citizens on whose behalf a treaty might have been negotiable by India with the East African states. But, as will already be clear from this introduction, the very poorest layer of overseas Indians was no longer to be found in Uganda after local Asian initiative as well as British restrictions on further immigration after the Second World War, while the second option could not be taken up by India because the overwhelming majority of East African Asians wished to become British rather than Indian passport-holders after the East African countries had become independent of British colonial control in the early 1960s.

The legal aspects of the resultant situation are surveyed by James Read but, in order to understand the paradoxical situation whereby many a Ugandan Asian kept his *man* (heart) in India and his *dhan* (wealth) in Britain while still managing to retain his *tan* (body) in East Africa, the whole symposium should be read. The symposium will not itself resolve the paradox but it will reveal some of its commonly neglected ingredients. For, besides the more publicized feedbacks into Ugandan affairs from British immigration policy, inputs from both the Indian and the East African situations were of more than minimal significance in shaping the destinies of persons of Indian descent living in Uganda during both the colonial and the post-colonial periods. Furthermore, from these particular vantage-points the actual manner in which 'the Asian problem' was finally dealt with in Uganda does not appear to have been inevitable. Another bout of anti-Asian agitation certainly seemed likely in 1972 but not a wholesale expulsion.

2

INDIANS ABROAD: EMIGRATION, RESTRICTION, AND REJECTION[1]

Hugh Tinker

Among the Indian communities overseas those in East Africa are not among the most numerous, whether the measurement is that of total numbers (cf. Ceylon with 1,234,126 resident Indians, or Malaysia with 810,000) or that of percentage of population (cf. Mauritius, Indians 68 per cent; Guyana, Indians 51 per cent). Comparative figures for all important Indian communities overseas in 1969 are listed in the table below, and it will be seen that in 1969 (before the recent exodus)

Indians Abroad, 1969

Aden	2,000	Mauritius	520,000
Afghanistan	20,000	Muscat	4,500
Australia	3,108	Netherlands	1,500
Bahrain	5,500	New Zealand	6,130
Burma	272,000	Nigeria	1,600
Canada	20,000	Philippines	2,516
Ceylon	1,234,126	Qatar	2,000
Congo	3,000	Rhodesia	10,000
Ethiopia	4,520	St Vincent	3,703
Fiji	241,000	Saudi Arabia	1,035
France	1,400	Singapore	125,000
Ghana	1,750	Somalia	1,360
Grenada	9,500	South Africa	614,000
Guyana	357,000	Spain	1,600
Hong Kong	5,000	Sudan	2,550
Indonesia	27,617	Surinam	101,715
Iran	1,000	Tanzania	105,000
Iraq	12,000	Thailand	18,014
Israel	23,000	Trinidad	360,000
Jamaica	27,951	Trucial States	5,000
Japan	1,141	Uganda	76,000
Kenya	182,000	United Kingdom	270,000
Kuwait	12,006	United States	32,062
Laos	1,800	Vietnam (South)	2,000
Madagascar	12,350	West Germany	4,681
Malawi	11,299	Zambia	10,705
Malaysia	810,000		

Note: This list is based on information contained in the *Times of India Directory and Yearbook, 1970.* Only countries in which there is a group of more than one thousand Indians are included. The *Times of India* figures have been modified where other estimates appear to be more reliable. The usual difficulty is encountered: that 'Indians' means, in one context, 'Indian nationals', and in another 'persons of Indian descent'. Thus the figures for Mauritius or South Africa are almost entirely composed of the latter category, those for Kuwait and the Gulf states belong to the former. The *Times of India* states that there were only 202 Indians in the Netherlands but there were also approximately 1,300 'Hindustanis', i.e. Surinamese—Dutch citizens—whose ancestors were exported to Surinam as indentured labourers. The list above attempts to combine both categories.

Since 1969 the Indian population in all the East African countries has diminished, while Indians in western Europe and North America have substantially increased.

Indians formed about 2.3 per cent of the population of Kenya and about 1 per cent in Tanzania and Uganda. And yet, over the last fifty years, the fortunes of the Indian community in East Africa—along with those in South Africa—have loomed large in the politics of the Indian subcontinent, in a fashion that has quite overshadowed the troubles of Indians in Ceylon or Southeast Asia. The cry uttered by Srinivasa Sastri in 1923, 'Kenya lost, everything lost', has echoed through the debates ever since. In reality, the grievances of Indians in Ceylon and Southeast Asia have been infinitely greater than of those in East (or South) Africa but the former's grievances were primarily economic—depressed working conditions—while those in Africa have been mainly political and social. It was because the Indian community in East and South Africa contained a sizeable urban, middle-class element that they were able to articulate their grievances and aspirations, whereas the Indians in Ceylon and Southeast Asia remained largely a rural, manual labour force, unorganized and inarticulate.

The Indians in East, Central, and South Africa emerged as sizeable communities during the early years of the twentieth century. They arrived in response to the demands of white pioneers and white settlers requiring labourers, contractors, and suppliers of stores. They were assimilated into a situation in which the high game of imperialism was being played out between rival European governments, while a more mundane form of imperialism was being advanced by white settler communities determined to establish their superiority over the local African inhabitants. The British Empire provided the framework which shaped the Indian communities of Africa and, although the Winds of Change have blown that empire away, post-imperial hang-ups still pursue the Indians. It is the argument of this chapter that Indian communities in all the overseas territories, but especially in Africa, were beckoned in three directions. In following the pull of three forces, the Indians found themselves following contradictory courses. In the end they had arrived nowhere and were unable to respond to the challenge and demand of African nationalism in the post-imperial era.

The signposts pointed in three directions. First, the Indians tried to become the equals of the whites; they tried to establish a claim to be British citizens in Africa. This effort was resisted and repulsed by the white settlers. Then they fell back on their Indian resources and tried to mobilize the support of the Government of India and of Indian nationalism. This move was strongly opposed, first by the Colonial Office in London and later by the Union government in South Africa. In return, the Indians were told that they must regard themselves as citizens of the lands where they now resided, though only meagre tokens of citizenship were offered to them. In some bewilderment the Indians passed through the last rapid stage before African independence north of the Zambezi, and total white supremacy in the south. They were not very well placed to respond to the last (or present) phase.

The theme of equality was first enunciated in a despatch issued on 24 March 1875, when Salisbury was Secretary of State for India. It was postulated that 'the colonial laws and their administration will be such that Indian settlers. . .will be in all respects free men with privileges no whit inferior to those of any other class of Her Majesty's subjects resident in the colonies'. This proposition was endorsed by Sir Henry Bulwer, Lieutenant-Governor of Natal, in a despatch of 7 September 1878, which reproduced exactly the same sentiments but twenty years later the first major breach was made when the few Indians qualified for the parliamentary franchise were *as a race* denied any further right to vote.

The Gandhian campaigns did something to halt the erosion of the rights of the South African Indians. But the Smuts–Gandhi agreement of 1914, seen by Gandhi as the first step towards the betterment of Indian conditions, was interpreted by Smuts as a compromise whereby most of the Indians would return to their homeland. The Government of India responded to this view by stopping indentured emigration to South Africa, and subsequently by abolishing the whole system of indentured emigration. The very last indentured emigrants embarked in January 1917. The long-established right of the self-governing Dominions to complete control over immigration was explicitly recognized at the Imperial Conference of 1918 (Australia had first imposed a restriction on coloured immigrants in 1855) but in return, at the Imperial Conference of 1921, the Government of India made a strong bid to persuade the Dominions to concede that Indians already resident in their midst should be given equal rights alongside the white British population. This proposal was pressed with immense vigour by Edwin Montagu, Secretary of State for India, and was argued persuasively by Sastri as the representative of India. New Zealand, Canada, and even Australia, were disposed to accept this new concept of Indian equality, in recognition of India's massive contribution to the war effort and in the light of India's new status 'as an equal member of the British Empire' (as the resolution stated). Smuts absolutely refused to agree. On 21 July 1921 Montagu wrote to Churchill (then Colonial Secretary, and Smuts' main ally): 'We claim that Indians should rank with Europeans and not with the natives [Africans] to whom no promise of Dominion or equal status has ever been given.' The resolution was passed, with Smuts dissenting, and Montagu went on to press Churchill to give effect to the resolution ('As a matter of principle the rights of citizenship of such Indians should be recognised') in the franchise of Kenya. He demanded that Indians become eligible for inclusion in a common electoral roll with the European settlers.

In this chapter we cannot follow the tortuous politics whereby this proposal was whittled away until, after both Churchill and Montagu had given up their posts, under the Devonshire award of 1923 the Kenya Indian community was given inferior representation on a separate communal roll, while the Europeans retained their privileged position.[2] 'Kenya lost, everything lost': Sastri travelled to London to plead the cause of equality, along with representatives of the Kenya Indians. In a dignified letter to Lord Peel, Secretary for India (20 July 1923), Sastri appealed against the acceptance of a colour bar in British colonies: 'Two, if not more classes of citizenship will thus become the distinguishing characteristic of the British constitution, classes based on colour—a distinction inimical to the destiny of the Commonwealth, the ideal of democracy and the hope of humanity.' But this was no match for Lord Delamere and the handful of white farmers (1,386 in 1920) who successfully defied the British government and forced them to back down. There was a small concession: the legislation, approved by the Kenya Governor, Coryndon, to place a virtual ban upon further Indian immigration was quashed. But the Indian bid to get a toe-hold in the White Highlands was also dismissed, along with their claim for electoral equality with the whites. Throughout the next twenty years all their efforts to get back to the 1921 position were a failure.

In the years between the wars Indians were absolutely excluded from settlement in all the white Dominions except Newfoundland and the Irish Free State. Southern Rhodesia exercised an administrative system of exclusion, though there was no legal exclusion, and in theory the small Indian community had the right to be registered as voters on a common roll on the same terms as the whites. In 1922, out of a total Southern Rhodesian white population of 33,620, the franchise was held by 18,640 (over half). Among the 1,184 Indians only 138 (12 per cent) had the vote, while of the total African population 35 African immigrants from the Cape were registered voters.

All but a handful of Natal Indians were deprived of the municipal franchise in 1925 but in a tentative way the Cape Town agreement of 1927 between the South African and Indian governments did recognize the Indians as potentially equal citizens. The agreement included the commitment of the Union government to the 'upliftment' of the Indians: 'The Union Government recognise that Indians domiciled in the Union who are prepared to conform to western standards of life should be enabled to do so.' But a large price was envisaged: Dr Malan and his colleagues confidently expected that a sizable proportion of the Indian population would return to India under the subsidized repatriation scheme, and the Government of India promised to assist with their resettlement. An Agent (later Agent-General) was to reside in the Union 'to interpret the wishes of the Indian community to the Union Government' and to 'watch the progress of the new scheme of assisted emigration, on the satisfactory working of which a great deal will depend'. The Agent was permitted a good deal more latitude than a normal diplomatic representative because he was, in the eyes of Malan —and Smuts—the leader of a community of people *temporarily* resident in South Africa, but essentially transients who could be encouraged to depart. India and the South African Indians put all the emphasis upon upliftment; South African whites thought only of return to India. When the repatriation scheme, after an initial spurt, declined into a trickle, other ways of dealing with the situation were adopted by Unionist and Nationalist alike.

Deprived of their expectation of attaining equality with the whites, most of the Indians turned away from the mirage of partnership. Only the Aga Khan continued to hope that expressions of loyalty would gain advantages for his followers. Even he became tired of buttering up British statesmen, and we find him telling the Marquess of Zetland (14 March 1939): 'In South Africa, and now in Kenya, Indians are humbled and harassed and so many humiliating restrictions are placed on them. . .that Tanganyika was a sort of haven of rest.' Long before, most politically conscious Indians had embarked upon a course of boycott and non-cooperation. This was less effective than it might have been because the East African Indian National Congress was riven by dispute and faction. There were Hindu-Muslim splits, Mombasa-Nairobi splits, and Kenya-Uganda splits. In this rather frustrating situation, the East African Indians turned in hope to India and the Indian government. The East African Indian National Congress tried to interest nationalist leaders in their condition, and such notables as Mrs Naidu and H. N. Kunzru were invited to preside over the annual congresses. But perhaps more importance was attached to the support of the Government of India. Appeals from organizations, or even individuals, often elicited a direct reply from the Indian government, who then went on to intercede on behalf of overseas Indians with the local Governor or with the Colonial Office, via the India Office.

For some time the Colonial Office acquiesced in this practice, which was highly irregular from a bureaucratic point of view. The Colonial Office itself was only prepared to receive representations from the colonies which were submitted, correctly, through the local Governor. Eventually, in May 1936, a more than usually abrasive politician, Ormsby-Gore (later Lord Harlech), became Colonial Secretary and he soon showed he was not prepared to put up with further interference from India. During the 1930s, the role of Indian middlemen in East Africa had been narrowed by a new policy of promoting government marketing boards. The policy was instituted to help the African producer of raw materials, but the Indians did not fail to note that the persons appointed to manage the new government agencies were invariably whites. Things came to boiling-point in Zanzibar, where a series of ordinances were passed, directed at the long-established Indian mercantile community. The Government of India despatched a senior official, K. P. S. Menon, to enquire into the changes, and he discovered the Zanzibar Indians 'in a state of panic'. Subsequently the Government of India decided to appoint a trade commissioner at Mombasa as a quasi-diplomatic representative. His task would be to 'watch local developments. . .that appear to concern the Indian community and to report such of them to the Government of India. . .as are in his opinion likely to justify their intervention at some stage to safeguard their [the Indians'] interests'.

When a copy of these instructions was transmitted to the Colonial Office Ormsby-Gore became very angry. He ordered his officials to reply (26 January 1937): 'Mr Ormsby-Gore is fully satisfied that the appointment of such an Agent would be most undesirable either now or in the future.' His instructions were 'open to severe and insuperable objections'. The Colonial Secretary went on to observe that the category of 'Indian' covered both persons of Indian domicile on business in East Africa and 'persons of Indian race. . .[who] have no connection with India'. Concerning the latter, 'It is very doubtful how far the Government of India ought to concern itself in their affairs. They may justly be regarded as citizens of the colonies in which they reside. . . While Mr Ormsby-Gore is fully prepared to admit that the Government of India has an interest in the Indians in East Africa who have not established a domicile there, he is unable to agree that the Government of India has a similar interest in the domiciled or long established Indian communities either in East Africa or elsewhere in the Colonial Empire.' The appointment of a Trade Commissioner under the terms envisaged 'would inevitably act as a stimulus to sectional political activity on the part of the local Indian community'. An official representative would encourage 'political aspirations in Kenya which in present circumstances it is impossible to satisfy'. Therefore only the most carefully defined trade agent would be accepted: 'It must be emphatically reasserted that the position of Indians in a colony is in no wise different from that of any other section of the community.'

Thus the Indians overseas had been nominated for another role: they were not the partners and equals of white British settlers, they were not Indians looking back in hope to the motherland; they were citizens of the colonies, 'in no wise different' from other local colonial peoples.

When, subsequently, the Government of India applied to appoint Agents in Fiji and the West Indies, the Colonial Office returned the same answer: the Indians in those territories were 'permanent settlers', enjoying 'harmonious relations' with other sections of the local population. In the West Indies the Moyne Commission declared that 'any measure which causes the East Indians to look upon themselves, or to be looked upon as a people apart will at once pave the way for inter-racial rivalries and jealousies'. This refusal to allow the Government of India to set up a listening-post in colonies where Indians were numerous did not apply to Ceylon and Malaya (nor to Burma, separated from India after 1937), where Agents were accepted. However, in these places the Indians were still in demand as an unskilled labour force, and the Agent functioned as a kind of trade union organizer-cum-welfare officer. The contrast was enough to embitter even the moderates in Indian politics: as Sir Girja Shankar Bajpai noted, it was believed that the Colonial Office 'is at least indifferent, and in all probability hostile, to Indians resident in the territories under its control...The cumulative impression...is...that the presence of the Indian in these territories is not welcome.'

In 1940, after Italy joined Germany at war, many Indian families were encouraged to leave East Africa, now a war zone, and return to India. Later, in 1944, the governments of the East African territories introduced stringent restrictions on immigration (ostensibly because of wartime shortages in housing, etc.) and anyone who had been away from East Africa for over two years forfeited the right to re-entry. This created an angry response in India. But most concern was felt about the South African Indian community, which—despite Smuts' promise of no legislation in wartime—was banned from occupying or purchasing any property within a European residential area, under the 'Pegging Act' of 1943.

For many years Indian politicians had looked for ways in which they could exercise counter-pressure on South Africa by forms of political or economic sanction against South Africans or South African interests. Draft bills were introduced in the central legislature but thanks to government indifference they all lapsed. At last a Reciprocity Act was passed in 1943 to enable the Government of India to institute counter-measures, though official opinion pronounced that it was 'virtually unworkable'. At this point a separate Department of Indians Overseas had been created as part of the central government and Dr N. B. Khare, a pugnacious former Congress chief minister, was in charge. Khare declared in the legislature, concerning the Pegging Act and other anti-Indian measures: 'Some means must be found for maintaining the dignity and prestige of Indians and the Government of India even in wartime. . .Had India been independent she would have considered this a casus belli against South Africa.' Once again we cannot uncover the tangled communications between Smuts, the South African Indians, the British government, and the Government of India.[3] Whitehall, led by Churchill and Amery, resisted any move to apply sanctions against Smuts and South Africa. The Viceroy—first Linlithgow, and then Wavell—although acutely conscious of the need to preserve Commonwealth unity in wartime, was also conscious of the concern and anger felt by all shades of Indian political opinion. Wavell 'stone-walled', as he put it, for as long as he could, hoping that Smuts would respond to his personal appeals based on consideration of the contribution of the Indian Army to preserving the wartime 'bastion' of the Middle East. The situation only deteriorated and the activities of the representative of the Government of India (now styled High Commissioner) became ever more frantic as he tried to push his own government further and also to galvanize the leaders of the South African Indians. The Union government reacted by repudiating their former acceptance of the Agent-General as a recognized leader of the Indian community in South Africa. Heavy emphasis was now placed on observation of diplomatic protocol and also on the status of the domiciled Indians as South African nationals.

When the Government of India issued a notice reducing the rights of South Africans resident in India to those of Indians in South Africa (which, all admitted, was only a symbolic gesture), the Union government retorted that in future India could have no grievance against South Africa as their policies were now identical. The additional question of denouncing the trade agreement between the two countries and enforcing an Indian embargo was taken more seriously.

A debate in the Indian legislature in November 1944 revealed a mood of chauvinism. Once again Khare announced: 'I wish India was in a position to declare war on South Africa. Some day or other. . .India will come into her own.' G. V. Deshmukh (Congress) said: 'I wish very much Indian regiments...could be sent to drive some sense into South African whites.' In another vein Hooseinbhoy Lalljee demanded the repatriation of all Indians from East and South Africa: 'another 200,000 of our own countrymen will not make much difference'. In January 1945, in a debate in the Kenya Legislative Council, the leader of the European group proposed that the British government should ask Smuts to convene a conference of all the British territories in East, Central, and South Africa. The proposition was opposed by all the Indian, Arab, and African representatives but it was approved by eleven votes (the Europeans) to seven (the rest).

Commenting on this move, Wavell reported to Amery (21 February 1945) that Indians had concluded 'that the general hostility to Indian immigrants in the East African territories was not an accident, but was part of a plan concerted with the Union Government'. Amery played down the notion. The Colonial Office was concerned to check the spread of South African ideas and practices into Central and East Africa: hence they might promote a Central African Federation to keep out South Africa. But 'anything like an attempt by the Colonial Office to enforce a drastic policy of overriding their [the white settler] point of view might very well incline their minds to look to the Union for moral support'.

And so, in the years immediately after the Second World War, the position of the Indian communities in East and South Africa was, in political and social terms, worse than after the First World War, while the white settler viewpoint, backed by the towering authority of Smuts, was dominant and the voice of black Africa was still ignored, for (as Eden wrote to Halifax in May 1943) their prospect of self-government was still 'many generations' distant.

With the advent of independence in 1947–8 in India, Pakistan, Ceylon, and Burma, the Empire moved into the transitional, much applauded, and fugitive phase of the multiracial Commonwealth.

The British Nationality Act 1948 symbolized the transformation. Lord Chancellor Jowett introduced the measure with some of the most elevated sentiments ever expressed in the House of Lords: 'Of all the remarkable contributions which our race has made to the art of government,' he said, 'the conception of our Empire and Commonwealth is the greatest.' The new concept of Commonwealth citizenship was 'not mainly important because of its material advantages. It is, if you like, rather mystical', and, on the whole, their lordships did like it. Lord Tweedsmuir (John Buchan) stated: 'I was very anxious to know whether it would be possible for a Dayak head hunter from Sarawak to land in this country and become chairman of the National Coal Board. . .I understand that he can in fact hold that office and in fact always could.' So that was all right. Of more immediate interest to the Indians, and other citizens of East Africa, the new Act introduced them to the legal status of citizens of the United Kingdom and Colonies. *Pace* Lord Tweedsmuir, this did represent a gain to many in East Africa. Uganda and Zanzibar were protectorates, and Tanganyika was a mandated (or Trust) territory, while the coastal strip of Kenya was also (legally) a part of the Zanzibar protectorate. The inhabitants of all these areas had previously been British protected persons, and this included all the Indians born in these areas (a quarter of the Uganda Indians were local-born by 1936) as well as Indians originating in an Indian princely state. Only British Indians, and everybody born within Kenya colony, had previously enjoyed the legal status of a British subject. The status of British protected persons was ambiguous in the extreme: according to the Foreign Office, they were 'aliens from the point of view of municipal law in this country [UK] but nevertheless equally with H.M.'s subjects British "nationals" when in foreign countries'. Under the 1948 Act all such people found it easier to acquire the status of British subjects/Commonwealth citizens—and, more important, citizenship of the United Kingdom and Colonies.

The decision to accord this status to the peoples of the British colonies was pressed intently from the Colonial Office point of view. The inherited Colonial Office suspicion of interference in the colonies by the Government of India was greatly intensified now that this government was completely Indian and national. A fear that the new India would attempt to mobilize all the communities of Indian origin throughout the British colonial territories, as a sort of fifth column, was a very real factor in urging the conferment of British citizenship as a counter-attraction on the colonial Indians.

In actuality Jawaharlal Nehru was insistent that Indians who had settled in British colonial territories must identify themselves with these countries. Wherever he went his message was that these Indian communities must not look over their shoulders to Mother India for assistance nor must they try to claim special privileges or a special status as Indians; they would only be accepted by 'the sons of the soil' when they demonstrated that they, too, were committed to the future of the country of their choice. Nehru's message was intended specially for the Indians of newly independent Burma, Ceylon, and Malaya, but he regarded the message as equally important for Indians in what were likely to be British colonies for many years still to come.

In characteristic ruminative fashion, Nehru discussed the question with the Lok Sabha in an exchange of 8 March 1948:

Now these Indians abroad, what are they? Are they Indian citizens? Are they going to be citizens of India or not? If they are not, then our interest in them becomes cultural and humanitarian, not political. That interest, of course, remains. For instance, take the Indians of Fiji or Mauritius: are they going to retain their nationality, or will they become Fiji nationals or Mauritians? The same question arises in regard to Burma and Ceylon. It is a difficult question. This House gets mixed up. It wants to treat them as Indians, and with the same breath it wants a complete franchise for them in the countries where they are living. Of course, the two things do not go together. Either they get the franchise as nationals of the other country, or treat them as Indians minus the franchise and ask for them the most favourable treatment given to an alien.

Despite the utterance of reassuring sentiments by Nehru (and it must be added that few other Indian leaders adopted Nehru's tone), the suspicions of the Colonial Office remained. Soon after independence the Indian government applied for representatives—Commissioners—to be stationed in East Africa, Mauritius, and Fiji. The British government acceded to this request only after demanding assurances that the commissioners would concern themselves entirely with Indian visitors and not with the permanent residents. The distinction proved impossible to observe in practice and the new commissioners attracted some obloquy from the still-British colonial regimes. Apa B. Pant, who has recently departed from London with a high reputation for helpful mediation between Indians and British, was appointed as the first commissioner in East Africa. He was accused of encouraging the local Indians to identify with militant African nationalism and when the Mau Mau phase developed in Kenya the government strongly objected to his activities.

The situation of Indian leaders in East Africa became increasingly fraught with difficulty, especially in Kenya, as the political situation polarized in different directions. Even the white minority began to appear irrelevant, and attempts by Michael Blundell and others to find formulae for a multiracial political dialogue within the 'Capricorn' framework faded out as soon as the British government decided to press ahead with independence plans. The Indians had attempted to gain some political mileage by supporting African nationalist leaders but these leaders did not really have a common interest with the Indians, and the last interregnum before independence was concerned almost entirely, in Kenya and Uganda, with the resolution of pressures between African forces driving towards regionalism and other African forces pulling towards unification.

Thus the strands of British citizenship, Indian relationship, and identification with Africa, had by no means been unravelled by the Indian communities when independence arrived for Tanganyika/Tanzania in 1961, Uganda in 1962, and Kenya in 1963.

Meanwhile, Indians in other parts of the world were finding extreme difficulty in accommodating to the nationalism of newly emergent nations. Disputes over treatment of Indian labourers brought labour emigration to a halt, to Malaya in 1938 and to Ceylon in 1940. Even before Ceylon attained independence the Ceylonese ministers made it clear that the Indian immigrants had no permanent place in their country. They were removed from the electoral roll, and only those whose parents had been born in Ceylon might compete for posts in the public services. As India and Ceylon moved into independence, the bulk of the Indians in Ceylon (about 600,000) acquired neither Indian nor Ceylonese nationality; they remained in a kind of limbo, notionally citizens of the United Kingdom and Colonies, although nobody proposed packing them off to Britain. The conundrum was never really solved. In 1954 an agreement was signed by Sir John Kotelawala and Nehru, which envisaged the granting of Ceylon citizenship to some Indians and the gradual repatriation of the remainder to India under a scheme of inducements, not then worked out. Little came of this agreement but in 1964 Mrs Bandaranaike concluded another agreement with Prime Minister Lal Bahadur Sastri whereby repatriation would be implemented through a Government of India rehabilitation scheme. It was envisaged that about a third of the million stateless Indians (as the number was now calculated) would return to India, a third would be accepted by Ceylon, and the remaining third would be subject to further negotiation. Once again the agreement produced no tangible consequences. But the Ceylon government took no drastic measures, other than tightening up on immigration—virtually reduced to nil.

The attitude of the government of Burma was less patient. Under Acts passed in 1948 and 1953 all agricultural land was nationalized: this included almost 3 million acres which had passed into the ownership of the Chettyars, the south Indian banking caste who had provided the infrastructure of rural credit in Burma. Although a plan for compensation was approved no recompense was ever given to the Chettyars, who were, in effect, expropriated. However, the Chettyars were a small group only, an embarrassment to Indian socialists such as Nehru who saw them as little more than neo-colonialists. The remainder of the 800,000 Indians in Burma comprised a small professional class, a large group of middle-grade technical experts (post office engineers, railwaymen, and the like), a small number of big entrepreneurs, a large number of small shopkeepers, and a mass of unskilled labourers. Their stay in Burma was made difficult by a tiresome machinery of registration and stay-permits, for all but the tiny minority who wanted to become citizens of Burma (and who could cut through swathes of red tape to achieve this). The gradual deterioration was suddenly accelerated when General Ne Win seized power in 1962. Under his 'Burmese Way to Socialism', all private enterprise was abolished, and all foreign employment in hospitals, schools, and other public services was terminated. Enormous pressure was put on the now unemployed, and unemployable, Indians to leave the country. They were permitted to take only Rs 50, and even personal jewels and valuables were confiscated (some said gold teeth were extracted on the dockside). During the early and mid-1960s some half million Indians left Burma to return to their motherland (a country which some had never seen). About a quarter of a million remain. A few have, as it were, 'disguised' themselves, taking Burmese names and wearing Burmese dress: this includes an essential few still needed by the government. Some continue as the dregs of the urban labour force, discharging menial tasks which no Burman would take on; and many are living in remote villages—some as agriculturalists, but most surviving in the vestiges of trade and small-scale industry which persist, despite the Burmese way to socialism.

The experience of Indians in Malaysia is vastly different; indeed, it may be said that their situation is the most favoured of any Indian community in the tropics. The major imposition is a tough immigration policy which prohibits even small children from joining Indian parents in Malaya, while an Indian who takes a holiday in India may forfeit his right of readmittance. By contrast, immigrants of the Malay ethnic group from Indonesia are freely admitted into Malaysia. Most of the community remain plantation workers and with the conversion of many of the former European rubber estates into small, peasant-owned plots for rubber production many are thrown out of work. Some are achieving social mobility through entering urban employment in factories, transport services, etc., but the Malayan Indians remain predominantly a rural, plantation-based population. In political terms they have to accept the role of camp-followers of either a Malay-dominated government or an opposition which is radical and Chinese. In a country where all the communities think of themselves as minorities, the Indians are especially conscious of their own vulnerability.

Returning to Africa, the sharpest contrasts are revealed in South Africa. A minority among the Indians have achieved a comfortable economic status, while enjoying no political rights at all; the majority are in transit from being a rural proletariat, as estate workers or small-holders, into becoming an urban proletariat in the Greater Durban area. Defiance of white dominance was broken by severe and sustained repression, and now the Indian community is (outwardly, at any rate) acquiescent, with a small and perhaps increasing number collaborating with white nationalism. There seems a possibility that, in the face of African resistance, the South African whites may seek to coopt the Coloureds and the Indians as allies, as the change in the balance of the population swings increasingly against the whites.[4]

The policy of the Indian government towards South Africa has not sustained the fervent demands of 1944-6. In June 1946 the Government of India placed the case of the Indians in South Africa on the agenda of the newly born United Nations, and the next month instituted a trade boycott against South Africa (this was before Nehru and the Congress took office as an interim government). Subsequently India obtained a vote from the United Nations (December 1946) ruling that 'treatment of Indians in the Union should be in conformity with. . . provisions of the Charter', but although the case came up before the UN time after time the South African government did not budge from its position. India could do no more: nothing further was heard of the cry to send Indian troops to South Africa after independence. Perhaps the only consolation obtained by India was the withdrawal of South Africa from the Commonwealth in May 1961—in the face of rejection by 'the new Commonwealth' (and also by Canada) of a philosophy of white racism. Yet, as Nehru told the Lok Sabha (24 March 1961), 'The evil continues and will continue in an aggravated form.' Independent India had had no more success than imperial India in modifying racist policies against Indians domiciled in South Africa—or in other countries practising overt discrimination.

Probably the South African failure has strongly influenced Indian policy towards emigration. As long ago as 1923, Tej Bahadur Sapru told an Imperial Conference: 'There is a growing sentiment in my country that we should not send our Nationals outside anywhere. . .I was probably the strongest exponent of the view that there should be no immigration [sic] from India to outside on any conditions whatsoever . . .There is plenty of scope for the conservation of the energy of my countrymen in my own country.' This attitude has continued to dominate official thinking. The issue of passports to Indians wanting to go overseas has been restricted and persons without qualifications have been refused passports. Prospective emigrants have been permitted to take only £3 out of India. Frustration at the inability of India to influence the immigration policies of other countries has reached a peak in relation to Britain: whenever restrictive immigration legislation has been introduced at Westminster (as in 1962 and 1968), the evidence shows that there was no prior consultation between Whitehall and New Delhi. In 1968 the very first news received by the High Commissioner for India was the Home Secretary's announcement of the new restric-

tions. Resentment at such treatment has been a factor in the Indian
government's reluctance to accommodate the 'British Asians' when
they wanted to return to India. In general India has accepted people of
Indian origin who wish to return to the ancestral motherland, without
qualification. There is an understanding that India's future and India's
peoples cannot be 'exported' as it were: unlike a country such as
Ireland (or Italy), India can never expect to relieve pressures by wholesale emigration. Indians overseas represent no more than one (or at
most two) per cent of total population. For the mother country, they
are only tiny offspring. Yet, in relation to the countries of settlement,
the Indians overseas have a significant potential in relation to future
development.

3

THE ISMAILIS IN UGANDA

Gardner Thompson

The Asians in Uganda did not form a homogeneous community but comprised a number of distinct sub-groups. This chapter selects one of these, the Ismaili community, and investigates its response to the changing situation in Uganda between 1958 and 1972: the nature and degree of its adaptation to British decolonization, African independence, and, finally, Asian expulsion.[1] The expulsion itself raises a number of issues. The historian needs to examine the two charges most commonly levelled at the Asians at that time—economic exploitation and social non-integration. However, the value judgements of 1972 must be avoided: the Ismailis were neither heroes nor villains.

The Ismailis were a minority within a minority. They formed the largest single Muslim Asian community, numbering about 14,000 in 1972, but the Muslims in Uganda were heavily outnumbered by the Hindus.[2] The Shia Imami Ismaili sect is defined, briefly, as those who accept His Highness the Aga Khan as spiritual leader.[3] Within Islam, the major division is between various Shia groups who believe that the Prophet passed on both his spiritual and secular authority, and the Sunni majority who deny any such succession. Of the Shia group, only the Ismailis believe that the succession of Imams has continued unbroken to the present Aga Khan, the forty-ninth Imam, and this belief has had profound practical consequences especially in the last hundred years. The Ismailis became distinguished from other Shias by their claim that the succession passed through Ismail, as seventh Imam, and from this they derive their name. The forty-sixth Imam was a Persian nobleman who acquired the title of Aga Khan. When he moved to India the British honoured him with the further title of 'His Highness', since which time the community has preserved both appellations for its leader. It must be stressed at the outset that, notwithstanding some common beliefs and practices, the Ismailis are regarded as distinctly heretical by other Muslims; their perspective has been well illustrated by a reference to the Sunnis as 'the sect not accepting the leadership of the Imams'.[4]

The modern emergence of the Ismailis begins in nineteenth-century India, and their subsequent achievements in East Africa can only be understood in relation to the developments of this earlier time. The Ismailis were then centred in the coastal city of Bombay and were commonly referred to as Khojas. A community of about 2,000 had migrated from Kutch and Kathiawar earlier in the century but their homeland may have been further north still. Originally Hindus, their conversion to Islam began in about the twelfth century and increased especially in the fourteenth and fifteenth centuries. In Bombay the Khojas outwardly practised Sunni rites for fear of persecution but they secretly continued to recognize the spiritual claims of the distant Aga Khan and to make financial offerings to him.

Migration to the urban setting of Bombay and the prosperity which accompanied it, as many small traders became important shipowners, put strains on the structure of the community. The most serious was the emergence of an educated and rich group who resented the claims of the Aga Khan to obedience and money, and who wished to 'reform' the Khojas by wholeheartedly adopting Sunni practices; this would not only sever the connection with the Persian nobleman but also improve relations with dominant Muslim communities in Bombay. It was in these years of the middle of the nineteenth century, however, that the Aga Khan came to be established without question as leader of the Ismailis in India.[5]

After an abortive rising against the Shah of Persia in 1838 the Aga Khan fled to India, and, having established himself in British circles by his assistance on the north-west frontier, eventually settled in Bombay. He was accompanied by over 1,000 relatives and dependants, and now his presence in the city enabled him to make his claims and exercise his authority with new force. There developed a deepening division between the 'reform' party, numbering about 800, and the majority of the Khojas who adhered to the Aga Khan. At last, in 1882, the re-formers had recourse to the British courts and filed a suit aimed at pre-venting the Aga Khan's interference in the affairs of the community, which had become especially marked with his instruction that his followers must declare themselves openly to be Shia. It was the recourse to British adjudication which resolved this internal crisis: not, however, by supporting the 'reforms' but by establishing the Aga Khan's position, confirming religious tradition by legal sanction. Sir Joseph Arnould ruled that the Khoja community 'has always been and still is bound by ties of spiritual allegiance to the hereditary Imams of the Ismailis'.[6] Arnould was not authenticating the line of succession but giving the community a legal definition in face of which the 'reform' party was forced to secede.

In several respects these developments represent a useful starting-point for a study of the Ismailis—the emergence of the Aga Khan and the recognition of his status both within and outside the community; the urban, commercial setting; the discarding of Sunni practices and of the doctrine of *taqiyya*.[7] Furthermore, prosperity was contributing to a concern for internal progress and order, and it was significant that the wealthier, better educated Shia Khojas who remained after the defeat of the 'reformers' took up the pursuit of change and improvement, especially in the areas of financial organization and educational advance. These all became dominant themes of the following century but already one other trend was becoming visible: Khojas had begun to migrate to other corners of the Indian Ocean.

In Zanzibar there were reported to be between 5,000 and 6,000 Indians by as early as 1860,[8] and the Khojas formed the largest single community among these. Indians had been active on the east coast of Africa for centuries but the nineteenth century was something of a pre-colonial golden age for the Indians, unrelated to the later arrival of indentured labourers for the British East Africa Protectorate with which Indian settlement in East Africa has so commonly been associated. Encouraged and patronized by the Sultans—themselves under increasing British influence—the Indians in Zanzibar had an almost total grasp on overseas trade as well as controlling retail trade; as customs farmers they were in a position close to the Sultans; and as creditors they financed both the huge Arab clove plantations on the coast and the trading caravans which were beginning to penetrate the interior. A prominent Ismaili, Tarya Topan, encouraged other Ismailis by his outstanding success as a trader and he also pioneered welfare projects by founding a school and, in 1887, the first general hospital in Zanzibar.

The most remarkable Indian figure of the period of European partition was an Ismaili, Allidina Visram, who operated first in this Zanzibar context but then moved inland. Indeed, he can be said to have pioneered the Indian impact on Uganda, his enterprise owing little to colonial protection and nothing to promptings from any quarter. He had established trading centres in many parts of Uganda before the railway reached Kisumu and in 1902 Frederick Jackson wrote that 'Allidina Visram is already prepared to buy up as much as the natives like to cultivate'.[9] He dealt in a wide variety of products, while his stores acted as banks and creditors. He diversified into small-scale manufacturing and processing, especially cotton-ginning. He displayed philanthropy as well as industry, contributing to a hospital in Kampala, a school in Mombasa, and, perhaps most remarkable, Namirembe Cathedral. By 1916, the year of his death, he had done more than any other Indian to realize the potential which Uganda offered the enterprising immigrant and at the same time he set a pattern for the subsequent activities of his community.

'By 1910, the scene in East Africa was more or less set...the picture did not substantially alter in the next 40 years.'[10] In terms of the location of power, the distribution of economic activity, and the three-tier racially-stratified social hierarchy, this observation of H. S. Morris is valid. But within that 'unaltering' context, the situation of groups and individuals was far from static, but fluid and dynamic. As far as the Ismaili immigrants were concerned, there was a constant evolution founded on a willingness to adapt for the sake of the community's progress. The so-called 'Asian community' in Uganda was by no means homogeneous, though frequently treated as a unit by both government and Africans. Far more significant, as Morris has stressed, were the communal sub-groups, and for these the Ismailis acted as pace-makers in the process which he has termed 'communal crystallisation'; moreover, it was at this level that Asians won concessions and achieved most. For example, the Ismailis soon insisted on their right to have exclusive burial grounds and exclusive title to land for their *jamatkana*, or mosque. Characteristically, the community was also the first to insist on, and build, separate schools for their children. Indeed, by the mid-1920s the Ismailis had succeeded in winning legal recognition as a separate community, despite the government's preference for dealing with the Asians as a single category.

Thus established, and with their numbers growing steadily by natural increase and continued spontaneous immigration from India, the activities of the Ismailis as of other Asians in Uganda became more varied. Partly through choice, partly as a response to colonial policies, Asians diversified over the next three decades into wholesale trade, service industries, small-scale manufacturing, and, as a return on educational investment, into office jobs and indeed the professions. What distinguished the Ismailis in this period is their institutional evolution and the foundation of various self-help projects, most of which were the personal achievement of Aga Khan III. It was he who confirmed the status of the Imamate which had been won in India. On the surface there is a paradox in the fact that he reinforced his spiritual position in the eyes of his East African followers while becoming a statesman of international reputation, closely linked both politically and personally with the West in general, and Britain and France in particular. Yet it was vision and experience gained in this way which led him to promote change among his East African followers and it was the secular evolution and material progress which resulted from these changes which in turn reinforced his religious position.

Earlier, the Aga Khan's authority had been in question in Zanzibar as it had been in India, and between 1880 and 1910 there were many defections,[11] especially to the Ithnasheris, a closely related Shia group which did not have a living Imam. The penetration of the interior, however, itself encouraged by the Aga Khan, changed this situation. In the 1920s the Aga Khan inaugurated a system of councils in Uganda, founding his community's organization on a written constitution according to the Zanzibar model which dated from the turn of the century. In 1937 he founded the Jubilee Insurance Company on the occasion of his fiftieth anniversary as Imam, making a substantial personal investment in a company which was to provide the whole range of insurance schemes for his community. Ten years later, in celebration of his Diamond Jubilee, he was weighed in diamonds, the value of which (£684,000)[12] he then donated to the community for the establishment of an investment trust which might invest in land and businesses and make loans to cooperatives, building societies, and related institutions of sums equal to their capital, while paying dividends to member investors in the trust. In the following decade, he launched a further project whereby all East African Ismailis might own their own homes by 1960. A building society was set up to provide mortgages for the better off and to acquire land and build houses in which less prosperous followers might take occupation as tenants but eventually pay back sufficient to become owners.

Thus we may agree that 'the progressive, prosperous, and united Ismaili community of present-day East Africa is virtually a creation of the late Imam'.[13] Moreoever, these developments represented a significant investment for a Ugandan future and contemporary emphasis on educational advance helped to confirm not only the community's commitment to Uganda but also their reputation as the most accomplished sector of what was, by the late colonial period, a most conspicuously prosperous Asian minority in East Africa.[14] Largely through the practical guidance of an Imam who could claim divine authority, the Ismailis solved the problem which has faced all Muslim communities in recent times of how to adapt to change and compromise with modernity.

The pattern continued into the decolonization period, a demonstration that the enduring organization still found practical expression. A brief examination of this organization is necessary since it was the foundation of the various community projects and it will serve to explain the corporate nature of the response of the Ismailis to the political challenge of decolonization.

'Religious' and 'secular' leadership were inseparable and centred on the person of the Aga Khan, the living Imam; but Aga Khan III ensured that there was an efficient organization below him and reaching down to each member of his community. The fundamental unit was the congregation, or *jamat*, in each of the towns in which the Ismailis dwelt. The *jamatkana* was in each case the focal point of the congregation, serving both as a place of worship and as a 'multi-functional community centre'.[15] The largest of the three Kampala *jamatkanas*, for example, comprised a hall for worship, a council chamber, a library, and a dispensary.

The constitution for the Uganda Ismailis, dating from the 1920s, was updated by the late Aga Khan in 1937, 1946, and 1954, and further modified by the present Aga Khan in the year of Uganda's independence, 1962.[16] By means of these constitutions the council hierarchy was maintained, with provincial and territorial councils working under an East African Supreme Council centred in Kenya. These councils, comprising prominent members of the community nominated from within the hierarchy but approved by the Aga Khan himself, 'directed, supervised and co-ordinated'[17] the activities of the *jamats*. Each council had a president and secretary and a number of officers responsible for different departments, for example, health, education, finance, and housing. The constitutions periodically reformed the code of Ismaili personal law, so that the 1962 version, for instance, explicitly forbade the betrothal of boys below the age of 18 and girls below the age of 16, a remarkable contrast to Hindu practice. At the same time, the wife's rights in divorce cases were laid down, while the explicit prohibition of polygamy pointed to one of the many contrasts between Ismaili and local African Muslim practice.[18] In these respects the community operated its own personal legal system, with its own structure of tribunals, within the host state of Uganda.

Social projects were financed by the regular payment by each adult of an eighth of his income to the mosque officers, the *mukhi* (treasurer or steward) and *kamaria* (accountant). This fundamental religious obligation predated the nineteenth century where, as noted above, it had contributed to a constitutional crisis within the community in India. The payments were deemed to be the Aga Khan's exclusive personal property but in practice the money collected—and collected also from gifts, initiation fees, and payments for ceremonies—was used to finance community services at the local level.

Also established in the constitutions were Ismaili Associations, in parallel with the councils but with responsibility for the religious life of the community. Although they played an important part in the East Africa Muslim Welfare Society, which will be discussed later, the Ismailis did not seek to propagate their faith to non-Ismailis in Uganda. The purpose of the Associations was, rather, to teach the community itself, explaining the Aga Khan's interpretations of Islam, reviewing the faith in the light of modern science, and continuing to cleanse belief and practices of superstitions, like the use of charms, which had been inherited from the Hindu past. Indeed the religious context of these constitutions, which were on the surface so secular in form and content, was made plain in the first two parts of the 1962 version, first the holy *firman* (verbal edict of the Aga Khan) by which the constitution was issued, second a clause to explain that nothing contained within it could be held to be binding on the Imam himself.[19]

Though appearing to constitute a state within a state, the Ismaili constitutions did not, in the light of the Aga Khan's guidance, have serious political implications. They served rather to clarify religious affairs and to found the welfare services, so conspicuous in the absence of state provision, on a solid organizational base. Local autonomy was preserved where possible but the wider the implications of any issue, the higher up the pyramid was guidance sought, with the Aga Khan always the ultimate authority. It would be hard to exaggerate the practical consequences for the Ismailis of having a living Imam, and this centralized, corporate organization which enabled successive Aga Khans to guide and effect change. First introduced by the young Aga Khan III, when he was called upon, in 1899, to settle problems both among his followers in Dar es Salaam and between those followers and the German authorities, the constitutions, in their revised forms, continued to regulate the communities' affairs and to confirm their separate identity vis-à-vis other Asian groups while binding them closer to other Ismaili congregations. Thus a young Ismaili's summary, 'our community has been taught to look after one another no matter what colour or nationality'.[20]

The central significance of the Aga Khan appears to be disputed by H. Amiji's contention that 'the community is basically ruled by a small plutocratic elite'.[21] The plutocracy existed, it is true. It included, for instance, Sherali Bandali Jaffer who, as a member of the UPC government, was perhaps the most prominent Ismaili personality in the 1960s, and a number of other prominent businessmen and property owners were reputed millionaires. Yet while undoubtedly forming an upper class within the community, these figures saw themselves as servants of the Aga Khan, they served in honorary capacities on the councils, and their rewards of titles and prestige were won from the Aga Khan and their proximity to him. They were partners in ruling, in that consultations were held with them before *firmans* were issued and in that the task of execution frequently fell to them. Nevertheless, they were subordinates to successive Aga Khans who could claim not only to possess divine authority along with their nineteenth-century predecessors, but also to have subsequently made unequalled personal contributions to the progress of their community. A further, minor, qualification to their status as an Ismaili 'upper class'[22] might be made. Distinctions of wealth and power within the Asian sub-groupings in Uganda and elsewhere in East Africa have tended to be overlooked by commentators though in fact representing yet further divisive criteria. Nevertheless it could be argued that the ordering of the Ismailis as outlined above minimized the class distinctions within the community, the rich contributing more to community funds and the poor receiving welfare payments; while, according to one member of the plutocracy, the Ismaili leaders sought 'to make the lower class middle class, and the middle class upper class, so that all might be equal at the top'.[23]

The significance of the community's formal organizational structure was that it worked in a practical way and the community visibly served its members—and, increasingly in the 1950s, non-Ismailis too. To take one example, education was compulsory for all Ismailis. Thus, on the one hand, the continuing emphasis on school building, such as His Highness The Aga Khan Secondary School opened in Kampala in June 1959, soon to become possibly the finest day school in Uganda; on the other hand, school fees were provided for children whose parents were too poor to contribute their own. Furthermore, this school was, from the outset, open to Africans, as were other Ismaili foundations since the early 1950s.[24] Attention has already been drawn to the housing scheme, which only narrowly missed its target in 1960 and which, meanwhile, accelerated the tendency towards nuclear family units. Estates were built and flats bought for widows and the destitute. Nor were these projects confined to Kampala: in 1960, for example, a similar project, for twenty houses, was inaugurated in Masaka.[25] A further illustration of the community in action lay in the social security payments which were of two kinds: emergency expenditure in the case of, for example, hospital fees; and regular supplements to the poorest members. Although the community in Uganda could not match Nairobi's Diamond Jubilee Hospital, they did provide a health insurance scheme which entitled subscribers to treatment there, and local dispensaries—again open to Africans. Thus the Kampala Health Centre, independent of government financial support, was reported in 1963 to have a 65 per cent African clientele.[26] Meanwhile the longer-standing institutions founded by the late Aga Khan continued to operate: there were 4,000 Ismaili shareholders in the Diamond Jubilee Investment Trust at independence.[27] These activities added up to a significant willingness to invest, and, while originally and predominantly serving the communities' own interests, became open to non-Ismaili participation under the auspices of the successive Aga Khans in the 1950s.

It has been remarked that 'the history of the Asian communities [in East Africa] is largely one of accommodation to the prevailing historical situation',[28] and this generalization was nowhere more fully illustrated than by the Ismailis' response to decolonization in Uganda. It is a mistake to assume that the withdrawal of the colonial power was an absolute hiatus in Ismaili history here. Rather, the Ismailis' accommodation at this time represented merely a further adjustment, consistent with their previous practice. Indeed, the succession of the present Aga Kan to the Imamate on the death of his grandfather, in 1957, heralded an era, not of defensive introversion, but of even closer involvement and identification with Uganda.

The events of the past decade in general and of the expulsion in particular hinder a balanced evaluation of the conditions prevailing at the end of the 1950s. For those who seek them, there are portents of disaster in these days; there is material to suggest that the Asians' position was precarious and must have been perceived as such: thus one commentator remarks upon the Asians' 'almost paranoic sense of vulnerability'.[29] There was, indeed, an uncertainty about the constitutional changes that were pending, both in terms of the timing of independence and the distribution of representation.[30] More alarming perhaps, the African political parties did not make clear their attitude towards the Asian community.[31] Meanwhile, events in the Congo, following the abrupt departure of the Belgians, included the flight of expatriates—among them Asians; while nearer home, indeed in the neighbourhood of Kampala itself, a boycott of non-African traders, 'politically inspired' and aimed mainly at the Asian businessman,[32] was accompanied, in 1959 and 1960, by acts of intimidation and physical violence, including murder,[33] and in March 1960 the Indian Merchants' Chamber reported that half the rural Asian traders in Buganda had been put out of business.[34] These events could be interpreted as the acceleration of an earlier trend seen in an anti-Asian ingredient in the rise of the Bataka party in the 1940s,[35] and the controversy over the installing of an Asian minister, in 1954.[36]

But these are the impressions of hindsight or of those who believed that because the Asians dwelt in Uganda they must necessarily have in themselves represented a further 'problem'.[37] The Asians were not, however, a central issue in Ugandan politics at any time: concentration was so focused on constitutional change in general, and the Baganda in particular—a far more important 'minority' than the Asians[38]—that not one editorial in the Uganda Argus was devoted to the Asian question in 1958. Undoubtedly the Asians were, as later events demonstrated, vulnerable: an alien trading community, dominating the towns, competing for jobs in the bureaucracy, yet politically weak through small numbers and lacking any mutual interdependence with the state. They had frequently been subjected to racial discrimination and intolerance; they were used to periodic anti-Asian invective; even the boycott of 1959–60 was limited in scope and linked to the essentially Baganda Uganda National Movement. Nor did decolonization involve a significant loss of political power for the Asians since they were essentially exchanging masters of one race for another. Above all, it was the Asians' own experience of material progress in even these, to some extent, unfavourable circumstances which minimized not only the call for constitutional safeguards on their part but also the flight of personnel and capital from the country.[39] With African political leaders beginning to woo the Asians as voters and indeed also to appoint Asian candidates for the urban seats,[40] even the boycott, which died away in 1960, could be seen as a temporary factor of trade recession or Baganda obstructionism, rather than as a threat, as such, to the Asian community.[41]

Only by retaining such a view of the process of decolonization in Uganda, one in which the situation held promise of continued well-being as well as the possibility of danger, can one understand the political response of the Ismailis, and of other Asian groups, to these changing circumstances. Decolonization involved a change from communal to national politics, from nomination to direct election,[42] and it implied an end to the conducting of Indian politics at an informal personal level between representatives of pressure groups and officials of government. As in Kenya, the central constitutional question for the Asians was whether to accept a common roll or to seek safeguards in the shape of separate seats for racial minorities. Though some voices, British[43] and Asian,[44] argued for the latter, there was a remarkable unanimity in the public expression of all Asian political organizations on the preference for the common roll—a unanimity which warns against making over-sharp distinctions between Ismailis and other groups. Again, as in Kenya, differences were of emphasis; indeed, they were generally lacking in substance so that rival groups were seen publicly to be disputing over trivia.[45]

The oldest political grouping of Asians in Uganda was the Central Council of Indian Associations (CCIA), founded in 1921 as a congress comprising members from the various local Indian urban associations. Weaknesses of internal inter-communal differences became explicit in 1947 and led to the Muslims breaking away to form the Central Council of Muslim Associations (CCMA) which immediately sought separate representation on the Legislative Council.[46] However, in the decolonizing period, these two formed something of a common front, a remarkable achievement in view of their past rivalry and, indeed, of what occurred later in Kenya where Muslims insisted on special seats.[47] It is wrong to suggest that the CCIA proposed communal representation at this time,[48] for in fact, by 1959, the Council was repeatedly rejecting such a proposal and finding the CCMA agreeing to a common approach.[49]

This degree of consensus did not prevent the emergence in early 1959 of the Uganda Action Group (UAG). The UAG claimed to be not a political party but merely an advocate for the total disappearance of a distinctive Asian presence on the Ugandan political scene. Since it, too, therefore accepted the common roll, friction with the older organizations concerned symbolic questions, such as the rate of electoral registration in 1960 or which Asian group had first preached identification.[50] The most serious criticism UAG members levelled at the CCIA and CCMA was that of using communalism, by their very existence, as a supposed means of abolishing communalism. Perhaps the brief prominence of the UAG is to be seen in terms of a frustration felt by young radicals at a time when the older Indian establishment still claimed to speak for all.[51] However, as Hilda Kuper rightly remarks, 'its own support was too limited and came too late to make a major impact on African leaders, or even to become known to the African masses'.[52]

As the largest single Muslim denomination, the Ismailis were naturally prominent in the CCMA—indeed it has been asserted that the CCMA was 'dominated' by the community.[53] But, as H. S. Morris remarks, the Ismailis 'were never firm in their allegiance to any other group',[54] and while it is valuable to see the CCMA as a distinct category, it may well have been a reflection of the Ismaili influence in it that no public mention of the CCMA as such in the Uganda Argus is later than September 1960; the CCIA, on the other hand, continued to articulate and influence Asian views well into the independence era. At the same time, in its total abdication from politics as a group, the Ismaili community perhaps most closely resembled the UAG. On the other hand again, distinguishing the Ismailis from, say, the CCIA may result only from an optical illusion—while the CCIA held mass meetings, spoke up on the question of the boycott and indeed attempted to counter it with a form of 'Home Guard',[55] the Ismailis were also exhorting their followers through their communal organization, away from the public eye.

The instructions of the Aga Khan were notably unambiguous. Though in some respects the 'secular' as well as the 'religious' head of the community, his existence posed no problem of political loyalty. At his installation in 1957, the young Aga Khan declared 'the position which I occupy. . .never will be a political one'.[56] Two years later at the opening of the Wandegeya Mosque in Kamapala, he repeated 'I have neither the wish nor the means to dabble in politics.'[57] His only political advice, he added, was that his followers should identify with Uganda and help to develop it. Consistent with his advocacy of the common roll rather than communal seats, he explained that 'although as a community the Ismailis will never be involved in politics, individually they may well play a constructive part in their countries' political developments'.[58] Such participation was illustrated by Sherali Bandali Jaffer and by Kassim Lakha who was soon to join him as a UPC member of government.[59] Nevertheless, in the brief period of successive popular elections the Aga Khan reiterated, 'to tell people to vote for X or Y is not the role of the Imam'.[60]

Perhaps a more productive distinction to be made between Ismailis and non-Ismailis than these differences of degree in disengaging from communalism in politics is to be found in the relative significance or weight of the exhortations made by different community leaders. As the UAG contested the claims of the CCIA and CCMA to be representative of Asian opinion, and the latter replied in kind, it became clear that the Ismailis possessed a leadership which enjoyed a different authority. The urgings of the CCIA that Asians should apply for citizenship or their claims that Asians supported the common roll appear unimpressive in view of remarks made by other Asians at the time. Thus in October 1959 the UAG declared 'the fact is that the mass of Asians in the country have never been represented by anyone. The most that these sectional bodies have ever succeeded to represent is the top, financially well-to-do 10 per cent of the Asians. . .The 90 per cent has seldom got within hearing distance of the conventional Asian "leaders".'[61] In the context of the colonial political structure this was not remarkable but even more critical was the voice of a newly elected committee member of the Kampala Indian Association itself who, in October 1960, admitted that that body 'speaks for only a couple of rich patrons. . .and is not an association of the people'.[62]

This debate highlighted the special nature of the Ismaili community, which was no more democratic than any other Asian grouping but which did possess an unquestioned authority at its head, whose political impact was hence of great significance. Thus, as with the question of citizenship, for example, it becomes more important to note what the Aga Khan's advice was than to note that given by leaders of other bodies, if one is to explain mass response; for while the content of the advice may have been similar in all cases, it was only the Ismailis who had an external leader whose authority was so widely respected. In the case of other groups the absence of a community of interests between the small prosperous elite, which had an easier and more varied set of options, and the mass of ordinary Asians, greatly reduced the significance of the instructions the former gave to the latter. Though, for instance, a degree of partnership existed between African and Asian members of the 'upper class', less prosperous Asians might perceive the frailty of African assurances and thus more seriously question their own supposed 'leaders'. While similar distinctions did exist within the Ismaili community, only they had the Aga Khan as a supreme source of guidance and, not least, the community itself as source of assurance. At a time of choice, it was Asians' identification with their own sub-groups which was of primary importance.

The Ismailis' confidence was vindicated by the political develop-ments of the early 1960s. Not only did political parties make assurances both before and after elections, as in 1961, but they competed keenly for Asian support,[63] especially in the towns where the introduction of direct elections to both national and local assemblies gave scope to the predominantly Asian electorates. To African leaders at such times 'the Asians' were not an issue; it was neither necessary nor wise to alarm the community though below this level of articulation views may have been different. Even 'Africanization' was at this time only a remote threat, usually seen in relation to taking over European jobs in the civil service.[64] Granted this context, the Ismailis' political stance was not remarkable.

From a slightly different angle of vision, one can see the Ismailis in this period continuing a process of identification with Uganda which again had many precedents from the colonial period. As the leader of a people without a homeland, the late Aga Khan had seen the wisdom of adaptation not only institutionally but culturally. As early as 1914 he had told his followers in Burma 'to identify socially and politically' with the life of that country and to adopt 'the names, habits and cus-toms' of the people there.[65] His advice to his East African followers was to make English their first language and to 'found their family and domestic lives along English lines'.[66] Successive innovations in their schools exemplified these trends in practice. English became the teach-ing tongue from the start of primary school and Gujerati was dropped; especially progressive was the accent on the education of girls; while even attempts to teach Luganda were made when the schools set an example by opening up to Africans in the 1950s. Other compromises were made, from the wearing of Western dress to the increasing inci-dence of non-arranged marriages. Certainly enough flexibility was displayed to question the assertion that the community was not 'emancipated', and the automatic equation between communal cohe-sion and being 'culture-bound'.[67] There was little that was specifically Indian in Ismaili 'culture' in Uganda by the time of the expulsion.

These moves towards identification were a feature of the colonial period but the young Aga Khan urged his followers to continue the process, albeit in a different manner, in the independent state of Uganda. He said they must 'live their lives not as a separate race but as part and parcel of their national community',[68] giving the same loyalty to the new government as they had given to the former one. It was consistent, then, with both his own and his grandfather's previous policy when he advised his community by a *firman* in 1962 to make the most conscious and outward sign of identification, the acquisition of citizenship.

How far the very high proportion of Ismaili applications was a response to the promptings of the Aga Khan is arguable, bearing in mind the readiness of the community as a whole to remain in Uganda.[69] While many became citizens automatically because they fulfilled the qualifications,[70] the application of others was a bureaucratic formality, merely an expression of their willingness to continue to live and work in Uganda which is not difficult to explain. Members of the community saw the question simply in terms of whether or not they would be allowed to live, work, and prosper as before. The prospects appeared favourable in the light of the smooth transfer of power and the immediate offer of citizenship. As noted above, the Ismailis' historic links with East Africa went back more than a hundred years and the late Aga Khan had inspired a corporate unity, an organizational framework, and indeed solid material achievement which it was calculated amounted to a thirty-million-pound investment in 1962.[71] Their infrastructure of houses, schools, and mosques was the envy of other Asians. Neither culturally nor in terms of economic potential were the Ismailis attracted to India, whereas Hindus and indeed the closely related Bohra Shias (whose spiritual leader, or *dai*, lived in Bombay) had deep religious associations with that country. Also, the description of the Asians as a British as well as an East African minority[72] is least applicable to the Ismailis whose status was that of British protected persons. Under British law, people of such status were aliens and had never had unrestricted rights of entry into Great Britain. With members of the community setting each other an example in determining to remain, in the hope of building on their already remarkable success in the country, the specific guidance of the Aga Khan may have been superfluous, except in achieving a remarkably high proportion of Ismaili applicants. As Sherali Bandali Jaffer pointed out shortly before the expiry of the two-year period for application, it was the 'lower classes' who needed persuasion while the upper elite had more options open to them and could make up their own minds.[73] Whatever the explanation, the charge of 'calculation'[74] which was levelled by Africans at the time of the last-minute rush of applications is least applicable to the Ismailis, since Kassim Lakha announced that over half of the community had already applied by September 1963.[75] Elsewhere in East Africa the Ismailis responded similarly, with 90 per cent of the community said to have joined TANU in Tanganyika.[76] Furthermore, the determination of the community to remain in Uganda even after August 1972 emphasizes that their attitude to citizenship a decade earlier represented a natural and reasonable attachment to their homes and commitment to their country of residence.

The most convincing sign of Ismaili good faith was the continuing programme of investment in Uganda, in which the Aga Khan again took a lead. No sudden break occurred in 1962, so the house schemes and the operation of the interrelated community institutions went on as before. Private investment could be seen in the building of 'The Fairway', a luxury hotel in Kampala opened only months before the expulsion. More significant, however, was the much greater degree of partnership and cooperation with African business and government which testified to the Aga Khan's conviction that, whether or not his community had an indefinite future in Uganda, it was wisest both for his followers' welfare and as a concrete gesture to African government, to be seen to be investing and sharing in the development of the country. Thus in 1961 he hired a German firm to investigate the economic climate of East Africa and offer advice.[77] The upshot was the setting up of Industrial Promotion Services (IPS) with its motto 'Partners in Progress'. The Aga Khan himself contributed most of the £1 million capital with which it was launched and ensured that it was staffed by young graduates like himself. It remained privately operated but its main object was to encourage selective local industrial development, along with African government and business, by contributing advice or capital. Many articles came to be manufactured in Uganda for the first time as a result, from suitcases to socks, fishnets to plastics. Another field was farming where in Fort Portal, for instance, tea, coffee, and poultry farming schemes were launched after a personal investigation of prospects by Prince Amin, the Aga Khan's brother. A later addition to the IPS network followed in the late 1960s in the shape of Tourist Promotion Services (TPS), at a time when Uganda's enormous tourism potential was becoming fully appreciated. TPS became jointly responsible with the Uganda Development Corporation for the construction of Mweya Lodge in the Queen Elizabeth National Park and for the operation of air charter services. The themes of these twin concerns, under the close personal supervision of the Aga Khan, were investment, cooperation, and diversification, and the contributions which the Ismailis were making won the recognition of the Uganda government.[78]

There were other illustrations of the same approach. To take another example from the educational field, in 1969 a second Aga Khan Secondary school was opened on Kololo Hill in Kampala. When the quota of Africans increased in the 1960s, there were insufficient places for all Ismaili secondary-school candidates at the school built earlier in Makerere Road. So the Kololo High School was built with community money to meet the need, though it, too, admitted African students. Even the problems of accommodation were dealt with, a multiracial girls' hostel adjoining the new school, while the Makerere Road complex included a boys' hostel along with the nursery school, primary and secondary schools, and teachers' flats.

An examination of one further area of Ismaili identification and cooperation will serve to illustrate still more vividly the nature of relations between the community and Uganda. In 1945 Aga Khan III founded the East African Muslim Welfare Society which had an apparently enormous potential for exploiting the religious bond of Islam and breaking down barriers of race.[79] The Aga Khan sought always to further the pan-Islamic ideal and his work in the creation of Pakistan was testimony to his breadth of vision. The East African foundation was part of that vision and to help realize it the Aga Khan not only contributed 3 million shillings at the outset but promised to contribute, shilling for shilling, sums equal to those raised locally by the Society.[80] The Ismailis remained the main source of finance for the Society which between 1945 and 1957 was responsible for 63 mosques, 75 schools, a training college, and a technical school,[81] an emphasis on the promotion of education which was charactersitic of the Ismaili involvement and which was emphasized increasingly in the later period. So great was the personal contribution of Sherali Bandali Jaffer as Vice-President that Prince Badru Kakungulu described him as 'almost a Muganda after all he has done for us',[82] at the opening of the Wandegeya Mosque in 1959 by the Aga Khan—who had himself contributed half the funds. The work of the Society, however, demands careful evaluation. Montgomery Watt's optimism in 1966[83] that the Ismailis would increasingly contribute to the progress of African Islam deserves qualification, especially since the contribution was essentially one of funds. There was little in common in temperament or religious practice between progressive Ismailism and traditionally conservative African Islam in Uganda, and the mutual consciousness of heresy has already been noted. Nor was there much scope for social integration at ground level, while Ismailis worshipped in their own *jamatkanas*, contributing only financially to worship in African mosques. Ultimately the barriers of race proved more important than religious brotherhood, as the events of 1972 showed when an overtly Muslim President, with the support, later explicit, of a strongly Muslim Nubian element ordered

the expulsion of the Ismaili community along with all Asians of whatever denomination.

This brings us to the most controversial issue of the pre-expulsion
days in Uganda: that of 'integration'. As Yash Tandon has recently
written, 'the very vagueness of the term "integration" is the source of
its most explosive potential in verbal dialectics'.[84] Theoretically there
are two extremes of interpretation—first, pluralism, which involves
'different sections of the community living side by side but separately,
within the same political unit...mixing but not combining',[85]
secondly, assimilation which 'rules out all diversities' and, as Hilda
Kuper has written, 'those who are supposed to assimilate the culture of
others are in fact expected to subordinate the culture that was their
own'.[86] What in practice were the different interpretations by Africans
and Asians? And how did the Ismailis, in particular, 'integrate'? Asian
tradition and also the colonial structure meant that, as H. S. Morris
accurately observed, 'few found it improper to think of living in a
society permanently divided into exclusive communities having
restricted relations with one another',[87] so their interpretation was the
pluralist emphasis. A characteristic expression of African sentiment,
on the other hand, was given by Tom Mboya in Kenya when he said
'we are demanding the maximum from a non-African'.[88] Specific
African demands tended to be related to the question of racial intermarriage; President Amin concentrated on 'this most painful matter'
at the Conference for Asian 'elders' in Kampala in November 1971,
while the only specific injunction in *Freedom and After* was similar.
The motivation or explanation of this concentration is not within the
scope of this chapter; what must be said here is that it was a demand
which not even the most progressive pluralists among the Asians were
ready to meet, as we shall shortly see. This being so, the Asians were
indicted, and even the expulsion itself effortlessly justified, in terms of
their failure to 'integrate'.

Many examples have already been cited of Ismaili identification and
cooperation with political, economic, and religious life in Uganda.
It is remarkable, indeed, that this most distinct and cohesive community, this nation within the nation, with its own constitution within
the constitution, was the Asian group which most closely 'integrated'
in Uganda with indigenous Africans. But a look at the nature and
extent of this integration resolves the apparent paradox. For what the
IPS, the EAMWS, and even the Ismaili schools had in common was a
degree of integration that was essentially financial and institutional,
though even this latter aspect must be qualified by the Ismailis' continued existence as a distinct institution in themselves. What was absent
was a significant degree of social integration at anything below leader-

ship level, and it was in this respect that the Ismailis were most similar to other Asians in their expression of pluralism. It has been argued that multiracial schooling was 'bound to lead to better race relations and to enhanced social contacts across racial lines'.[89] In practice, however, common attendance was not enough, since, in the Kampala secondary schools immediately before the expulsion, for example, streaming tended to divide the high-ability Asians from up-country African students who had serious linguistic disabilities to overcome, while casual social intercourse outside the classroom was generally on ethnic, indeed even tribal, lines. In such conditions, the stereotypes through which each group viewed the other could persist and even harden. On balance the contribution of the Aga Khan schools was to widen further the gap between Ismaili and African attainment.

The Ismaili distinctiveness, symbolized by their exclusive constitution, and so concretely translated in the two residential housing estates in Kampala, extended to the question of marriage. Sharing as they did with other Asians the dominant role in employer-employee, master-servant, relationships and lacking avenues for social mixing even in their various projects of investment and cooperation, the Ismailis had no social base on which intermarriage might have taken place. It is incorrect to speak of 'rigid' endogamy within the Ismaili community[90] for not only was the 1962 community constitution equivocal on this point[91] but many examples since then have shown a certain flexibility in the community's attitude. But the three incidences of intermarriage in the case of one family demonstrate the limited extent of this flexibility—in each case the non-Ismaili partner was from another Asian community and in each case the Ismaili continued to attend the *jamatkana* and to be treated as a member of the community.[92] Thus the ultimate African demand for integration was not met—Ismaili girls reacted with horror at the suggestion for accelerated intermarriage made at the Asian conference convened by President Amin in December 1971—while for the community, not only racial but religious integrity would have been lost, along with their identity as an immigrant minority of 'strangers'[93] which they held to so closely. To conclude, whatever the substantive as opposed to the symbolic content of this issue in 1972 and before, the Ismailis' failure at the level of social integration led them to be associated merely with the general Asian category and can be said to have somewhat undone those other achievements which, on their own, present the Ismailis as at the same time the most distinct yet the most 'integrated' of the Asian communities in Uganda.

Much of the distinctiveness lay in the nature of Ismailism as a religion and the place of the Aga Khan in, or above, the community. In the

1960s, notwithstanding the specific projects outlined above, the community continued to look, from the outside, less like a religious congregation than a mutual benefit society. The Ismailis were therefore at the same time outward-looking and yet introverted towards their own affairs. The young Aga Khan himself said 'Islam is concerned with the whole life of the faithful, not only their religion',[94] and both the content of his leadership and the activities of the community in Uganda gave practical expression to this conviction. To the extent that they were seen to be building their kingdom in this world—in Uganda— the Ismailis fell short of the African expectation that the balance of their energies could be tipped in favour of outward-looking investment to the benefit of Ugandans as a whole.

Both the social exclusiveness and, as far as government was concerned, the financial features of this, came under scrutiny. The two, indeed, closely interlocked. Second to acknowledging the Imam, allegiance and obedience to whom superseded the other duties of non-Ismaili Muslims, the most important religious obligation of the community was payment of the 'eighth'.[95] This, and the attendance at the *jamakana* which went with it—itself serving a social function though not, as one observer has suggested, 'compulsory'[96]—was the cornerstone of weekly religious practice. Other, non-financial, religious obligations were few, and moral injunctions, for example, covering drinking and smoking, were flexible—hence an Ismaili's observation that 'our religion changes with the times'.[97] Considering the presence of an Imam, the community permitted remarkable scope for personal choice, and religious sanctions were few.

'Religious' and 'secular' departments of life became increasingly fused over time, as fused as were the 'religious' and 'secular' roles of the Aga Khan. An early parable lies in the story of the young Eboo Pirbhai in Kenya, to whom the late Aga Khan, on a visit to East Africa, said 'I give you my blessing for your business'; Eboo prospered and, as Sir Eboo Pirbhai, became President of the East African Supreme Ismaili Council.[98] Another illustration was the weighing in diamonds of the late Aga Khan at Dar; this celebration of a religious occasion, the sixtieth anniversary of the Aga Khan's succession to the Imamate, resulted in the foundation of the Diamond Jubilee Investment Trust. Further day-to-day examples could be cited: the relative prestige and position of Council, rather than Association, members; the English translation of the two central *jamatkana* officials, as 'treasurer' and 'accountant'. Ultimately, it becomes an artificial and purposeless question whether the community was held together by a religious bond or by the fact that it served its members' material interests.

So, too, with the Aga Khan, whose position, as described above in the case of the late Aga Khan, has been such that material leadership and spiritual authority have reinforced each other. Since 'an outstanding feature of recent Asian history [in East Africa] has been the lack of inspired leadership',[99] the position of the Aga Khan deserves a little more treatment. Since the Imam acted as a religious and non-religious focus, articulation of the relationship between him and the community has found different forms—from the prayer which reads, 'from thee is my strength. . .thou art the Imam, the Truth, the Perspicuous, at mention of whose name prostration is due'[100] and the suggestion that as 'virtually an incarnation of the Deity'[101] he can 'not only interpret but even abrogate'[102] the Quran; to the perception of his functional value as a figure of international standing who can negotiate with national leaders on the community's behalf.

Leadership of this more practical kind has taken different forms, but its significance has lain in its giving direction to the operations of the community, or, in terms of the 'balance' referred to above, periodically recharging the outward-looking content of those operations. The Aga Khan led his community in Uganda in the 1960s by exhortation and *firmans*; by frequent visits; and, not least, by his own example in investing large sums from his own funds in Uganda projects. 'Identification', as noted above, was a consistent theme; 'diversification' was another. Fearful of the economic roots of racial tension, he advised his followers as far as possible to withdraw from trade and move into industry[103] and agriculture, where the IPS took the lead, and to take up the professions.[104] So, in October 1959, he not only urged followers to become teachers and nurses but increased the number of scholarships he was awarding for engineers, economists, and accountants. This advice to seek such specific goals, however, though heeded, had little chance to effect great change in the community in the single decade after independence, in view of the traditionally large numbers of *dukawallahs* (shopkeepers) and *fundis* (artisans). Thus there was no absolute distinction in occupational terms between Ismaili and non-Ismaili at the time of the expulsion; although by that time diversification had already come to include 'diversification' beyond Uganda, as the international nature of IPS and the personal affluence of individual Ismailis in Britain after the expulsion, for example, testify.[105]

It is difficult at the present time to look at the independence decade as anything other than a prelude to the expulsion order of 1972 but it is dangerous to argue inevitability and historically unsound to assume either that events were leading to a general Asian exodus or that the Ismailis in particular felt this to be so. As noted above, the transfer of power in Uganda was delayed by primarily African political problems while the 'Asian problem' was seldom even acknowledged to exist. Similarly,

Obote's first years of power saw the continued prominence of almost exclusively African issues, notably the position of Buganda. When, towards the end of the decade, Obote gave more attention to the Asians, his enactments discriminated between citizen and non-citizen categories, thereby causing little concern to Ismailis, whose citizenship, if not acquired, had been applied for by at least the great majority. So the 1969 Trade Licensing Act required all non-citizens to possess a valid licence from the authorities in order to carry on business—and the Immigration Act of the same year required them to possess an entry permit,[106] in the absence of which they were liable to deportation or heavy fines. This, then, was the perceived value of citizenship—whatever the degree of 'calculation' in the 1962–4 period, citizenship was felt to be an insurance, and, until the 1972 crisis which discriminated in effect in terms of race, enactments and official statements sustained such a feeling. It is true that 'Africanization' as opposed to 'Ugandanization' was practised, but such moves were isolated and sporadic, such as some early seizures of business property in Kampala;[107] discrimination at Makerere University;[108] or, more far-reaching, the final demise of Asian participation in cotton-ginning, which they had pioneered.[109]

There were in the 1960s, therefore, no particular periods or fields of tension for the Ismailis, little affected as they were by the dramatic political developments. An element of caution and secrecy became more marked, however, and some readjustments were necessary. The continued identity of the Ismailis and all its manifestations led to a fear by members of the community of being 'misunderstood'. They became particularly sensitive to public scrutiny of their financial operations and, when government attempted to regulate exchange control, the financial officers of the community had to show that the money collected from the community in Uganda was being retained in the country and not, as tradition demanded, exported to the Aga Khan. Indeed, in 1970, Obote caused more concern than previously with his avowed intention to work towards 'African socialism'.[110] Although this never passed the stage of rhetoric, it did remind the community of the Tanzanian model which had already included nationalization of property—a move which would have affected many Kampala Ismailis —and encouraged members of the community to leave that country.

Herein lay the reason for the Asian welcome to the Amin coup in January 1971, representing not only a change from Obote's implied threat but also better relations between Uganda's government and Great Britain.[111] This calm was disturbed by the Asian census of October and the conference in December. The census was an examination of status, the conference a series of denunciations, with the Madhvanis' and Mehtas'[112] personal contributions rather than the communal

Ismaili achievements cited as exceptions. Moreover, though citizenship status issued 'properly' before the coup would be recognized, any outstanding applications would have to be re-submitted. In the following February, recognition for the Ismailis was publicly given in the *Uganda Argus*, now unmistakably a government mouthpiece, but even the assurance that 'the Asian Ismailis who are citizens and fully pledge their allegiance to the country have nothing to worry about' was qualified by a demand for more social integration.[113]

Nevertheless, citizenship was still regarded as sufficient insurance to render the ninety-day expulsion order of 4 August 1972 inapplicable to the Ismailis who had never regarded themselves as 'British Asians'. The announcement appears to have been received with a mixture of surprise and complacency, amusement and disbelief. Reaction was even more confused in the following weeks as Amin's decrees multiplied. In a decree of 19 August even citizens were included, only to be reversed three days later. Thereafter the citizenship question was rendered irrelevant. The Ismailis found themselves in a similar position to other Asians of whatever status: mass rejection of citizenship claims on technicalities such as late renunciation of British citizenship coincided with a campaign of terror such that, in a typical case, an Ismaili family, though in possession of citizenship papers which had survived official scrutiny, decided to leave the country on hearing of the murder of a relative. In such a way, the hope that Amin might change his mind rapidly gave way to the fear of being the only Asians left in the country. The role of the Ismaili community officials in this crisis could only be one final act of 'accommodation' to circumstances: leaders held their own censuses—the community numbered approximately 12,000[114] in September; offered advice which, for citizens rendered stateless, included that focus on Canada which resulted in the 5,000 total of Asians admitted to that country comprising over 60 per cent Ismailis; and giving financial assistance to those who needed to buy air tickets.[115]

At present one can only conjecture to what extent the expulsion came as a surprise to the Ismailis. One must simply point out that there were signs both of surprise, and of fatalistic acceptance of an end previously anticipated. As far as the former is concerned, one can point to the complacency resulting not only from citizenship status but also from the illusion that all necessary steps, under the guidance of the Aga Khan, had been taken as a precaution against such a day. Yet one must recall the awareness of the Aga Khan that his followers might not have an indefinite future in Uganda,[116] the precedent of Tanzania, and perhaps above all the discreet export of money which, as is now openly acknowledged,[117] was widespread and in which Ismailis undoubtedly shared. In view of these instances, the surprise occasioned by the events of 1972 could be seen as that of timing rather than substance.

In the event the Ismailis' separate identity was ignored in their identification as 'Asians'. The positive pluralism that they had displayed was not enough to counter the historical legacy, the racial stereotypes, the economic relationships, the political weakness and physical conspicuousness of the Asian minority. As traders and competitors for jobs, as aliens and 'strangers' (even 'criminals'), the Asians in Ugandan society were acutely vulnerable to an expulsion order. The Ismailis in particular found that, in the absence of political power or the presence of the external protector, their economic or political moves towards an alliance with the local African leadership—which as one observer pointed out could never be a partnership of equals and was thus unlikely to endure[118]—proved an inadequate substitute. The Ugandan Ismailis had to seek new countries of adoption but they could do so with a reputation as good citizens and as an accomplished and adaptable community, which their expulsion from Uganda, in spite of the individual human suffering it involved, did not destroy.

4

THE GOAN COMMUNITY IN KAMPALA

Jessica Kuper

THE FORMATION OF THE GOAN COMMUNITY

Although, before their expulsion, the Asians comprised just over one per cent of the total population of Uganda,[1] they dominated the urban centres. Their impact on Kampala was very striking: nearly all the stores in the centre of the city were owned by Asians; there were several suburbs which were almost exclusively Asian residential areas; the architecture of most of the older buildings throughout the city was Asian; and women in saris were an integral part of the local scene. One frequently heard an African comment resentfully that Kampala was becoming 'just like Bombay'. Despite this superficial identity and impact, the people classified as Asians were an agglomeration of several different and distinct communities, broadly differentiated on the basis of religion and language, with further distinctions according to area of origin in India or Pakistan, and caste or sect. The majority of the 80,000 Asians were Hindus, from various castes and mainly of Gujerat origin. There were fewer Muslims, but they too were organized into a number of different sects. Finally there were small communities of Asians outside the main religious groupings, Sikhs, Jains, Parsees, and some Roman Catholics, the most important of whom were the Goans.[2]

This chapter is a picture of Kampala Goans based on research done between January 1968 and September 1970. The research focused on the structural features which distinguished Goans from other Asian communities in Kampala, and also on the principles of segmentation within the community itself.

Goans displayed significant contrasts to other overseas Indian communities which had already been studied, in East Africa and elsewhere. They came from the former Portuguese colony of Goa, which was situated on the Indian mainland and was finally taken over by India in 1961. The Goans who came to East Africa were virtually all Roman Catholics, although in Goa itself more than half the population was Hindu. Thus in Uganda they were cut off by religion from their fellow Asians and by race from fellow Ugandans. They did not fit readily into any broad category, though obviously in a racially stratified society they were assigned to the Asian sector, despite their cultural distinctiveness.

Goans formed the only significant community of Christian Indians living in Uganda. (Mangalorians, who were culturally similar, were the only others who were represented in sufficient numbers to be organized in a community, but it was a small one, comprising about twenty-five families.) Goans were also the most 'Westernized' of the Uganda Asians, immediately distinguishable from the Asian majority, bar the few other Christian Asians, by a combination of European dress among the women (practically all Asian men in the city wore Western-type clothes); their Portuguese names; the fact that in general their first language was English; and their distinctive occupational niches.[3] Many Goans worked as clerks in government service, banks, and private businesses—more than half the Asian civil servants recruited during the Protectorate were Goans. At the other end of the social spectrum were the Goan artisans—tailors, cooks, stewards, and carpenters, and, more recently, photographers. The Goan tailor was familiar to all Ugandans, and immortalized in the term 'Gomesi', a name given to the modern, cotton version of the traditional Ganda woman's dress, designed by one Goan tailor, Gomes. Like the clerks, Goan tailors once enjoyed a virtual monopoly. The contrast with the general Asian pattern of economic activity was therefore marked—the Goans were clerks and specialized artisans, while the majority of Asians were small businessmen, or employees of Asian businesses. Few Goans owned businesses, and few worked for other Asians.

Like the other Asians, Goans started coming out to East Africa in significant numbers towards the end of the nineteenth century but, unlike the rest, relatively few came to trade. The majority were recruited on contract to fill low-grade clerical positions in the British East Africa Company, the King's African Rifles, and the railways. Many Goans settled in British India were employed in similar posts. However, writing of the first Goan settlement, in Zanzibar, established in the mid-nineteenth century, Sir Charles Eliot noted: 'The Goanese number some large merchants in their community but are mostly cooks, of which trade they have almost a monopoly. They are also employed extensively as clerks in Government offices.'[4] The successful traders later established branches of their businesses in the coastal towns in East Africa, and gradually some of the more enterprising ventured further into the interior. Goans continued to talk nostalgically of the old days when there were important Goan traders all over East Africa, but while there were indeed successful businessmen they never accounted for more than a small proportion of the total Goan population. The greater significance of the occupational pattern in nineteenth-century Zanzibar was the recruitment of clerks in the administration, for the precedent set here was later followed elsewhere in East Africa.[5] Goans migrated to Kampala itself at the turn of the century. As elsewhere, the self-employed were shopkeepers, while those with less education and of lower caste were tailors, cooks, and stewards. The rest, the majority, were clerks. The pattern of immigration from Goa and from other parts of India where Goans had settled remained remarkably unchanged over the years. At first no documents were required but a new immigrant simply had to be vouched for by someone already living and working in Uganda. Some of the early civil servants were recruited directly in Bombay, but more often Goans did not follow the official channels but found jobs on arrival, generally through the influence of relatives, friends, or fellow villagers who were already employed in the administration. The fact that Goans from a particular village and caste group constituted the majority in certain of the government departments reflects this personal method of recruitment, which the British seem to have encouraged. Thus when a post fell vacant, or a new one was created, a Goan working in the office might be asked by his European superior to suggest someone to fill it. A person from one's own village was often also a relative and from the same caste, a point to which I shall return later. Ties to fellow villagers remained very strong throughout the period of settlement and were even perpetuated among the younger generation of Goans born and brought up in Kampala as a consequence of the form of their parents' network of friends, and through the annual celebration of village feasts.

Goans in business in Kampala adopted a similar procedure of sending for people from Goa, and usually paid their passages, in return for which the new arrival would work for them for a stipulated period without receiving any pay. The immigrant was not, however, permanently bound in a relationship of patron to client. In the early years, when tailoring was a Goan monopoly, many of the tailors were brought from Goa by large shopkeepers, and in these cases sponsorship went across caste lines, for tailors and other artisans were all low caste. Some of the more enterprising tailors would in turn establish their own businesses and recruit as their new assistants caste mates from Goa. Cooks and stewards, also predominantly Goan at first, were traditionally employed as cabin staff on the various shipping lines in the east— hence their nickname, 'shippies'. In East Africa, aside from finding employment with other Goans, they usually worked on the railways.

The early businessmen were Brahmins and Chardos, members of the two top castes. The general Goan view was that the businessmen of their community had provided mainly for the needs of the Europeans in East Africa, a view substantiated by Mangat for Nairobi, where, he noted, 'some of the leading European stores were run by Goans'.[6] Business enterprise per se was not particularly respected by Goans but the European orientation of their commercial enterprises provided them with a certain prestige which they thought the other Asian businesses lacked. In turn, the decline of Goan businesses was generally blamed on the others, the 'Indians' (i.e., all other Asians) who in their crafty way had cheated the scrupulous Goans! What really happened is not clear, but few of the early businesses survived the depression of the 1930s.

By 1921 there were 474 Goans living in Uganda, mainly in Kampala and the Protectorate capital Entebbe, where nearly all the civil servants were stationed. Then there were the Goan district clerks in remote country districts who were 'crucial to the smooth running of the administrative machine'.[7] Men were disproportionately represented, for it was still a time when Africa was regarded by many foreigners as a highly unsuitable place to bring women and children. When the attitude changed, and whole families began to immigrate, women might be sent back to Goa for their confinements and children were still educated at mission schools in Goa or British India. Leave was granted every four years to the civil servants, bank personnel, and even to some of those employed in the private sector. This meant that even for Goans born and brought up in Uganda, Goa was not some remote spot on the map from where their parents had once come but a country which was also likely to have some connotations of 'home'.

For nearly all the early Goan immigrants, the plan was to come out to Uganda to find employment but ultimately to retire to their village in Goa. This was generally still the normal aspiration of older members of the community as late as 1970. One rarely heard of an elderly Goan in Kampala who did not have plans to retire to Goa.

In 1970 there were approximately two thousand Goans living in Kampala (the capital of Uganda since independence), and a further thousand were scattered around Uganda, mainly in Entebbe and Jinja. As a community they could be characterized as predominantly lower middle-class. The business sector had become insignificant, while there was a growing number of university-educated professionals. But the majority were still clerks—using the term in a broad sense, to include both low-grade clerical workers and qualified book-keepers. Most of them would have fallen between these two extremes. Most Goans drew salaries. Few owned homes or had other investments in Uganda, and not more than 250 of the 3,000 Goans were citizens of Uganda. (This is an estimate, and in addition many other Goans had applied for Ugandan passports after independence but their applications were never processed.) Of the rest, there were about an equal number of British and Indian (previously Portuguese) passport holders.

At the economic extremes there was one enormously wealthy family who owned a hotel and cinema and had other major investments in the country. (They were Ugandan citizens but they too departed in the exodus, to Canada.) Then, at the other end of the scale, there were a number of very poor Goans, hardly earning sufficient to live on, whose impecunious circumstances were generally coupled with social difficulties, and who received small financial benefits from Goan or Catholic charities. Most of them lived in Mengo, which was mainly an African suburb, and were tailors by profession. By the time of my enquiries, however, the position of nearly all these families had been ameliorated, since their children were old enough to take jobs and supplement the household income.

Most family incomes were also augmented by the wives going out to work, which they did to a far greater extent than other Asian women. They were mainly secretaries, clerks, and primary school-teachers, but there were also a few graduates in the professions and teaching in secondary schools. The fact that most Goan women worked was also a key factor in their relative emancipation. They often commanded high salaries, and the household budget was usually crucially dependent on their earnings.

By the 1960s, education had become an important avenue to success for the Goans, particularly since there were so few Goan businesses in which the young people could be absorbed, while the lower-grade clerical positions were now being filled by Africans. A Goan needed special qualifications in order to be sure of a livelihood. At the same time it became more and more common for Goans to be educated entirely in Uganda, although a few parents continued to send their children to secondary schools in India.

After Uganda's independence, in 1962, the Goan community began to diminish in size. In the normal course of events, older people retired outside Uganda, and there was also a small exodus of people who feared that Uganda might be the scene of 'another Congo' and post-independence anarchy. Moreover there were virtually no new Goan immigrants to Uganda, as a result of new restrictions on entry and work-permit legislation. After 1968 the position of the Asians deteriorated, and many Goans started to make serious plans to leave. Some were forced into such decisions as a result of being made redundant in their work, usually as a consequence of work-permit restrictions. By 1970 there was a steady flow of non-citizen Goans from Kampala, and 'vouchers' (for entry into Britain), work-permits, and citizenship applications had become staples of conversation in the community.

The older and generally less educated usually returned to Goa, where nearly all of them had some property, or to other parts of western India. Others joined their children in England or in Canada as dependants. The younger people, particularly those with skills, and who had lived all their lives in Uganda, were more inclined towards Britain or Canada. (In 1970, already, there were two Goan clubs in London and one in Toronto which had been established by Goans from East Africa. These were the main cities to which Uganda Goans went.) Finally, there were those Goans who had become Uganda citizens and, in 1970, wanted to stay on in Uganda. After the expulsion, in 1972, hardly any, even these, remained in the country.

GOANS AND ASIANS

Classified for racial purposes in pre- and post-independence Uganda as 'Asians', Goans were nevertheless regarded by the British administrators as somewhat different from the others, and culturally closer to themselves. In some contexts they were indeed recognized as a separate group, as in the censuses. For their own part the Goans retained a strong sense of separate identity, despite the divisions and tensions within their community. This was a multiplex sense of identity, based on ties to Goa, religion, culture, occupation, and language. Although Goans basically accepted the broadly defined and ranked racial categories of colonialism, they saw themselves as the top-ranking community within the Asian section, by virtue of their European-ness. (Other Asian communities also regarded themselves as superior, on the basis of other criteria, e.g. business success.) For the Goans, the 'others' were 'Indians', while the 'Indians' in turn joked about the Goans as 'Brown Europeans'.[8] Goans thus stifled anything in their culture and their communal life which smacked of 'Indian-ness', at least in the presence of outsiders.

Their refusal to see themselves as Indians stems partly from the fact that until 1961 Goa was indeed only geographically part of India, and the bulk of the Goans in Kampala at the time were citizens of Portugal. When Goa was taken over by India, or 'liberated', as some of the more pro-Indian Goans refer to the event, this did not alter the self-image of the Goans, who still had other grounds for regarding themselves as more like 'Westerners' (as they sometimes put it) than 'Easterners'. Even the tiny minority of Goans who did refer to themselves as 'Indians', and who were politically in favour of India's takeover, often differentiated themselves from other Asians in the Ugandan context.

The British were said to have preferred the Goans for cultural reasons; the Africans were thought also to prefer them to other Asians, because they could not be regarded as economic exploiters. These claims were a combination of fact and illusion, and, ultimately, their differences from the rest did not help them at all.

Goans' friendship networks were nearly always concentrated within the Goan community, though naturally Goans were forced into contact with non-Goans in their work, neighbourhoods, and so on. Other Asians were the outsiders with whom they felt most comfortable, in spite of all their prejudices and show of antipathy. It was pressure from the wider community which forced a man to act as an Asian rather than as a Patel, Ismaili, or Goan and, according to one anthropologist, it was this externally imposed recognition that the Asian communities were similar in one dimension, if different in others, which resulted in the elaboration of joking relationships between communities.[9]

By 1970 there were still Goan clubs and a Goan primary school. None of these was exclusively Goan any longer but they were predominantly so, in numbers and in flavour. When the clubs were opened to non-Goans (largely as a result of government pressure to dissolve 'communal' organizations), the Goans may have hoped to attract Europeans but, in fact, most of the new members were other Asians, with only a handful of whites and Africans. On the other hand, the few marriages which took place outside the community were more often with Europeans. Perhaps religion was the principal limiting factor in this case.

Finally, Goans and other Asians were brought together in various organizations, as in the pre-independence Legislative Council, which had Asian representatives, but no member specifically represented the Goans. Goans felt strongly that they should be granted separate political representation,[10] and were never happy to have their identity submerged in an all-Asian association. In a letter written to *The Goan Voice*, the Goan weekly newspaper in Nairobi, this commonly held view was stated: 'It is a fact that the whole Goan outlook and culture is the result of what Portugal has been able to impart. . .[and it] makes us so different from others.'[11]

Few Goans were ever politically active in Uganda. This can partly be explained by the fact that government employees were not allowed to engage in local politics, and by their greater political interest in events in Goa itself. Few Asians, moreover, were optimistic about their fate in independent Uganda; they feared the worst and had no desire to see the end of British rule. Once independent, African rulers in Uganda hardly encouraged Asian participation in the affairs of the country. But despite the increased pressure exerted on all Asians, there were still no signs of unity being forged between the Goans and the other Asian communities, or even among Goans themselves.

DIVISIONS WITHIN THE COMMUNITY

Goans complained constantly about the antagonisms and discrimination which divided the Kampala community. They cited lack of facilities to help poorer Goans and the quarrels which had bedevilled practically all Goan organizations, and they remarked that if one Goan did well, it was seldom due to any help he had received from other Goans. This was perhaps an overstatement but it was true that the community in Kampala suffered from much friction and factional strife.

Caste was the major force which divided the community. Nearly all the Goans in East Africa were Catholics, and Goa had been forcibly Catholicized by the Portuguese in the sixteenth century. For four hundred years, however, Catholic Goans continued to observe some of the rules of the Hindu caste system, and allocated themselves to caste categories in the traditional Hindu idiom. In Kampala they divided themselves into four main castes. These were Brahmin and Chardo (Kshatriya), the upper castes, Sudir (Shudra) and the untouchables, the lower castes. Instead of several sub-castes constituting the untouchable caste, in Kampala there was only one out-group in this category, the Mar (Mahar), traditionally weavers by occupation. This caste hierarchy almost replicated the traditional Hindu *varna* classification, but lacked the third *varna*, Vaishya, the merchants. There was yet a further category, Gauddo, usually ranked below Sudir in the hierarchy but above Mar. However, many younger Goans did not know about the Gauddo, while a few people insisted that this was not a caste at all but rather represented the original tribal inhabitants of Goa.

These major caste categories were not normally subdivided into sub-castes. Only at the lower levels were such distinctions recognized. Thus a Sudir might refer to himself as Sudir by caste when discussing his status vis-à-vis the whole community, while on another occasion he might be a Render (toddy-tapper) as opposed to his Sudir neighbour, who was a Kharive (fisherman), and such sub-categories were also ranked. These subtle distinctions were not usually relevant in the context of Uganda, where the *varna*-type categories operated for purposes of marriage and status like typical Indian sub-castes (*jati*). Brahmins distinguished themselves only in terms of origin in Goa, a factor tied up in turn with wealth and 'aristocracy', but not amounting to sub-caste identities. Goans did not use Indian terms for 'caste', using the Portuguese/English term 'caste', and sometimes even 'class', when referring to these categories.

Caste was regarded mainly as an ascriptive status category, and there was no religious sanction behind its perpetuation, a crucial difference from a Hindu caste system. Still, as among Hindus, a person who was a

Brahmin, or even a Chardo, started off with a built-in advantage in Catholic Goan society, and his status was usually bolstered by a better economic position. Status could also be achieved through education or wealth, but a wealthy or educated Sudir was unlikely to be admired by most members of the higher castes. The latter would not usually barter their status for wealth through an arranged marriage, and there were cases in which the successful low-caste man would move away from the community and seek and be granted respect from non-Goans.

Most of the older members of the community were able to place others according to their caste. Even if they were not acquainted with a particular person, they claimed to be able to tell his caste—from the way he spoke Konkani, the Indian language that most of the older people could speak or understand, and which had definite local as well as caste dialectical variations; from his village of origin, for certain castes predominated in certain villages, particularly among the immigrants to Uganda; and from the way in which he conducted himself in society, the assumption being that lower-caste people were 'rougher', while those from the higher castes were more 'cultured'. Even dress was believed to be a give-away, for Sudirs, according to the Brahmins, liked gaudy colours. Younger Goans were less adept at telling the caste of their associates, and showed less interest in caste, although sooner or later most of them picked up the cues, and caste matters became more relevant to them in their adult lives. Others who knew that the caste system operated in their community might not even be able to name their own caste, and said that they belonged to 'caste one' or 'caste two', whatever the case might be. In very rare instances they did not even know that much.

From the early days caste formed the main basis of division within the Kampala community. Moreover, the system was reinforced by the fact that caste and class were so closely correlated. Thus when a few Goans, mainly Brahmins, got together and started the Kampala Goan Institute (which changed its name after Uganda's independence to the Kampala Institute), in the first decade of the century, they excluded tailors, cooks, and stewards, and others who were illiterate in Portuguese or English and were not of 'high social standing'. These were the ostensible reasons for exclusion but what was also crucial was that thereby these rules effectively excluded most of the low-caste Goans. The majority of those excluded were tailors, who then decided to start their own club, accepting tailors as full members, and others as honorary members. The St Francis Xavier Society of Tailors continued to exist in 1970, despite the fact that the Kampala Institute had by then modified their membership rules so that practically any Goan could join. Still, tailors themselves, other artisans, and even their children who had usually moved into clerical positions continued to feel discriminated against and shunned by other Goans and felt more at ease with their own kind. They were always at a disadvantage in the Kampala Institute. For example, they could not have aspired to any key committee positions because they were seen as inferior 'tailor people' who would never really escape their lowly origins, and they were generally treated with disdain by all other Goans of high status.

The two clubs represented two almost distinct sub-communities among the Goans, but the separation of high-caste and low-caste Goans was not absolute, for there was always a small proportion of Sudirs, who, from the beginning, were clerks and were allowed to join the Kampala Institute. I was told that in the early days of the Kampala Goan Institute, the Brahmins held most of the important positions on the committee, but a Chardo who had become a prominent member of the community could also aspire to be club president. Within the Institute factions used to form constantly on the basis of caste, and fights based on caste recur in the annals. This was no longer the case in 1970 but caste prejudice still existed among some members and it was still possible to pick out a few cliques which were practically uni-caste.

About two-thirds of the Kampala Goans were members of the Kampala Institute. The clubhouse was a two-storey building on Buganda Road in an area densely populated by Goan civil servants. Every evening the bar was opened, and men gathered there after work to chat, to play cards or snooker. Other sports brought people together in the late afternoon. A tombola game was held nearly every Sunday evening, there were frequent dances, and occasional week-end sports competitions against Goan clubs from Nairobi, Entebbe, and Dar es Salaam. In certain weeks of the year, like 'Ladies' Week' and 'Married Week', different activities would be organized on every day, usually culminating in a dance on the Saturday night. Christmas and New Year were a time for special festivities. On most occasions, except dances, whole families would usually turn out, and it was not unusual for the different generations to be seated together for the gathering. Small babies were often included: they would be brought along, beautifully dressed, and passed around from one admirer to the next. The elderly members of the community continued to attend the dances, in order to watch the spectacle, meet their friends and, perhaps most of all, to keep an eye on their children. Friendship between boy and girl across caste lines was their main fear and preoccupation.

Although in principle Goans could have joined many other organizations after independence, including formerly European clubs, the

Kampala Institute continued to be a thriving social club. The tailor club, on the other hand, had seen its heyday some years before. The club had been established around 1910, but it was only in the 1930s that the tailors built themselves a clubhouse in Old Kampala, an area where Asians concentrated, and very close to Mengo where most of the tailors lived. Their club was renovated and expanded in the 1950s, with funds received from the Portuguese government, but the building was considerably more modest than the Kampala Institute. It had no sports facilities, and generally in its latter years was occupied solely by a few men playing cards and drinking. It was dedicated to St Francis Xavier and some members of the tailor community would make regular visits to the club to pray at the elaborate altar in the main hall. During the 1950s the club had been the social centre for the members and their families, who would gather there frequently. The language among the adults was generally Konkani, in sharp contrast to the Kampala Institute, where English was used almost exclusively. But in 1970 there were less than thirty tailors left in Kampala, and very few cooks, stewards, and artisans, formerly honorary members, and not all of these were enthusiastic club-goers. Old age, arguments, and scandals kept some people away, and in the event there were usually not enough members to form a quorum at meetings. Moreover, bitter arguments used constantly to flare up between the regular committee members, often provoked by the disappearance of club money. Since non-tailors were not allowed to become full voting members of the club, they could merely observe the mishandling of affairs with increasing fury. Disillusioned, and powerless to effect a change, they lost interest. The once celebrated events at the tailor club, the annual Ladies' Day Carnival, the Konkani concerts, were no longer held. Only the feast of St Francis Xavier, an important religious occasion for most Goans, was still celebrated and attended by many Goans, even non-tailors. The hall continued to be booked for private occasions, however, for weddings or christenings of members of the tailor community. Another reason for the decline of the club was that the children of tailors and other manual workers, having received some education and therefore better placed occupationally, now wanted to win acceptance from other Goans. This was not easy, although they could now join the Kampala Institute, and their marriages were predominantly within their own sector of the Goan community. While younger 'tailors' did often make use of the sporting facilities of the Kampala Institute, their parents, less at ease and less acceptable, were satisfied with the fact of membership. At the Institute they sat in small, self-contained groups. Their reason for becoming members was that membership of the Kampala Institute enhanced their status within the tailor community but once accepted they seldom went to the Institute, where they continued to feel shunned and humiliated.

Caste exclusiveness was most evident in relation to marriage. People who were fairly liberal about caste matters and did not restrict their friendships on a caste basis often lodged objections when their children wished to marry outside the caste, particularly into a lower caste. Even younger Goans, who were freer from caste prejudices, tended to oppose intercaste marriage.

In the past all marriages had been arranged, and were within the caste, except in a few instances when a lower-caste family had acquired wealth or education and was able to marry up. In 1970 there were still many arranged or 'proposal' marriages among Kampala Goans, although the bulk of marriages were by then what the Goans called 'love marriages'. Most girls brought some form of dowry with them, and even these 'love marriages' normally involved dowry and were intra-caste, despite the rationalization that it was a love-match, resulting from a free choice. There were many cases in which parents vetoed their child's first choice on grounds of caste. Children might then decide to marry against their parents' wishes but more frequently they submitted and either looked for a person who was of the same caste or accepted an arranged match. (Goans also explained the fact that love-matches were generally intra-caste on the grounds that people of the same caste were naturally attracted to one another because of cultural factors.)

Marriages that did occur between members of different castes were mostly between adjacent castes, a Brahmin-Chardo match being the most usual. The children of an intercaste marriage belonged to their father's caste. One might therefore expect more women than men to have married upwards but there was a more or less equal proportion of hypergamous and hypogamous marriages. Members of the tailor community tended to marry within their community, which was largely coincident with the Sudir caste.

Caste was significant in yet another field of social organization, the village unions. Goans referred to other Goans who originated from the same village as *gaumbau* (village cousin). This tie was often cited as the basis for friendship, even between two Goans who had lived all their lives in Uganda. In many cases common village origin also meant common caste, at least among the immigrants to East Africa; in fact, where this was not the case, shared village membership was not a sufficient basis for friendship. There were a few villages which were exclusively represented in Kampala by Brahmins, and members of these villages displayed the strongest esprit de corps. Co-villagers formed themselves into associations called village unions whose main function it was to organize a feast and a Mass to celebrate the feast day of the patron saint of the village. Any Goan who could claim direct descent from a villager through either parent or grandparent was eligible for membership of the village union. Not all villages represented in Kampala formed the basis for these corporate groups, the limiting factor being the size of the representation and its caste composition. It was significant that the effective unions were predominantly uni-caste in composition and that other villages represented in Kampala by both high and low castes were often not able to organize themselves at all.

Generation was another basis of differentiation within the community. Breakaway sports and social clubs were formed by younger Goans, and some of these, significantly, received enthusiastic support from the sons of tailors. However, most members of such breakaway clubs as the Horizons and Kololians were also members of the Kampala Institute, which meant that the clubs did not really threaten to divide the Goans along new lines. A factor which might one day have become important, however, was that many of the younger Goans who were active in these breakaway clubs were Uganda citizens.

In addition to these recreational clubs, to at least one of which most Goans belonged, there was the Kampala Goan Association, which aimed to give financial help to needy Goan families, and also to unite the Goan community and to foster understanding between Goans and other communities in Uganda—and furthermore, to preserve Goan culture and traditions. However, its achievements were somewhat limited, and it lacked funds and interested members.

During the 1950s the Portuguese government donated Shs 50,000 to the Goans in Uganda, through a body called the Central Council of Goan Associations. This was the period preceding the Indian takeover of Goa, when the Goans in Uganda were split into two camps, based mainly on opposing sympathies to the Indians and the Portuguese. Both factions set up their own committee and claimed to be the rightful representatives of the Uganda Goans. Despite court proceedings and attempts at arbitration by respected members of the community, the dispute remained unresolved, and in 1970 the Portuguese grant was still frozen in a bank account. It is worth noting that while the pro-Portuguese faction was led by a low-caste lawyer and was supported by most tailors, it was not possible to categorize the two factions solely on the basis of caste or any other social criteria. This was a particularly disruptive incident, and yet one could almost believe that the Goans were eager to get involved in disputes of this kind in their public life, irrespective of the consequences.

The other charity organization to which Goans could appeal for assistance was the Catholic society of St Vincent de Paul which also helped several needy Goan families in Kampala with money, food, and clothing. The Kampala Goan Association gave a small donation to this society, while most of its key members were Goans, who were usually entrusted with those Goan cases that came up—but it was not a specifically Goan or Goan-organized body.

Among Goans, every organization had its factions based on differences of caste, class, political attachments, age, and, finally, citizenship. This was in striking contrast to the Ismaili Khojas, whose leader was the Aga Khan, and whose communal organization was the essence of cohesion and cooperation.[12] There were several important reasons for the success of the Ismailis. They were a wealthy community and under the quasi-divine guidance of the Aga Khan they were obliged to donate some of their private funds to communal causes and to help poorer Ismailis. Miscreants were liable to strict public censure and fines. Furthermore, the Aga Khan had insisted that they become local citizens. Consequently they had to adjust more radically to the coming of independence. Thus in 1970 they were, ironically, the only community which thought of themselves as being secure in Uganda, and who could therefore plan for the future. (When the bulk of Ismailis left with all the other Asians, their resettlement abroad, mainly in Canada, was conducted with the efficiency that had marked all Ismaili affairs in Uganda.) Finally, the Muslim Ismailis were not divided by caste.

Clearly the Goan community fared very badly by comparison. Yet it would be wrong to ignore the features which did create a feeling of unity among Kampala Goans for, despite all, Goans did retain an identity distinct from that of the other Asian communities. Sporting achievements were a great source of pride to Goans, and on the playing field more than anywhere else Goans felt united and shared a common goal. Religion was another binding force. The fact that Kampala Goans were Catholics distinguished them from other Asians in Uganda and provided them with a feeling of solidarity. Most Goans in Kampala attended services at Christ the King, an attractive church close to the city centre which was usually referred to as the 'Goan church'. Goans spoke very disparagingly of the few members of the community who had lost their faith or who had embraced a new religion.

Finally, death was said to bring the whole community together at the graveside of the deceased. Many Goans told me how they would make a special effort to attend any Goan funeral, whatever the status of the deceased and regardless of whether or not they had any social or familial connection with him. This was not often true, however, for only the well-known, well-placed and well-liked had large funerals in Kampala. When such a person died in particularly tragic circumstances, then all the more people would come to mourn for him. However, it was very rare for upper-caste Goans to attend the funeral of a 'tailor'. As a low-caste Goan priest remarked bitterly, 'You can tell who has died just by looking at the crowd gathered around the grave.' A man's death was rather more likely to unite the members of the sub-community, and it was a time when personal animosities were forgotten; but the wider claim that it united all Goans was an exaggeration.

Practically all Goan organizations had their factions. The Goan Brahmin doctor who was appointed to the Legislative Council in Uganda in 1957 as a representative of the whole Asian sector made a special plea to members of his own community to 'sink all differences, discard petty jealousies and work for the welfare of the community',[13] but somehow Goans never could.

Nairobi also witnessed the failure of many Goan schemes due to personal enmities of the same kind, based particularly on caste. In fact the Nairobi Goans were even more divided than the Kampala Goans. The sheer size of the Nairobi community—about 3,000—facilitated the multiplication of Goan organizations and encouraged the greater exclusiveness of the different castes. But the smaller number of Goans in Kampala enforced greater interaction, which many might have preferred to avoid. Morris, writing on the emergence of castes and sects as communities in East Africa, stressed the importance of numbers: 'Whenever the members of a particular caste or sect grew large enough for its members to consort mainly with one another, it was not long before they emerged as a distinct communal group.'[14] This argument could also be applied to the emergence of intra-community sections. In the smallest Goan settlements in East Africa, Goans of all castes appeared to get along with each other: Brahmins reported having been friendly with tailors in Iringa and Tabora, both small towns in Tanzania where there were only a few Goan families.

Among other Asians in Uganda almost every caste or sect was the basis for the emergence of a community. Attempts had been made to unite all the different communities under an umbrella body, the Central Council of Indian Associations, but as all the constituent communities had their own separate communal aspirations, the plan was doomed to failure.[15] At the level of the Goan community, similar processes operated. The Central Council for Goan Associations tried unsuccessfully to unite Goans at a time when the tailor community and the Kampala Goan Institute association had already solidified.

Had the Kampala Goans formed a united community it would have been scarcely less surprising than to find Patels, Lohanas, and low-caste service Hindus forming a viable Hindu community. This did not happen, since these castes represented different and unequal sectors of the total Hindu population in Uganda, which had always been separated from one another socially, and which were endogamous, and economically unequal. On the other hand, since there were comparatively few Goans, it was not possible for separate Goan caste-based communities to emerge for all purposes. Endogamy could be maintained, as could two clubs, but all Goans had to attend the same church and primary school. The broad differentiation which existed between the top two castes and the lower castes, roughly equivalent to the class divisions within the communities on the basis of education, occupation, and income, was perhaps the limit of practical differentiation.

Moreoever, the Protectorate government had insisted on treating Goans as a unit while accepting, on the other hand, that it was impossible to ignore the internal differences among Hindus and among Muslims, whose separatist aspirations they reluctantly accepted. If their attitude towards Goans had been different, for example on the issue of schools, as in the 1930s when the two sectors of the Goan community tried to set up their own schools, this might have fostered rather than thwarted the fission in the community. But instead they imposed a degree of cooperation and interaction.

More broadly, the development of the Goan community must in the end be seen in the context of the development of Ugandan society. This is particularly true in respect to their efforts to maintain a distinct identity and forge a distinct destiny for themselves. The British had defined an 'Asian' category but the Asians preferred to identify themselves in communal terms, and in some contexts the British were forced to treat with them as communities. When African rule succeeded colonialism the new government alternated between imposing a categorical opposition based on citizenship, and attempts to mobilize populist sentiment on the basis of race. The racial definition, perhaps the most indelible legacy of colonialism, came to override all the rest with bitter and irreparable consequences. This was one logical development of the colonial creation of a plural society. Class factors were mediated by this primary racial definition, and at no stage was there any real choice for the 'Asians'. The variant adaptations of the different Asian communities were in the end irrelevant.

One can speculate about the growing communities of Goans in London and Toronto. Informal reports so far indicate that disagreements have already led to splits in the new clubs, and these reflect the underlying tensions I have already discussed. But there are other factors which alter the situation: the new and different external context, the relative dearth of older Goans, and the increased difficulties in the way of visiting Goa, all of which favour the diminution of the significance of caste. To many Goans in Kampala, the frame of reference was frequently Goa. In England or in Canada the frame of reference has become Kampala or Uganda, or East Africa. I hope that the description of the Kampala Goans given here will help in the future understanding of the Goan refugees from Uganda in these countries.

5

THE HINDUS OF BAKULI[1]

Rohit Barot

Although the Indians[2] have been uniquely distinct in East Africa, and even though their participation in each East African country has had far-reaching social, economic, and political consequences, only a handful of sociologists and anthropologists have studied them. Systematic microsociological studies of Indian groups in the tradition of African sociology and anthropology are unknown. Consequently Indians have only a small place in the ethnographic literature of East Africa. Besides some journal articles and a small number of papers presented at Makerere University, published work on Indians includes five studies. Earlier works of Hollingsworth[3] and Delf[4] comprise useful general surveys which remain almost entirely descriptive, while a later collection of essays[5] has six contributiors among whom only one is a social anthropologist. The volume represents once again a general survey of Indians in East Africa with some reflections on their future in the area. Morris[6] presents a partial overview of the Indians in Uganda with specific reference to religion, caste, family, and kinship among several Hindu and Muslim groups. Morris and Bharati have contributed essays on caste among the East African Indians to a volume on overseas Indian communities[7] and recently Mangat's detailed historical study[8] is a scholarly addition to the growing body of literature on East African Indians.

This chapter is primarily an exercise in historical sociology as most Indians have left Uganda following their expulsion in 1972. While the conference from which this volume has emerged focused attention primarily on a number of historical and contemporary issues, not much attention was paid to differences relating to internal distinctions within the Indian population. The material presented here attempts to shed some light on this issue by outlining how the Hindus used folk categories and how they discerned the realities of caste in Kampala.

As for the important question of the relationship between castes and the dynamics of local economics and politics, what is generally evident is that Indian dominance in trade and commerce was a conspicuous feature of life in Kampala and other Ugandan towns. What much less is known about is the relationship between a particular dominant caste, such as the Lohanas, and their control over specific aspects of trade and commerce in Uganda. Unfortunately this is not something on which research has yet shed much light.

A topic the conference participants did discuss briefly was the degree to which the organization of Indian castes and sects was a factor which may have contributed towards their general exodus from East and Central Africa and their sudden expulsion from Uganda in particular. In the Ugandan instance, apart from the post-colonial isolation of Indians, the complexity of internal Ugandan politics would have to be taken into account in order to isolate the main factors which brought about the expulsion decree. While a detailed discussion of this topic also falls outside the scope of my contribution, it is worth mentioning that the development of social structure in colonial East Africa—a structure marked by the three-tier system of Europeans at the top, Indians in the middle, and Africans at the bottom—created a harsh and unjust pattern of inequality for the indigenous population. Before caste and sectarian communities proliferated, colonial segregation had already effectively restricted Indians to urban areas.[9] The development of caste and sectarian communities then reinforced and enhanced the exclusiveness and insularity of the Indian population as a whole. There is no doubt that this privileged exclusiveness on the part of Indians made them particularly vulnerable to African criticism, especially when they were non-citizens. On this matter, although it is possible to argue that there is some relationship between closed Indian community life and the expulsion of Indian communal groups from Uganda, in my view this relationship is of secondary importance in the total process of post-colonial economic and political change in Uganda. This said, the rest of this chapter will focus on the data on caste I collected in the Bakuli neighbourhood of Kampala. In discussing this, I have retained the use of the ethnographic present as a useful heuristic device.

First of all, I introduce the Bakuli neighbourhood. Secondly, I attempt to present some material on caste from the perspective of Hindus who lived there. Since the Portuguese introduced the term caste in Goa in the sixteenth century, it has been freely used to describe the organization of Indian society. Used in a general non-specific sense, caste as a ranked endogamous category tends to be ambiguous and confusing, especially when it obscures levels of segmentation relevant locally. As I conducted my research in Bakuli, I gradually became aware of the vernacular folk categories Gujerati Hindus use in their everyday discourse to define specific realities of caste. I documented these as my investigation went on. I also collected supplementary information from *Lohana Sandesh*—a Gujerati magazine published from Jinja in Uganda dealing with the social affairs of East African Lohanas. As anthropologists view their findings in a comparative context, I have also made some comparative remarks on this issue in the concluding part of the chapter.

BAKULI

Bakuli used to fall outside the Kampala City Council boundary and was under the formal control of Mengo Town Council. After the latter was dissolved in 1967, the extended boundary of Kampala included Bakuli and other areas previously under the Mengo Town Council. Though Bakuli is now incorporated into Kampala city, some of the old contrast between Kampala and Mengo remains. Bakuli Indians are well aware of this. They know that the better-off Indians living in Kololo and areas close to the city centre often see Bakuli and the surrounding parts of Rubaga, Kisenyi, and Makara as 'slums'. The Bakuli residents themselves view the situation differently. Although they grumble about *murram* roads, red dust discolouring their houses, overflowing septic tanks, often untended rubbish heaps, and an almost total lack of street lighting, they also point out several amenities they enjoy over those living in Rubaga, Kisenyi, and Makara. The adjacent area of Old Kampala has a primary and secondary school easily accessible to children of Bakuli residents. Similarly the proximity of Mengo hospital, a bus station, a vegetable market, and some small shops offset other disadvantages. Thus Bakuli residents see themselves as living in a better area than those living in Kisenyi where living conditions are far more impoverished.

An old Ganda resident of Bakuli explained that Bakuli refers to Barclays—an Englishman whose name was rendered Bakuli over the course of time. Officially the area is known as Namirembe Estate—a nomenclature only known to those few unwilling to identify their residence in Bakuli. Bakuli refers to a fairly large city ward so that expressions such as 'upper' Bakuli, 'lower' Bakuli, and 'their' Bakuli establish differences as residents perceive them within the area. My study only extended to two streets in Namirembe Estate. These streets constituted my research unit viewed within the wider context of urban life in Kampala.

THE INDIANS OF BAKULI

Almost all the Indians of Bakuli came to Uganda from Maha Gujerat (comprising Gujerat, Kathiawar or Saurashtra, and Kutch), Punjab, and Goa. Migration from these specific regions has enabled the Hindus to achieve a degree of cultural uniformity in East Africa. To outsiders this uniformity appears to characterize all Indians. As a result one tendency has been to see Indians as belonging to a single undifferentiated community. For instance, Morris describes how the Protectorate colonial administration viewed and treated Indians as a single group.[10] In the initial period of settlement in Uganda, the Indians presented a united front to the colonial authorities. Only as time went on did separateness and differences between groups become publicly known. From 1910 onwards these groups demanded separate graveyards, mosques, and temples. The unique identity of each party also came out well in the field of education. Early on the Protectorate government had set up an Indian school in Kampala. Later, especially in the 1950s, in order to meet growing educational demands each Indian section established a denominational school for itself. Consequently at the level of elementary school education there came into being a Sanatan Dharma Mandal School for the Hindus, a Ramghria Sikh School for the Sikhs, a Goan school for the Roman Catholic Goans, a Muslim school for Sunni Muslims, an Ismailia school for the Ismailis, and an Ithnasheri school for Ithnasheris. In the process of differentiation which has marked the development of Indian groups, Shia Imami Ismailis, under the direction of their spiritual leader, the Aga Khan, were particularly successful in demonstrating and establishing their unique separateness through a complex of interlocking Ismaili associations and other organizations, especially in the economic field. Some of the semblance of unity that the Indian community had maintained earlier was thus shattered as Hindus, Muslims, Sikhs, and Goans emerged as separate communities. Each attempted to further its own interests rather than those of the Indian community as a whole, which by then hardly existed with any kind of corporate solidarity. Morris describes the emergence of these groups and sects as a process of 'communal crystallisation'.[11]

The Indians of Bakuli come from all the major categories of the Indian population in Uganda: 107 households are divided into 49 Hindus, 7 Sikhs, 13 Sunni Muslims, 22 Shia Ismailis, 3 Shia Ithnasheris, and 13 Goans. These households are of varying complexity, from a Goan bachelor who lived by himself to joint families made up of husband, wife, and their married children, or two brothers with their wives and children, which are the more common.

Apart from the Indian families I was concerned with, a large number of Baganda families live in Bakuli. In the streets where I carried out my work, a small number of Baganda families lived at the back of a large building occupied by Indian families. Although Bakuli is often regarded as an African area, social contact between Indians and Africans, apart from their brief encounters in shops, is non-existent. During my stay there was not a single instance of an Indian knowing an African as an equal or a friend. Separation and distance between the two sides is a marked feature of life in Bakuli.

Among the Indians in Bakuli, cultural differences are typical in the neighbourhood. For example, Hindus in Bakuli are Gujerati-speakers from Gujerat, Kathiawar, or Kutch. Even though some might come from one of these cultural areas, they still retain among themselves minute differences revealing which specific part of Gujerat, Kathiawar, or Kutch they come from. Similarly Sikhs from the Punjab area maintain a distinct cultural identity of their region in language, religion, dress, and food habits. Depending upon the part of India or Pakistan they come from, Sunni Muslims are either Gujerati-speakers or Punjabi/Urdu-speakers. Shia Muslims—both Ismailis and Ithnasheris—though religiously distinct from the Hindus, share many Gujerati cultural attributes with them. In contrast the Roman Catholic Goans by and large dissociate themselves from other Indian groups.

Even though the social network of one's own kith and kin is usually the central focus of one's activities, people do maintain contacts and relationships outside this social universe. Deriving from the physical fact of nearness, Bakuli Indians in the two streets share an orbit of community character in many activities. Consequently, many face-to-face relationships in the neighbourhood build up. For instance, to establish a code of conduct, close neighbours from different backgrounds invoke a kinship idiom. In other words, using a common set of kinship terms they weave intimate patterns of social relationships. Neighbours cooperate and participate in activities of common interest; they organize security arrangements and share the expense of hiring watchmen and contribute funds to keep the surroundings clean. In the event of marriage or death, neighbourhood participation is quite usual. On festive occasions like Diwali, Christmas, or Id, individuals from different groups join in common festivity.

I concentrated my research among the Hindus who form the majority Indian population in Bakuli. Divided into 11 different birth-ascribed endogamous groups, they make up 49 households and invariably remain an important part of life in the neighbourhood. The numerically dominant groups are Lohana and Patidar, respectively numbering 17 and 14 households. Rapid communication has enabled the members of such groups in India to form wider regional entities. Srinivas has termed such process 'horizontal solidarity'.[12] This concept can also be applied to East African Indian groups such as the Lohanas who have sought to unify themselves in East Africa under their central East African Lohana Supreme Council. This does not apply to Patels coming from Kutch and Gujerat who have maintained separateness in East Africa by prohibiting intermarriages between them.

In sum, the Hindu groups in Bakuli enjoy a high degree of cohesiveness and internal solidarity. Apart from their participation in the neighbourhood, members of each group spend a considerable time together in business and recreational activities. In the final analysis the group one belongs to takes precedence over the affairs which affect one as a member of Bakuli neighbourhood.

VARNA, NĀT-JĀT, AND ATAK

In the classical Hindu scriptures, caste is conceived in the sense of *varnas*. According to this well-known fourfold classification, among Hindus the highest category is that of Brahmins or priests, below them come Kshatriya or warriors, then Vaishya the merchants, finally followed by Shudra, usually known as workers or servants. The untouchables, who are left outside this classification, form a separate fifth category. What is important to note is that this classical scheme does not refer to specific groups as such. With the exception of Brahmins who occupy the top place at the local level, warriors, merchants, and workers do not exist as corporate groups. What is the relevance of the *varna* scheme for East African Hindus? To answer this question, first of all something should be said about the usefulness of *varna* in India. In the subcontinent it enables people from different regions to discern each other's identity in all-India terms. In other words, to take a hypothetical example, a man from Uttar Pradesh and one from Kerala can place each other according to the *varna* classification without having to find correspondences between two otherwise very dissimilar systems of ranking. Thus *varna* as a traditional category has a pan-Indian relevance.

For the East African Hindu *varna* seems to have had little or no meaning for defining social relations. This does not mean, however, that awareness of *varna* is totally absent. During my fieldwork in Bakuli several Lohana elders I talked to called themselves Kshatriya, describing themselves as men of action, adding that, as Kshatriya, they were descendants of Rama, the hero of the Hindu epic Ramayana. Similarly, in a pamphlet published at the inauguration of a Hindu temple in Kampala in 1961, the Lohana secretary of the religious body Sanatan Dharma Mandal called himself a Kshatriya whose duty it was to protext the Brahmins.[13] Apart from such occasional references, not much importance is attached to *varna*. It is usually the older East African Indians who are familiar with it, rather than the young for whom it has no bearing in everyday life.

Distinct from *varna* in each Indian region at the local level are birth-ascribed endogamous social groups known as *jatis*. The Gujerati-speaking Hindus refer to these groups as *nāt-jāt*.[14] In a traditional setting such groups are arranged in a hierarchy with the Brahmin at the top, the Harijan (untouchable) at the bottom and the groups such as merchants, farmers, craftsmen, washermen, oil-pressers, and leather-workers occupying intermediate positions which are more or less well-defined. That is to say, except for the Brahmin at the top and the untouchable at the bottom, disagreement often prevails between adjacent groups as to what their proper place is on the local social ladder. The ranking order depends on the opposition between purity and im-purity which defines separation between groups and their approximate ranking on the hierarchical order in relation to the Brahmin at the top. In addition, the economic interdependence between the groups is marked by each *jāt* group following its traditional hereditary occupa-tion.

How far do the East African Hindus observe the norms of the traditional hierarchy of *nāt-jāt* groups? Once the members of *nāt-jāt* groups leave their local area either to settle in cities or overseas, a basic change takes place altering the nature of caste relations outside its local setting. First of all, as David Pocock has shown,[15] the hierarchy does not emerge in East Africa as the Hindus living there are drawn from widely different areas and do not share a set of consensual ideas about what a hierarchical order should be in East Africa. As a consequence they have failed to develop in East Africa a replica of the graded ranking order. Free from the traditional constraints of a hierarchical order, they have also largely abandoned the values of purity and impurity which only acquire real meaningfulness within the context of a local area in India. While it is migration and overseas settlement that brings about this basic change, some ideas about hierarchy and purity do nevertheless remain. For instance, a diffuse awareness of some people being higher (*unchā*) and others being lower (*nichā*) finds expression in Bakuli, though it does not relate to a structurally constituted system of statuses such as is found in traditional India. Similarly, values of purity and impurity find some residual continuity in certain rules observed within the household. In Bakuli members of a family would refrain from drinking water from the same glass. Once used, it would be regarded as having become 'unclean'.

As for the hereditary specialization of occupations, only a small number of goldsmiths, carpenters, and barbers follow their traditional calling. Its pursuit is not obligatory as hierarchical constraints through economic interdependence between *jāt* groups is lacking in East Africa. Besides, the main preoccupations of Gujerati Hindus, trading and com-merce, have remained relatively free from pollution. If a merchant sells meat, fish, or eggs, this may be regarded as undesirable and unclean. No objections, however, are raised to grocers who sell spirits, canned meat, and fish which are traditionally polluting in India. Once the values of purity lose their structural relevance, almost all trading and entrepreneurial activity are regarded as legitimate and free from stigma, traditional or otherwise.[16]

How do *jāt* groups define their identity in the absence of hierarchical organization, values of purity and impurity, and the hereditary specialization of occupations? *Nāt-jāt*, as the Hindus understand it in East Africa, is chiefly expressed in rules of endogamy. In the absence of other attributes of traditional relations marriage within one's own *jāt* becomes a crucial mark of one's *nāt-jāt* identity. In my experience in Kampala, marriages across the *jāt* boundary are few and far between. In Bakuli there was not a single instance of a marriage between members of two different *jāts*.

It is within the bounds of *nāt* or *jāt* that a Hindu may have his or her largest number of social relationships. When one Gujerati meets another, traditionally one may ask the other: *Tame Kai nāt na cho?* (what is your *nāt*?) or, *tame kai jāt na cho?* (what is your *jāt*?). The answer typically may be: *Hun Patel chun* (I am Patel) or *Hun Luvano chun* (I am Lohana). The questioner may further ask what one's *atak*[17] is, *tamāri atak shun che?* (what is your *atak*?). The response will be as follows: *Hun Luvano chun ne mari atak Dattani che*, namely that I am a Lohana (by *jāt*) and my *atak* is Dattani. While *jāt* refers to endogamous boundary, *atak* refers to a number of units or sections within a *jāt* which are exogamous. Among the Lohanas this means one would not marry anyone bearing the same *atak* as oneself. The members of the same *atak* claim a common ancestry and a marriage within an *atak* is regarded as incestuous. Within one's *nāt* or *jāt*, however, one may marry a member of another *atak* without any adverse sanctions.

The Gujerati Hindus use the following scheme to distinguish between *varna*, *nāt-jāt*, and *atak*. A distinction can be made between a latent unit of reference and an operational unit of reference. Accordingly, *varna* is a latent category in so far as it is rarely used in day-to-day discourse to determine the boundary between two categories of people. On the other hand, *nāt-jāt* and *atak* are operational in that people use these terms and have a clear awareness of what realities each stands for. Some ethnographic accounts of East African Indians state that the Hindus use no vernacular terms to identify social groupings within their own society. The above formulation illustrates that such a view is inconsistent with the data on *nāt-jāt* and *atak* as presented below (p. 78).

In studies of Indians in East Africa the term caste is often used in a way that masks *varna*, *jāt*, and *atak*. For instance, Bharati says 'Whenever young Asians in East Africa speak about caste, they consistently use the English word, regardless of whether they are speaking English, Gujerati, Panjabi or Hindustani. They *never* use the Indian term. The

reasons for this practice are diffuse. In the first place very few Asians
are quite clear about the proper vernacular word. The correct term is
jāti (literally birth).'[18] This statement does not apply to Bakuli. The
Hindus I worked among there were not only aware of *varna*, *nāt-jāt*,
and *atak*, but also made clear distinctions between them. Contrary to
Bharati's description of the situation in general, Gujerati Hindus in
Bakuli use the above concepts in their day-to-day discourse. Educated
and anglicized East African Hindus also use the English term caste. But
to suggest that Asians *never* use the Indian term is untrue as regards East
Africa. What is perhaps true is that Hindus in Uganda seldom use the
term caste in its fourfold sense of *varna* but they do differentiate between
jāt and *atak*.

Atak Divisions among the Hindus in Bakuli*

Nāt-jāt group	*Atak*	No of households
Lohana	Sedani	1
	Kakkad	1
	Pujara	1
	Sad	1
	Kotak	5
	Jobunputra	2
	Karia	2
	Pattni	2
	Thakrar	2
Brahman	Vyas	2
Vaniya	Shah	1
Mochi	Solanki	1
	Total *ataks*	21

* Of 49 households, the *atak* divisions are relevant in the above 21 cases.

In the dimension of *atak*, Bharati's picture of the Lohana is not mirrored in Bakuli. He says, 'Although there is a large number of sub-
castes among the Lohanas, and though their sister community in western India preserves village exogamy, none of these seem to have any
bearing on the community in East Africa. Among one hundred parents
who had arranged marriage for their sons and daughters within the
prescribed Lohana fold, village exogamy had been considered in two
cases only and subcaste endogamy only once. The matches were not
made in conventionally undesirable subcastes; rather concern for
arranging most of them in conventionally permissible subgroups had
not entered in the negotiations.'[19] Bharati's account of *atak* as an exogamous variable, however, leads to difficulties. Whether *atak* is coter-
minous with village exogamy or not is an undetermined empirical
question. What is most significant in the East African context is the

absolute preponderance of *atak*-determined exogamy within the Lohana *jāt*. Out of 261 marriages and 147 betrothals reported in 20 issues of *Lohana Sandesh*, not a single instance of a marriage or betrothal within an *atak* has been reported. Given the nature of *atak* and its consequences for marriage among the Lohana, Bharati's use of subcaste endogamy is surely conjectural. Elsewhere Bharati uses the terms 'caste group', 'caste corporate group', 'caste mates', and 'caste surnames'.[20] He presumably uses these terms to mean *jāti*. However the terms are undefined and blur the distinctions Gujerati Hindus so clearly make between *varna*, *nāt-jāt*, and *atak*. His comment 'the caste system— whatever that means to East African Indians'[21] is more confusing than helpful as regards the sociological understanding of caste among East African Hindus.

In contrast to Bharati, Morris outlines his use of caste with insight and clarity.[22] First he distinguishes between *varna* and *jāti*. He also makes a clear-cut distinction between *jāti* as a subcaste category on the one hand and as a subcaste group on the other. This shows the way transition can take place, changing a category into a group. Although Morris equates caste association with *jāt* (his subcaste), it is not clear whether he regards them as synonymous or not. Further, he suggests that all four types of groupings, namely *varna*, *jāti* (his subcaste category and subcaste group), and caste associations are locally referred to simply as caste. That the different realities of caste are not simply referred to as 'caste' is surely clear from the foregoing discussion. Though he has recorded Patidar and Lohana as comprising 72 per cent of Hindu traders in Uganda,[23] Morris makes no reference to *atak*—an important aspect of Lohana social life.

What are the dynamics of *atak*? What are the political and economic consequences of *atak* among the Lohanas? Do some *ataks* form an upper stratum within the Lohana *jāt*? These and other related questions must be the subject of further research. At this stage *atak* would appear to be identical with the social network within which a man can mobilize political support, draw resources to set up a business, and explore inter-*atak* links to arrange marriages and other activities of importance. It must be admitted, however, that these speculations only suggest possibilities of further enquiry.

The term caste has been used in a variety of contexts and any attempt to define its meaning rigorously is unlikely to be fruitful.[24] To describe an endogamous kin group, English writers use the term caste or subcaste.[25] In so far as such usage is precisely worked out in a specific ethnographic context, then the term caste or subcaste will stand for clearly recognizable levels of reality.

For the comparative study of caste in the East African context, first of all, detailed studies of dominant groups like the Lohanas are not available. Secondly, the use of caste and subcaste tends to be vague, inconsistent, and misleading in existing studies of East African Indians. For example, confusion arises when the writers using the same English terms have different social realities in mind. Morris makes a distinction between caste and subcaste, meaning *varna* by the former and *jāti* by the latter, Bharati uses 'matrix' of *jāti* to mean caste.[26] The same term caste refers to the sociologically distinct realities of *varna* and *jāti*. This can only lead to confusion if any comparison is attempted. For example, when marriages between members of two different *jāt* groups are under discussion, the same phenomenon will be called inter-subcaste marriage by Morris and intercaste marriage by Bharati. Bharati's use of 'subcaste endogamy' brings the same point home. Here, in the context of Lohana *jāt*, he has in mind splits within the group, though he is not aware of these as exogamous *ataks*. According to the meaning imputed by Bharati, subcaste endogamy would be marriages within a subsection of *jāt* while for Morris this will be simply marriages within a *jāt* and not within one subsection of it. Two meanings expressed by the same term subcaste endogamy refer to two totally different social entities. A comparative study based on such loose categories may well therefore prove to be confusing and fruitless. The purpose of this chapter has been to suggest the usefulness of folk categories to discern realities of caste among the Hindus of Uganda, with particular reference to the Hindus of the Bakuli neighbourhood in Kampala. Gujerati Hindus in general and Lohanas in particular define differences between *varna*, *nāt-jāt*, and *atak* to establish three levels of social reality.

6

BLACK ATTITUDES TO THE BROWN AND WHITE COLONIZERS OF EAST AFRICA[1]

Dent Ocaya-Lakidi

Have black Africans in Uganda and in East Africa had a definite set of attitudes towards the Indians and Asians[2] in their midst? What have these attitudes been? And how can they be explained? The first two of these questions are obviously empirical ones, as they posit the problem: what are the facts? Unfortunately there is hardly available a serious, systematic study of the subject. Indeed even the general study of the Asian community in East Africa could still, as late as 1969, be claimed to be under-developed. Given the expulsion of the Asians from Uganda in 1972, such a study can now hardly be properly undertaken since African attitudes and opinions have been affected in a definite way by the expulsion and the manner in which it was done. In the writing of this chapter, therefore, the author was forced to fall back substantially on his personal knowledge of Asian-African relations as a native of Uganda, and on the few published sources.[3]

In the eyes of the three African social classes relevant for our analysis —the politically aspiring educated middle class, the economically aspiring middle class, and the lower class participating in the money economy—the Asians came off worst in almost everything when compared with the colonizing white Britons, except, perhaps, in their political roles. This was a rather peculiar and painful position for the Asians to occupy and, on the surface at least, it appears an unfair overall assessment of the Asians relative to the whites or 'Europeans'. The real and proper colonizers of East Africa after all were white Britons, not brown Asians. The white colonizers were, moreover, culturally arrogant, politically dominating as well as patronizing, and economically exploitative. Yet in the end they came to be more highly regarded than the politically powerless, culturally aloof though sometimes arrogant, and economically weaker, though equally exploitative, Asians. Why?

The reasons are to be found in the nature of the colonial context in which the Europeans, the Asians, and the Africans found themselves in East Africa. Colonialism, in terms of the kind of stratified society it ultimately produces, may be one of several kinds. There is a simple version of it, where one race or people are colonized by another race or people. White Britons imposing themselves on the Indians in the Asian continent is a case in point. Secondly, there is a compound form of it where three, rather than two, 'colonial layers' are involved. East Africa was typically illustrative of this. The Asians were 'colonizing' immigrants to East Africa, even if under direct British supervision, in the sense that they came to be above and to dominate the indigenous people of East Africa in many sectors of life. Yet they themselves were a colonized people, both in East Africa and in their original homeland, notwithstanding their talk of being British citizens. The significance of a compound or three-tier colonial context is, for our purposes, to be found in the phenomena of 'buffer', 'middleman', or 'intermediary' whose essential and inescapable nature, more than anything else, was to condition the attitudes of a large section of the African population towards the Asians. Finally, it is possible for a colonial context to assume a complex form. This happens when more than three 'colonial layers' are involved. We are, however, concerned essentially with Uganda and East Africa—a case of a 'compound-type' context.

It is at once clear that black African attitudes and views of the Asians arose largely out of the social, political, and economic dynamics generated within such a context. The dynamics were themselves manifestations of the self-interests of each of the three groups involved although it is always well to remember that one of these was a controlling power. In this regard, three sets of factors account for the manner in which the Asians came to be regarded more negatively than the Europeans. First, a great deal of the so-called African attitudes to Asians are in fact European attitudes assimilated and internalized by the Africans. It was often in the interest of white Britons in East Africa's colonial context to have the Asian appear in a certain way to both the natives and Britons at home in England. Various leverages were open to white Britons in this regard and they used them effectively. Secondly, the Asians themselves, being a colonized people and politically weaker than the British, were manipulated to serve the colonizers' economic interests by acting as middlemen between the white colonizers and the black Africans. By becoming the individuals who put colonial exploitative policies into effect, they inevitably came to take the blame for an exploitative colonial system while the real authors of the system, operating often invisibly behind the buffer, remained relatively free from black African hatred. Finally, a factor in generating certain black African attitudes towards the Asians were the Asians themselves in a more direct way, without being manipulated by a third party. Of particular relevance here are certain of their social customs and way of life. For the middle-class Africans with other grounds for resenting the Asians, these were additional grounds for further resentment. For lower-class

Africans, they were often as important in colouring attitudes towards the Asians as more concrete Asian roles in the economic sphere of their lives.

There are at least two ways in which the collective image of the Asians suffered in East Africa as a result of the activities of white Britons in various capacities in the colonization of East Africa. Firstly, in so far as the white colonizers were able to ensure a more positive image of themselves with the natives of East Africa, the Asian collective image dimmed by comparison. Secondly, it happened more directly by opinions being manipulated against the Asians.

Both the British colonizers and the Asian immigrants to East Africa were largely motivated by self-interest in their various activities in East Africa. Nevertheless there were always some important differences in their postures to the black Africans there. The British operated under the guise of a mission to civilize the natives. This made their economic interests and activities less obvious. If they were not there clearly or solely for the salvation of the natives, neither were they there clearly or solely for their own economic gains. Or so it could be made to appear. Lord Lugard put it succinctly:

Civilized nations have at least recognised that while on the one hand the abounding wealth of the tropical regions of the earth must be developed and used for the benefit of mankind, on the other hand an obligation rests on the controlling power not only to safeguard the material rights of the natives, but to promote their moral and educational progress.[4]

The possession of a philosophy of civilizing the natives subsequently made white Britons an attractive species in East Africa for, while the philosophy was partially empty in being only part of the reason for British presence in East Africa, it was nevertheless effective or ultimately became effective for it was backed up by an impressive material culture at home in England. Can one absorb a new material culture without at the same time absorbing also some of the philosophical and social values which go with it? Evidently not, and the British must have been aware of this. For they set about using their technology and material culture to win for themselves a permanent place of honour in the hearts of black Africans and not even African wars of resistance to white rule in some parts of Africa were to stand in the way of the Anglicization of the black man.

It was a slower process than Sithole would have us believe. Nevertheless his dramatic manner of describing the matter is apt for a process which was to transform the black African psyche itself: 'The first time he ever came into contact with the white man, the African was simply overwhelmed, overawed, puzzled, perplexed, mystified, and dazzled.

The white man's "house that moves on water", his "bird which is not like other birds", "his monster that spits fire and smoke and swallows people and spits them out alive". . .' Then there were the white man's 'motor car, motor cycles, bicycles, gramophones, telegraphy, the telephone, glittering Western clothes'.[5] Those who would object that this is an exaggeration might be right; but it is also well to remember that whole territories in Africa were bought and sold for the price of a looking glass. These things had often never been seen by the African before. They were beyond his comprehension, quite outside the realm of his experience. Consequently, he 'saw. He wondered. He mused. He trembled at the sight of the white man, whose prestige soared sky-high and left the African bowing before this new white god. . .'[6] And 'the new white gods were conscious of the magic spell they had cast over the Africans, and they did everything to maintain it. They demonstrated their control of lightning by firing their guns regularly, and this, to the ears of the Africans, sounded like thunder in the sky. *There was hardly anything that the white man did which had no god-like aspect to it.*'[7] A symbolic and dramatic rendering of the methods applied by the white man during the formative years in Africa, perhaps. They were to be modified as time went on.

A multi-pronged attack on certain indigenous values, way of life, and institutions soon replaced the crude pretence of godliness. At the same time various methods were instituted to civilize the native. It increasingly made sense to the natives themselves to try and become British and white,[8] an attitude which is still being fought by independent African states today. The English language, religion, culture, education—all these became highly attractive to the natives of East Africa. The editor of *Dobozi lya Buganda* (Voice of Buganda) was reflecting the sentiment of most Africans when he wrote in the 1920s: 'If he [the European] tries to give us what they call "African education", we shall oppose him tooth and nail, and we are determined in this. To attain the highest education the native must leave his country when young. The talk of natives coming back "de-Africanised" is all rubbish.'[9] In other words, European education in Europe at all costs. It is instructive here to note that formal education, in Uganda at least, ultimately came to be 'too literary', substantially ignoring technical subjects and agriculture, not because the missionary educationists did not concern themselves with practical and agricultural education but because black Africans were going in, not for something they themselves already knew, but for new kinds of things—not agriculture, but writing and the English language.[10]

But when all else has been considered, the decisive factor in the Anglicization of Uganda was British political authority over the

Africans. Without this their possession of a civilizing philosophy, their access to an impressive material culture at home, and their use of this culture for Anglicization in Uganda would have failed. Political power made all the difference.

In Uganda progress in the colonial society came to depend on what the colonizing power wanted it to depend on and they often wanted it to depend on a knowledge of the English language. This was British colonial policy from the beginning of the history of Uganda as an identifiable entity. 'So far from wishing to shut the Baganda out of the Government of their own country', Governor Sir Harry Johnston declared in 1900, 'I want to encourage them to enter into that Government. I want their boys to learn English so that they may take the place of the Indian clerks in the Government offices.'[11] The road to offices and key to advancement and, later, even to political power was to be through the English educational system.

If the Asian collective image was to dim comparatively because of the zeal with which Anglicization was forced on to and accepted by the natives, it was to suffer an even worse fate as a result of directed propaganda by pioneering Britons in East Africa to discredit them before both the East African natives and white Britons in England. In this connection Mangat's citation of the slave trade case is illustrative. Just when East Africa was being opened up to colonialism, the Asians came to be singled out as the worst offenders in the trade. 'The accusations of Livingstone and Burton were denied by Speke, Rigby, and Kirk. But Livingstone's highly coloured accounts of the trade and of Indian complicity in it aroused public opinion and led to the appointment of the Frere Mission in 1873 to investigate the whole issue. . .Sir Bartle Frere's detailed inquiry into East African slave trade revealed, so far as the Indians were concerned, that they had been quite unfairly singled out for complicity in this traffic. . .'[12] But the harm had been done already. 'In the final analysis', Mangat concludes, 'the adverse criticisms of the Indian community were to provide a precedent for the future and the tendency to use the Indians as a "scapegoat" was to continue.'[13] The adjectives that black Africans were to use in describing the Asians decades later were first used by white Britons at the East African coast. The Asian then had been described as crafty, money-making, cunning, someone with his soul bound to his body by the one laudable and religious concern to turn his coin to better advantage; the local Jew; unscrupulous and single-minded in the pursuit of gain; a user of false weights and measures, a receiver of stolen goods, and a 'Banyan' contemplating his account book.[14] How would these opinions fail to be internalized by black Africans immersed in a British educational system, reading Livingstone and Burton in English?

Asian-African interaction stood in stark contrast to European (British)-African interactions during East Africa's formative period. First, the Asians had very little claim to a civilizing mission in East Africa. Their collective image was, in comparison to that of white Britons, at best neutral, at worst negative, carrying the labels 'illiterate', 'inferior in education to the Natives',[15] 'uncivilized', or 'without culture'. But the Asians clearly had culture and civilization and it is quite true that some aspects of both might have benefited the natives, as some Asians were bold enough to point out: 'The Native who will be the product of the assimilation of two cultures will be a better, more enlightened, and more cultured man than one who may live and learn only under the influence of the Western civilisation...The Eastern civilisation has its own message to give to the world and I think that without it the National [Native] will surely be the poorer.'[16] This may be quite true but in fact the Asians had made no serious attempt and for reasons internal to their culture could not possibly have passed on to black Africans the essential messages of Eastern civilization.

In Uganda part of the reason for successful Anglicization is to be found in the fact that colonialism had been spearheaded by missionary activities. No eastern 'missionaries' ever walked the broad length and width of Uganda preaching and converting. The contending foreign religion in Uganda, indeed in East Africa, Islam, did not have anything distinctively Indian about it nor was it associated with India in its origins. And, although prominent Asian Muslims emerged on the Ugandan scene in later years, they were unable to secure for India the kind of African allegiance the Christian religion had generated for England. Most black African Muslims looked to Mecca and Medina and the Arab world rather than to India. But even had the Asians sent Hindu teachers among the natives of East Africa, where was the impressive material culture in India or Pakistan to back up their teaching? Was the black man to abandon his own native religion for a new one when those who preached this new religion could not even promise a better material life in this world?

It is true, of course, that the Christian religion itself promised, not a better life now or a better material life, but a better life in the world to come. But Christian missionaries could and did promise a better material world now; at least that is how a great many Africans came to look at the matter. Thus Watson was to discover that 'the intelligent pages in the Lubiri (Kabaka of Buganda's Palace) were quick to link education with religion and their interest in Mackay's technical and agricultural schemes was only a means to this end. The ability to read the written words became the overwhelming passion of the quick Baganda...'[17] Hinduism, indeed even Islam, was no avenue for either

education or clerical jobs and the material culture of the Indian sub-
continent at the time of the British colonization of East Africa was
incapable of promoting the Asian collective image in East Africa.

And what aspect of Indian civilization or culture could the Asians
have hoped to impart to the natives of East Africa? It is true of the
Asians, for example, that 'viewed from a moral aspect they are perhaps
the most remarkable people in the world. . .They breed an atmosphere
of moral purity which cannot but excite admiration. . .'[18] Yet can
moral uprightness be easily taught, especially if it is the property of an
exclusive group? Might not moral puritanism itself have repelled
Africans and could it not be that western culture was immediately
acceptable to the Africans because of its in-built potentiality for individual freedom and its tolerance for a great deal of what, in a society
emphasizing group morality, would pass for immorality?

As has been suggested already, it was new kinds of things rather than
merely new things that appealed to the Africans in their process of
Anglicization. Asian collective purity would appear to be much like
African collective morality and, for this reason, might not have been
very attractive. It might be that in cultural borrowing, as in magnetism,
unlike poles attract each other more than do like ones. In any case,
having accepted a substantial dose of western culture, the black man
was often quite unwilling to remain open to other influences. As an
African group itself was to put it: 'Our education and training has been
carried out on Western lines. . .Being the best for advancement. . .or
. . .[for] taking share [sic] in the government of our country, as well
as filling the position of clerks, trained and manual workers. . .Can
this be possible under two opposing civilisations; one Eastern and the
other Western, leading to a confusion of ideas on conduct, morals,
etc.?'[19] The Asians as civilizers were, on this view, just too late. The
Africans were firmly on the way towards westernization and nothing
was to divert their attention from this path. And it was the right path
because it led somewhere: to eventual economic and political power.

This brings us to political power as a crucial leverage absent in the
Asian process of penetrating East Africa. In the interplay for political
power in East Africa among the three groups, Yash Tandon has observed that 'Sanctions were. . .an important ingredient of European
power in Africa, and an element completely lacking on the Asian side
. . .it is not too difficult to believe that had the Asians in East Africa a
sanction machinery to back any bid for power, they might have staked
their claim as well as the Europeans.'[20] Tandon was referring to the
fact that, whereas the Europeans had powerful England to back them
up, for the Asians India was either also controlled by Europeans or,
when independent, too weak or too unconcerned to back up the Asians.

This is a fundamental point, because political powerlessness itself ultimately meant the Asians lacked a crucial leverage for staking a claim for a better collective image among the Africans.

When the Asians became an established economic class in later years, they already had a tarnished collective image among the Africans. The formative years had seen to that. Their economic activities were to add fuel to the fire. But here again we are still concerned with the attitudes of the educated or middle-class Africans.

In terms of the expulsion of the Asians from Uganda in 1972 and their gradual elimination from East Africa generally, critical African opinions and attitudes towards the Asians have derived substantially and directly from the economic activities of Asians as middlemen. But we cannot begin to understand the reasons for Asian behaviour in this sphere until it is fully appreciated that the role of middleman was not a voluntary one in a free market but one imposed and controlled by the white British colonizers. It is therefore Britain that must ultimately bear responsibility for what happened to the Asians in Uganda in 1972 and what is happening to them in Kenya today. This conclusion holds even when one takes into account those other Asian activities, resented by black Africans, which did not arise directly from their middleman role.

But black resentment of the Asians did not develop overnight with the establishment of the Asians as substantial holders of economic power in Uganda. Grace Ibingira had outlined in his perceptive work *The Forging of an African Nation*:

The comparatively few enlightened Africans who could have been in the van-guard of mass mobilisation found full satisfaction in the pursuit. . .of offices in the local governments of their respective tribes. . .There were [also] no political or economic issues of the magnitude essential to arouse massive opposition to foreign rule. There was no land problem such as that in Kenya 'highlands'; if the average African was poor, he was not destitute. In fact, he had most of the necessities to enjoy the simple life he and his next of kin lived. . .*This is one reason why the Asians could amass enormous wealth while the African looked on with little or no concern. . .*[21]

But some Africans did in fact begin to agitate against the Asians. They were what one might call the 'lumpen aristocracy', those who had lost any hope of economic ascendancy through the fast-disappearing tradi-tional political hierarchy and yet saw civil service jobs as either below their dignity or demanding qualifications they lacked. The Young Baganda Association was substantially such a group. Their war cries against the Asians were to become the war cries of the aspiring economic bourgeoisie after independence.

It is instructive to note that when the final crisis came, it was again a *lumpen* group, what Professor Mazrui has aptly termed the 'lumpen militariat',[22] that ultimately kicked out the Asians of Uganda. The expulsion of the Asians from the most profitable sector of the country's economy might thus have been inevitable, waiting only for a *lumpen* class which had no reason to be contented with the *status quo* to acquire effective power in the country. This happened in Uganda with the coming into power of the military. It is in this context that the earlier lament of an African correspondent in a colonial newspaper should be understood: 'As we have no power (as yet) to command Indians to get out of our country, we must protest and dispute every inch of the way so that they shall not get what they want in our country.'[23] The feeling that the Asians were the obstacle to African advancement gradually gained ground from the formative years, when this comment appeared, to the expulsion of the Asians in 1972. The Asians also came under fire for allegedly exploiting the Africans as middlemen in commerce, as employers, and as exporters of the country's money to foreign countries.

From the 1920s onwards, members of the Young Baganda Association and other Baganda launched a campaign against the Asians in the country, charging that they were blocking African upward mobility. But the campaign was confined largely to protest through newspapers. Indian migration, a correspondent protested in 1936, 'is inimical to the interests of the native...for [the] Indians of this type are the very people who...occupy positions which should have afforded outlets for Africans...'[24] For another correspondent in 1939, the Uganda Africans were poor because of the Indians;[25] and many blamed both the Asians themselves and the Protectorate government for this state of affairs. It is not at all far-fetched to regard the 1959 movement to boycott Asian trade in Buganda as a culmination of the gradually rising frustration among a certain class of Baganda from the 1920s. Recent research into the Uganda National Movement and trade boycott of 1959–60 tends to support this contention: 'The UNM was in many ways the culmination of frustrations of those African nationalists who were generally outside the "Establishment" of the Legco. Socially and educationally, they did not on the whole belong to the political elite. But their demands reflected the old grievances of diverse groups many of whom had been politically active since the early 1950s. When these economic and political grievances converged, they created the UNM philosophy.'[26]

After independence, pressure against the Asians intensified and found a sympathetic response from the government. But no satisfactory solution to the problem was to emerge till 1972 with their expulsion. The reason for this, as we shall see presently, is that those who might have acted to solve the problem of African upward mobility in trade and commerce were in fact the former politically aspiring bourgeoisie of the colonial era. Having gained political power, they had found ready access to the country's economic resources and thus were inclined to moderate behaviour vis-à-vis the Asians. The lumpen militariat logically applied very drastic solutions to the problem.

The Asians came under criticism from the Africans for exploitation on two grounds: as employers and as middlemen in commerce. One recent quotation must suffice for Asians as employers: 'Asians in industries', an African recently alleged, 'are more apt to keep to their own caste. . .whether there are qualified fitters, mechanics or electrical engineers and others of Ugandan origin; Asian employers would underemploy Ugandans at Shs 400 per month while an illiterate Asian artisan or mechanic would draw Shs 2,000 or more a month.'[27] As for the Asian as an exploitative middleman, African complaints and criticism span the whole of the colonial era as well as the independence period. For a great many Africans, the concern was with the Asian as a middleman in the cotton industry, the cash crop which in the greater part of the country was the sole cash-earner for the Africans before the Second World War. Certain sophisticated Africans were not blind to the true source of Asian behaviour in this connection but for the majority the Asian was the concrete entity that put the colonial system's exploitative policies into practice.

One must agree with Yash Tandon when he writes 'Often the problem of the Asian minorities in East Africa is presented as if it were a bilateral problem between the Africans and the Asians. Indeed the whole controversy on who is to "blame" (as if it is necessary to do so) for the bad race relations in East Africa. . .is often debated in purely bilateral and racial terms. But this misses out a third very important dimension of the problem, namely, the colonial dimension.'[28] But Tandon is wrong to insist that there is no need to apportion blame for the point is precisely that one cannot understand these relations without understanding the role of British colonialism in the matter, and one cannot understand this role and yet fail to blame, even condemn, Britain for what eventually happened. There are two main reasons why British colonialism is to blame. First, it was Britain that first shipped hundreds of Asians into East Africa for the promotion of British, not Asian, economic interests. Secondly, when Asian economic interests had to be taken into account, this was done at the expense of African interests. Again the primary aim was British economic interests. By placing them as middlemen between Africans and Europeans, Asians lost African goodwill. By being middlemen they were the concrete individuals who put into effect colonial policies resented by the Africans. Let us take these two issues in turn.

The story of the Asian penetration of East Africa must, naturally, begin with the construction of the Uganda Railway, for, as Mangat points out, when the decision was taken in 1895 to build the railway it was decided to construct it along Indian lines and chiefly by using Indian coolies.[29] Consequently 32,000 Indians had been imported to work on the railway by the turn of the century.[30] Later, British colonialism helped and encouraged Asian penetration of the interior. Asian traders and semi-skilled labourers began to establish themselves in the interior, including Uganda. The rationale behind the move to encourage the Asians into the interior had been largely anticipated by Lugard when he wrote that 'From the overcrowded provinces of India especially, colonists might be drawn, and this would effect a relief to congested districts. From them we could draw labourers, both artisans and coolies, while they might also afford a recruiting ground for soldiers and police. The wants, moreover, of these more civilized settlers would . . .very greatly add to the imports, and the product of their industry to the exports. . .Moreoever, the methods of agriculture. . .would soon be imitated by the Africans.'[31] A practical consideration guiding British policy during the formative years was that Uganda had been most reluctantly colonized. Consequently the colonial government there 'saw its immediate task as the production of local revenue which would emancipate it from subservience to a parsimonious British Treasury. Less urgently. . .official policy was motivated by the desire to prove that Uganda was an economic asset and not merely a strategic and evangelical acquisition.'[32] In pursuance of this policy, the taxation of Africans either in produce or in labour was found inadequate to meet the protectorate's financial needs. It became clear that the only solution to the problem lay in 'the establishment of an exchange economy'.[33] Hence the introduction of coffee, cotton, and tea as cash crops in Uganda; hence also the encouragement of the immigration of the more 'civilized' settlers into the country.

Though both Uganda and Tanganyika escaped the influx of white immigration that occurred in Kenya, that was not for lack of effort on the part of the Colonial Office. When Hayes Sadler was appointed Uganda's Commissioner, he was instructed that 'every encouragement is to be offered to capitalists and settlers'.[34] Despite this, however, and despite official encouragement, very few settlers showed up in Uganda. Nevertheless, by 1911 there were some twenty alien estates in the country, with rubber as the major crop. With the exception of the Asian-owned sugar plantations, however, the plantation economy as such was not very successful in Uganda. This was partly because of world market conditions. But it was also because 'the people of Uganda were, on the whole, able to satisfy their subsistence needs through the traditional economy. Their demand for cash was increasing

...but was tempered by natural reluctance to work as unskilled "porters" (a word of humiliating connotations).'[35] A possible way to force the people into cash employment and thereby make the plantation-type economy successful would have been to undermine the basis of African traditional economy—land. But the British had accepted that Uganda was a 'protectorate' to be developed in the interests of the indigenous Africans there. Consequently various agreements, in which land guarantees figured most prominently, were concluded with African traditional authorities over much of the country.

Two alternatives now remained open to the colonial regime: to promote the African commerical and industrial sectors or to rely on the 'more civilized' colonial immigrants, the Asians. They chose the latter alternative, no doubt because some Asians were already fairly skilled in commerce and industry. But the Asians were also allies, albeit subordinate allies, in colonization. From here the colonial government moved quickly to the principle, so well enunciated and practised by the colonial government in Kenya, that 'people who contribute capital and enterprise to the country must not be allowed to fail'.[36] Accordingly various means were worked out to make sure that the Asians would not fail, for on their success depended or appeared to depend the success of the white colonizers. 'By 1910', H. S. Morris has written, 'the scene in East Africa was more or less set. Administrative and agricultural development were thought to be European occupations; trade and craftsmanship were relegated to Indians; and Africans were encouraged to work in the European agricultural system and to supply cheap labour in the towns that were developing in response to European and Indian activities. The picture did not substantially alter in the next forty years.'[37] The important thing here is that the situation did not just develop. On the contrary, 'a fairly clear racial division [was] envisaged between African growers, Indian middlemen, and European ginners'[38] as far as primary commodities went. When in the 1930s some Africans in Uganda formed a company to buy cotton with the intention of setting up their own ginneries, they were told that 'they were inexperienced and incapable of entrepreneurship, "eager to run before they could walk"...'[39] As late as 1955 the Royal Commission on East Africa wrote, assessing African economic advancement: 'The system of state-directed trade...has also been accompanied by a network of trade regulations and restrictions designed to protect those Africans who were anxious to enter the field of distribution against certain risks to which they were said to be exposed. It may be recognised that the native trader and producer are generally at a disadvantage with the traders and producers of other races...In so far as the development of the co-operative movement is an attempt to overcome exceptional

disadvantages which lie on the side of the Africans, it may. . .be worthy
of special support. . .'[40] But in Uganda, Africans, far from being given
special support, were discouraged and restricted in economic entrepreneurship. At the same time Africans saw protected Asians getting
rich, but rarely saw the supreme manipulator behind the scene: the
colonial government.

Such was the case with cotton, for example, where Asians were given
ginning monopolies and Africans had to sell to them at controlled
prices. Such also was the case with the virtual award of the monopoly of
the towns to the Asians for commercial and, eventually, residential
purposes. In 1938 a trading ordinance excluded the Asians from trading
in the countryside, confining them to the towns and trading centres.
No doubt the colonial government thought it was protecting or even
promoting African commercial interests. But how? Nothing was being
done about the Asian entrenched position itself. In any case, as Jack
Parson and Dharam Ghai have pointed out, this was 'negative in its
impact rather than. . .a positive encouragement to the commercial and
entrepreneurial activities of the Africans. It prohibited trading by
Asians in certain areas but it also implicitly ensured the position of
Asians in townships and trading centres',[41] and the 'concentration of the
Asians in the urban areas, for which they themselves were not responsible, aggravated matters; it prevented racial integration, pushed up
prices of property in urban centres making it difficult for Africans to
start enterprises there, and made the Asians appear as a privileged group
of town dwellers where all the facilities were located'.[42] In other words,
the Asians again found themselves face to face with black African
resentments for reasons not of their own creation.

However, it would be most unfair to the British and even to the
Asians themselves to argue that all Asian economic activities resented by
black Africans were the results of white British manipulation. For, at
least in two areas, the source of anti-Asian resentment was the Asians
themselves. While the African elite have resented most bitterly the
Asian practice of investing money earned in East Africa abroad, the
ordinary African has been resentful of the alleged Asian habit of cheat-
ing his buyers. The well-known case of capital flight from East Africa
and African outcries need not detain us much. There is hardly any
dispute about the extent to which the Asians indulged in this practice
and the fact that it has cost the Asians the goodwill of the East African
political leaders. It created the impression that the Asians are 'get-rich-
immigrants-in-transit', people without the interests of East Africa at
heart. As for the common man's economic view of the Asian, the
source of the problem would appear to be 'bargaining', a practice
perfected to a fine art by Asians. 'These people', a black Ugandan

pointed out in 1972, 'have and are still exploiting the sons and daughters of Uganda in many ways; e.g., when one goes to buy a dress you find there a written price of 140/-. As you go on bargaining you will surprisingly find that you have bought the dress at 100/-; which means that they are never straightforward to us at all.'[43] Dharam Ghai has pointed out in defence of the Asians that the practice of bargaining in Asian shops is not peculiar to the Asians in East Africa. 'Any system of bargaining must inevitably lead to the charging of different prices to different customers, and thereby complaints of exploitation and racial discrimination.'[44] But he does admit that 'It is perhaps true that many Asian traders have shown themselves more interested in quick profit rather than in steady long-term gains, and have not hesitated to exploit temporary scarcities to make windfall gains.' And yet, 'none of these practices are peculiar to Asian traders in East Africa; indeed they are the stock in trade of businessmen all over the world, especially in under-developed countries'.[45] This is certainly the case. But, if so, why should it have led to the kind of views expressed by black Africans about the Asians in East Africa? Race and ethnicity should not be ruled out here. The fact is that those who sell and those who buy are of two different racial stocks or at least of different colour. Naturally where there would ordinarily only be complaints about overcharging there is likely to be resentment instead, especially if the race that sells is generally 'above' the buying race who, however, happen to be the predominant 'owners' of the country's resources.

What we have considered so far are largely views of Asians such as may have been held by the middle-class and educated Africans in Uganda, those who no doubt were bent on improving their own economic standing in the country but who also were capable of forming a comprehensive view of the place of the Asians in East Africa. But to the ordinary man in the street and in the countryside to talk of Asians was to talk of brown town-dwelling shopkeepers. And these are people they have never admired. Some of these people's opinions of Asians may appear 'stupid' or 'trivial' to the sophisticated mind. Nevertheless, such opinions have been and continue to be held and our survey of African attitudes is incomplete without at least a mention of some of them. The ordinary African had probably never thought Asians could or would leave his country, just has he never thought the white man would. And he probably had no ambition to replace the Asian shopkeeper. Nevertheless, he had certain definite views of Asians.

First of all, he shared with his more sophisticated countrymen the view that Asians were cheats. The case of the Asian as an artful bargainer has already been referred to. But the African's resentment of the Asian was often all the more pronounced because the Asians appeared to him a lazy lot, earning money 'for doing nothing'. To the African in East Africa *work* has a special meaning. It excludes activities where one wears nice clean clothes and stays away from the burning heat of the sun. To work is to sweat. Yet was it not the African 'boy' who was doing all the sweaty jobs in Asian shops? Paradoxically, however, Africans have identified with precisely the kind of European who wears a clean shirt, a colourful tie and jacket, and sits around in an office apparently doing nothing. This must surely show the extent to which Africans were prejudiced against Asians in Uganda right from the beginning. The second African attitude which might be mentioned is the belief that Asians are a prolific race. The fact that they and they alone appear to occupy the towns, through which they lazily roam in large numbers during the week-ends especially, only strengthens this conviction. From this arose in turn the fear that unless something was done, Asians were bound also to 'take over' the country one day through their sheer numerical strength. A related opinion has linked Asian numbers and their concentration in the towns with dirt and unhealthy living. To add to this, the average Asian is seen as a weakling, suffering from the metabolistic consequences of his 'hot' diet. His habit of constantly coughing and spitting, often in the street, is perhaps the most obvious distinguishing mark of the Asian to the ordinary African —and it further confirms Asian weakness and incapability to work. Asians are also seen as rich, showy people: riding their long new cars recklessly and twirling dust in the eyes of African pedestrians. Finally, the Asians have been criticized for their social exclusiveness and often their arrogance. The African manual labourer, for example, has resented the manner in which the Asian looked down upon him, calling him 'boy' and 'stupid'. In sum, the Asians are viewed by the ordinary African as a low sort of human being who, though rich, live in con-gested quarters, and are dirty and weak. African charges of Asian social exclusiveness need, however, to be examined in rather more detail.

In recent years much has been made of Asian social exclusiveness and, sometimes, also their political exclusiveness and inactivity. It is pointed out that very few Asians made friends with black Africans sufficiently close for social visits at home. Attention has also been focused on the fact that very few Asian-African marriages have taken place, whereas there have been many African marriages with Europeans. If only the Asians were more open, more integrated with the rest, if only they intermarried more, all might have been well. Thus Yash Tandon has written: 'In retrospect it would seem that if the Asians in East Africa had shown the same amount of exuberance for freedom, and if they had completely identified with the African aspirations, and still more, if they had started the initiative to start the struggle against colonialism even when the Africans were not ready themselves, then the Asians might have reserved for themselves a position of respect and leadership among the Africans today.'[46] Grace Ibingira recently wrote: 'It is. . . regrettable that while the Asian community fought for constitutional rights, they made the great mistake of not appealing to Africans for support. Had they done so, they would probably have forged an indissoluble alliance in the protracted struggle for ultimate sovereign power. Consequently, instead of living side by side with the Africans as they do today, they would have been completely integrated and accepted in African society, and would not constitute the minority problem that the Uganda of today faces.'[47] Peter Nazareth, an Asian novelist, would appear closer to the truth than either Tandon or Ibingira. In his *In a Brown Mantle*[48] he paints a fairly realistic picture of a Mr D'Souza, an Asian politician, who completely identified with the Africans and the African cause during the struggle for independence in a fictitious African country, only to be dumped and forgotten when power had been won and was being parcelled out among the African nationalists.

In the social sphere, President Amin himself was critical of the Asians for their social exclusiveness. Addressing those citizen Asians who had the conviction and courage to remain behind after the expulsion on an occasion when he made them practise the march-past in preparation for the country's tenth anniversary of independence, he said: 'This is the spirit of the Second Republic of Uganda. If you had done like that long ago, what is happening now [referring to the expulsion] would not have happened. You must now come out and identify yourselves with Ugandan Africans. You must go with them and stop isolating yourselves. . .I want to see Africans marrying Asians and vice versa. I will attend those weddings myself.'[49]

Often enough in trying to defend themselves against such criticism Asians talked as if they themselves were indeed to blame. But surely they were powerless to behave otherwise. The fact of the matter is that most black Africans had such a low opinion of Asians that they would not have wanted to associate too closely with them. This fact is graphically illustrated in the manner in which black African males, especially, look at any 'loose' black girl who goes with an Asian. That the woman is already 'loose', a prostitute, ought to mean that she is already written off as far as being a proper member of the African community is concerned. Yet should such a girl go with an Asian, she can still create considerable revulsion among black African males. By going with an Asian she is seen to be sinking even lower than the lowest African can go. It follows that for a 'clean' or good African girl to want to marry an Asian is just unimaginable. As for the black males themselves, no doubt the idea of 'testing' a 'brown skin' is attractive but none would stoop to marry an Asian.

African views of Asians in Uganda have not been entirely negative. Some Africans have gratefully acknowledged Asian contributions in opening up East Africa for commerce and trade. In Uganda such pioneering Asians as the late Allidina Visram and a tycoon like Mulji-bhai Madhvani have been acknowledged as creditable Asians. But on the whole Africans have had and continue to have very negative attitudes towards Asians. The reasons for this are not to be found merely in what the Asian has been and what he has done. Instead one must also look at the structure and nature of the colonial system for an explanation.

7

THE UGANDAN CIVIL SERVICE AND THE ASIAN PROBLEM 1894–1972

Nizar Motani

It has been a commonplace of politicians and journalists as well as scholars that the unpopularity of the East African, especially Ugandan, Asians was due to their control over retail and wholesale trade and the failure of the Africans to compete with them in commerce.[1] After the 1940s commerce was undeniably the crucial province of racial friction. In the preceding period, however, the civil service was somewhat more responsible for the origin of some of the anti-Asian outlook of Uganda's African leaders. Antagonism between African and Asian staff in the civil service during and since the 1920s had already soured relations between them, as will soon become apparent. Many of the future chiefs and politicians commenced their careers as Protectorate government employees.

Numerically, there have always been far more Asians in commerce in Uganda than in the public services. Therefore the larger trading community was naturally in greater contact with the African masses. The Asian shopkeeper–African customer relationship, on the one hand, and the master (Asian housewife or commerical employer)–servant (African domestic or shop employees) relationship, on the other hand, not only hindered good race relations but also shaped attitudes to each other and created racial stereotypes.[2] However, a survey of the Uganda civil service (UCS) is also necessary for the proper understanding of the 'Asian problem', because in addition to Asian shops and homes the UCS was another significant arena that bred mutual dislike.[3] It is profitable to start the survey from the beginning of British rule in Uganda so as to identify the main types of early Asian personnel in the UCS and to follow their fortunes to the post-independence era.

Once Britain assumed imperial responsibility for Uganda in 1894, the need for many kinds of personnel had to be satisfied. At that time the most practicable and economical solution seemed to be a three-tier system under which each of three racial groups in the British Empire would contribute according to its ability. The absence of educated or skilled Africans in Uganda would cause the middle tier to be filled by the Asiatic peoples of India. On climatic, racial, and financial grounds the top-tier would be very small and reserved for the members of the European (ruling) races. To the Africans would fall the menial and unskilled tasks associated with the bottom tier.[4]

While native affairs could be left in African hands, administration of justice to foreigners and other scientific and technical matters required special expertise. In each of these fields, the British needed subordinate technical and clerical personnel. Naturally such people could either be trained locally or brought from outside. The skeleton staff of British officers was too preoccupied with other governmental duties to find either the time or the inclination to undertake the training of Africans. Thus the impossibility of obtaining locally men familiar with western concepts of administration made Britain turn to India and other parts of her empire in search of suitably efficient and cheap subordinate staff.

In 1896, the first Protectorate government official visited India specifically to recruit such employees. He returned with six clerks and eighteen artisans, having concluded arrangements to later receive two hospital assistants and five compounders (dispensers).[5] Thereafter Uganda required an increasing number of clerks, medical assistants, and artisans. Thus began the process of 'Indianization' of certain junior establishments of the Uganda civil service.

The British had detected great eagerness for education among the Baganda and they were described as the artisans of the future as well as suitable replacement for Asian clerks. However, lack of training facilities in English and Swahili or the skilled crafts hindered their employment as junior clerks, interpreters, or artisans.[6]

By the early 1910s the Indianization of the economy and the subordinate services of Uganda and Kenya had occurred. The Indian element had become firmly entrenched into the middle grades of the government, railway, and postal systems. The availability of Asians[7] with years of experience and previous training kept the Africans in the background as spectators watching the British and their Asian collaborators carry out a wide range of exotic and seemingly complicated activities.

This Indian participation in the government departments from an early stage had multiple effects. The British officers soon became accustomed to receiving reasonably well-trained, economical, and usually reliable manpower from India. It spared them the strenuous and patience-exhausting task of familiarizing essentially tribal peoples with novel ideas and occupations pertaining to a post-industrial society. The Asian staff was more expensive than the Africans would have been but the Protectorate government saved substantial sums of money by not providing education or other social services. Therefore coaching Africans for duties executed by Asians did not become very urgent.

However, in 1912 a senior Secretariat official, G. Lyall, was disturbed by the prevailing government recruitment practices regarding clerks. The backwardness of Uganda's educational facilities had made the country a kind of paradise for Indians and Goans who had any experience of clerical work. They could immediately obtain employment in the expanding government machine. It was the expense of employing them that worried Lyall and he offered the first official view, backed by a blueprint, on Africanization of the clerical service. Lyall thought it 'eminently necessary' to devise a training scheme for 'native clerks with the ultimate object of the Civil Service of Uganda being composed only of Europeans and natives'.[8]

Accordingly, in December 1913, Governor Jackson appointed a committee to consider and implement Lyall's scheme. This committee also favoured the replacement of Asian clerks with Africans but the outbreak of the First World War and the attitude of the imperial government in London prevented any further action. Moreover, immigrant, especially European, opinion of Africans tended to be suspicious of their integrity, for there had been several incidents of embezzlement of funds by African employees in certain government departments.[9] As things stood in 1919, the success of the native clerical services—intended slowly to eliminate Asian clerks—depended on winning the complete confidence of a majority of European officials (since they helped formulate policy) regarding African character. It also depended on improvement in the educational system and a clear demonstration of reliable work from the Africans to satisfy European requirements in Uganda.

In the meantime, in March 1918, eighteen African clerks and interpreters in government service took the unprecedented step of petitioning the government for stabilized terms of employment and equality with the Asian staff. They were dissatisfied with their position as casual and least privileged employees.[10] The petitioners included three names which later became influential in African politics and protest: Joswa Kamulegeya, the Budo-educated son of an important *saza* (county) chief; Sepiriya Kadumukasa, the British-educated son of the chief minister of the Buganda Kingdom; and Joseph Bampade, a Ganda clerk with the Provincial Administration. This petition also set the pattern of African political activity in the UCS. It was to be followed by numerous supplications demanding equality with the Asians and expressing resentment at British partiality towards the Asians.

When the report of the second Native Civil Service Committee (NCSC) was presented in 1920, the government desire ultimately to

Africanize the entire subordinate service was reiterated. Thus it can be seen that Africanization of the subordinate UCS was a fairly old topic in Uganda's colonial history, though very little was actually done to realize this hope until the 1940s. The NCSC also pointed out that no institutions existed in Uganda where a native could acquire the necessary education or training to 'make him a first class clerk, or a skilled mechanic, or a carpenter, etc. . . .'[11] And here again the situation did not radically change until the 1940s.

These post-First World War British thoughts about Africanizing the subordinate civil service were accompanied by African pressures and political action. These principally manifested themselves through small tribal or intertribal groups. Of relevance to this chapter are the African efforts to obtain better education, a fair chance of employment, and equality with the Asians in the UCS.

The Young Baganda Association (YBA), founded in 1919, made public one of its letters to the Indian Association of Kampala to bring about a change in the attitude of the Indian community towards the Africans in general and the educated[12] Baganda in particular. The YBA complained that Indian firms did not engage enough Baganda clerks and shop assistants and deprecated the views of a leading Indian transporter, expressed to the Uganda Development Commission (1920), that Baganda car drivers and mechanics were uneconomical![13] Indeed, and as will become more apparent later, competition for positions in commercial firms and the civil service between Africans and Asians had created considerable friction. This rivalry, which preceded competition in retail trade, was to be an important and early cause of dislike between the two races in Uganda.

A more radical shade of Baganda opinion was projected from Nairobi, through *Sekanyolya*—a Luganda newspaper launched in 1920 by young Baganda working there. It advocated the expulsion of Indians, who were branded 'exploiters', from Uganda. The editor, Zefaniya Sentongo, accused them of undermining the country by sending money to India and was convinced that their presence was detrimental to the Africans:

Indian artizans and fundis. . .oppose an almost insurmountable barrier to the native who wishes to engage in skilled labour. If the European Community would establish technical training schools, accept some of our young natives in the workshops as apprentices and promise to employ trained native workers wherever possible, the standing menace of the Indian to native advancement would be killed in a few years.[14]

Evidently General Amin's feelings expressed during 1971–2 were not unprecedented, nor was his solution to the 'Asian problem' particularly original. The significant difference was that in Sentongo's time Asian subordinate personnel were viewed as the principal obstacle to African, especially educated African, aspirations. But in 1971–2 Amin faced a situation where the commercial community posed the major hurdle and African eyes were fixed on the business sector. What needs to be emphasized here, however, is that the educated Africans' resentment against the Asians seems first to have been generated by the Asian preponderance in the junior and middle-level clerical and technical posts in the public and private sectors. Jealousies and wider antagonisms resulting from commercial rivalries belong to the later decades.

In the year following Sentongo's fierce bombardment of the Asians, thirty-eight African employees of the Protectorate government, led by Yusufu Bamuta and Erasito Bakaluba, privately denounced British favouritism with regard to the Asian clerks,[15] while Joseph Bampade publicly exhorted the government to commence Africanizing the clerical service.[16] The government, however, lacked suitable educational facilities in Uganda and was averse to Africans studying abroad mainly for political reasons. Moreover, during the 1920s Africanization—already regarded by the government as a gradual and protracted process—was further confined to fields where the repeatedly mentioned moral weakness of the Africans would not jeopardize the public interest. It was commonly stated that 'only in exceptional cases' had Africans 'acquired that sense of responsibility necessary where the accounting of considerable sums of money was involved'.[17]

Though not doing anything effective about Africanization in the early 1920s, the British continued to assure the educated Africans that they would replace the Asians within a short time. Consequently many African clerks and interpreters became disillusioned. Frustration with bad conditions of service and poor prospects in general gave birth to the first truly intertribal association in Uganda, the British Government Native Employees Association (BGNEA), in 1922. British equivocation regarding Africanization of the subordinate bureaucracy made the BGNEA and its successors deeply suspicious of the Protectorate government and resentful of the Asian staff. Moreover, the BGNEA remained very active throughout the interwar period and equipped many of its leaders—e.g. Y. Bamuta, E. Bakaluba, Petero Serumaga, and Mikaeri Kintu, to name just a few—with political and organizational experience. And, as these clerks and other ambitious African employees left the civil service, they took with them this experience as well as an acute dislike of the Asians. The diversion of educated Africans to the tribal governments served two purposes: making the native administrations more efficient as well as pacifying the African elite, because there it could rise to the top.

As far as the Asians were concerned, this policy virtually guaranteed them permanent government employment but at the cost of becoming unpopular with the African staff. In the civil service the group corresponding to house servants were office messengers. The former often suffered indignities at the hands of Asian employers while the latter frequently complained about arbitrary dismissals suffered at the hands of Asian clerks. They were also unhappy with European officers for devising a system whereby the African staff had no access to them, except through the agency of Asian clerks.[18] This made the Indian position in the bureaucracy even more uncomfortable.

By 1928, though Makerere had produced many field assistants of several types, junior clerical vacancies continued to be filled by ill-prepared pupils drawn from the intermediate schools. This failure of the educational system to train African clerks further complicated matters for the Asian supervisory personnel. Young African pupils who were suddenly removed from the intermediate schools and transplanted to government offices for clerical work frequently ended up as office messengers or interpreters. Moreover, they had to be corrected by Asian clerks and doubtless they were abused for lack of clerical knowledge which they were supposed to have already acquired. Another result of this was that it confirmed the belief of the Asian staff in its own superiority over African office staff.

One of the rare early tangible steps towards Africanization, taken in 1929, dismayed the Asian representatives in the Legislative Council. They were categorically told that Asian clerical appointments would, from that year, be on a temporary basis so as to facilitate the future Africanization of that particular branch of the UCS. Though the future of the Asian clerical establishment was thus clarified in 1929, the position of the Asian community as a whole remained ambiguous to the Asians as well as to the British. While the Protectorate government regarded the Asians as 'permanent inhabitants' of Uganda, the Africans were described as 'still more permanent'.[19] The 'rootlessness' and the post-independence 'statelessness' of many Asians was actually a condiing obtaining throughout the colonial period and official policy did little to lessen it.

In 1930, with the introduction of the African Civil Service (ACS), racial discrimination in the UCS—with pay and privileges generally distributed in descending order to Europeans, Asians, and Africans—was further endorsed. Throughout the 1930s the most painful thorn in the African staff's flesh was the glaring British partiality towards the Asian clerks at a time when there was so much official talk about doing away with them. E. Musoke effectively conveyed the general African mood at that time: 'I think East Africans are very much suffering from flooding of the Indian civil servants. Indians are ruled subjects and as such they must serve in their own country and let East Africa be served by Europeans and Africans.'[20] The Protectorate government justified this discrimination, above all, on the grounds that Europeans and Asians were 'overseas civil servants' while the Africans belonged to a 'home civil service'.[21] Especially in the long run this discrimination and the British practice (with Asian collaboration) of excluding Africans from the clerical service was more inimical to the Asians. When the colonial administration handed over power to the independent Uganda government in 1962, European officers ceased to be a barrier to African advancement. Most Asian civil servants, however, only exchanged masters and were visible as a legacy and a reminder of the unhappy African days in the UCS.

Returning to the thirties, the Protectorate government kept up its periodic public professions of the desirability of Africanizing the junior service, to the discomfort of the Asian community. Since Africanization could no longer be questioned on either moral or economic grounds, the Asian representatives urged that this policy be modified on grounds of efficiency. Also, like the Africans, the Asians were unhappy about racial segregation in the UCS as this barred them from many higher posts and privileges normally reserved for the Europeans. At this time the Asians believed that their future would be best safeguarded by the creation of a non-racial local civil service (LCS), entrance to it being by competitive examinations and its terms of service being equally applicable to African, Asian, and European members. Thus Asians as well as Africans supported the idea of a LCS.[22]

During Philip Mitchell's remarkable governorship (1935–40), the LCS idea received serious consideration. Mitchell was committed to making optimum use of local manpower, the accent being not only on Africanization but also on localization.[23] Furthermore, secondary education received a tremendous boost. Not only did more Africans get secondary education after 1938 but in many cases obtained higher passes than Asians in the Cambridge School Certificate examination.[24] Hitherto the Asians had had to acquire their secondary education in Kenya or overseas as there were no such facilities for them in Uganda. From 1938 they could acquire full secondary education at the Indian schools in Uganda.[25] Both the Africans and the Protectorate government could then justifiably feel that there should be similar terms of service for the locally educated Africans and Asians. However, although African educational standards had demonstrably improved, Africans were not yet, in the late 1930s, credited with the same reliability and experience as the Asians.[26]

The birth of the LCS in 1940 then seemed a major dent in the racially structured UCS but in retrospect it appears to be only a minor one.

The LCS which was 'open to all candidates irrespective of race' comprised a higher section (First Division) and a lower section (Second Division).[27] Asians on overseas or other terms and pensionable African civil servants (members of the ACS) were given the option to convert to the LCS. The Asian response was negative. In fact they disliked the LCS since it had split the Asian staff into 'the favoured and the unfavoured' classes.[28] Asian discontent, effectively conveyed to the Protectorate government by the Asian members of Legco, together with government fears of inefficiency in the bureaucracy as a result, brought about some changes which removed part of this dissatisfaction. Asians thereafter normally entered the First Division while Africans would be appointed to the Second Division, thus showing that Africans continued to suffer discrimination.[29] This could hardly improve relations between the African and Asian staff.

Moreover, even in the late 1940s, the Protectorate government did not generally consider the Africans fit for the European-held posts and senior African staff continued to be transferred to the native administrations.[30] Their dislike of the Asians presumably accompanied them, wherever they went.

However, British paternalism in Uganda was slightly relaxed after 1945. Three Africans were appointed to the Legislative Council in that year. Asian as well as African representatives were allowed to sit on the Local Civil Service Board (LCSB) for the first time, also in 1945.[31] Thus, when in 1948 the Holmes Commission rejected the non-European demand for 'equal pay for equal work' on the ground that each race had an unequal 'sense of responsibility, judgement, application to duty. . .' and recommended a racial salary scale,[32] a marriage of convenience occurred between the Asian and African staff. Its purpose was to secure a single meritocracy for all government servants.[33] This became a likelihood after Andrew Cohen became Governor in late 1952. He initiated several schemes to increase African participation in the central government institutions, especially the senior civil service. However, the irony of his dynamic governorship was that Uganda's rapid social, economic, and constitutional development made the government machinery not only more complex but also swelled the number of expatriate staff. Africanization of the senior posts correspondingly became harder and proportionally remained static.[34] Nevertheless, in 1955 a single UCS was introduced, geared to local recruitment, with some necessary inducements for overseas staff.

Cohen was thinking ahead of his time and did not really enjoy the support of his senior officials regarding his Africanization programme. Whether it was hidden race prejudice, fear of forfeiting the comforts of expatriate status, or a wrong assessment of the probable date of self-government for Uganda is rather difficult to state categorically. European officials and the non-Africans generally were sceptical and paternalistic about Africanization at higher levels and urged a policy of *festina lente*.[35]

Furthermore, the African members of Legco, though always keeping the question of Africanization alive in the 1950s, were largely in harmony with the non-Africans about the necessity to maintain standards and the efficiency of the civil service. The leaders of the newly emergent nationalist movements, while critical and suspicious of British intentions concerning the Africanization of the senior service, did not themselves clearly envisage self-government in the immediate future.[36] They often lapsed into Baganda provincialism, thereby arousing the suspicions of the non-Baganda who were not very eager to see a rapid Africanization of the UCS since the educationally advanced Baganda would reap most of the benefits.[37]

The 1950s were also relatively free from African hostility towards Asian civil servants as attention had then shifted to the more senior posts held by Europeans. Moreover, Africans did not want to see the expatriate characteristics of the top establishment changed. Thus the legacy for the future was to be seen in the growth of a class of indigenous expatriates, namely those Africans enjoying conditions of service appropriate to overseas personnel.[38]

One of the colonial practices that had incensed African civil servants, as has already been seen, was British partiality towards Asian staff. With the attainment of independence in 1962, this particular cause of anti-Asian feeling could be and indeed was removed. However, memories of Asian arrogance when dealing with African subordinates or peers survived when many former subordinate African employees had attained senior political or government positions. Non-citizen Asians in the civil service did not constitute a permanent barrier since their posts would eventually be Ugandanized. It would be the brown Ugandan public servants who would be regarded as long-term rivals by the African staff and the independent government would have to formulate a clear policy towards them.

Independence had vastly altered the three-tier character of the UCS. While there would still be a large African subordinate establishment, there was now an African government in power. The British masters had been replaced by African lords. It may be assumed that psychologically the Africans as well as the Asians were not in a position to run the immediate post-independence UCS in a healthy, cordial atmosphere. A reasonable period of adjustment would be necessary to enable the Africans to forget or forgive Asian arrogance and their real or imagined obstruction of Africanization during the colonial era. The Asians would have to get accustomed to having Africans as their new departmental heads and superior officers. Furthermore, Asian morale would depend on whether they received equal consideration with regard to promotion and new appointments. It is also likely that Africans would resent promotion or high-level appointments of even competent Asians, since independence to some Africans meant redressing the balance by discrimination in their favour. Government policy would likewise have to be harmonized with public opinion. It is against this background that the working of the UCS in the post-colonial period becomes more comprehensible.[39]

The circumstances that ushered in independence were such that there was no intense public pressure for Africanization of senior, and especially professional, posts at the expense of standards. The clerical cadre no longer ranked important with the Asians who by then increasingly sought entry into the professional branch of the UCS. As far as the expatriate staff was concerned, there was no significant difference between the policy of the Obote government during its first few years and that of the colonial government since 1952.[40] As far as the Asians were concerned, the official policy was 'Ugandanization', i.e. equal opportunities for all citizens. In practice, however, a subtle 'Africanization' programme was followed. Up to 1966 the UCS had a large number of unfilled vacancies, and the dearth of skilled and high-level manpower was 'aggravated by disinclination to make full use of the capacities of educated Ugandans of Asian origin'.[41] Neither the skilled manpower situation nor the reluctance to recruit and promote professional citizen Asians had changed noticeably in 1970. The government was in a dilemma. It rightly wanted to increase African participation in the public service at all levels. If Asian citizens were appointed to fill vacancies, they could not legitimately be removed later. But if expatriates were contracted for short periods, Africans could take over at some stage. Such devices only lowered the morale of the Asian staff still further.

Since independence the behaviour of many Asian civil servants, like that of the Asian commerical community, has been censured by the government. While they could not be accused of 'economic sabotage' or 'milking the economy', Amin did reprimand them for absolute disloyalty to the UCS.[42] The implication seemed that the Asian professional staff was being indifferent to government employment simply because the employer was African. This charge of 'disloyalty' and its causes need further consideration. The Asian attitude to the UCS appears to have been conditioned by their assessment of their future prospects in the UCS in the light of government policy and by fluctuations in the labour market. Their response to these factors does not seem to differ in essence from the African response to government service before and since independence.

Ex-President Obote's 'Communication from the Chair' in April 1970 embodied several measures designed to bring the UCS, with its many 'expatriate' features, into conformity with the new egalitarian society envisaged by his 'Common Man's Charter'. Obote emphasized the idea of service and curbed the benefits that had been associated with government employment.[43] Given the widely held Asian belief that they already suffered discrimination in the public service, Obote's commendable and necessary austerity measures,[44] though some eight years too late,[45] possibly increased disheartenment still further.

Since these retrograde measures would affect all established officers, many an ambitious public servant would be compelled to explore alternative openings in the private sector. It is a law of nature that the introduction of retrogressive terms or withdrawal of privileges will draw a negative, if not hostile, reaction from those affected by them. The history of the ACS abounds with such incidents. For example, the African clerical staff denounced government proposals of 1934 to dilute African salary scales and replace free pensions with a contributory provident fund. Those Africans who had better prospects with the native administrations left the Protectorate government.[46] The Asians, not having 'tribal' governments to seek refuge in, turned to private commercial and professional firms for alternative employment. The 1970 austerity measures, moreover, were applicable to a 'public body' the definition of which was greatly enlarged.[47] Thus to many highly qualified Asian professionals public employment probably became less lucrative after April 1970.

Asian resignations from the public service to join the private sector or to emigrate in the last resort were subsequently interpreted as 'disloyalty' to the government.[48] Emigration was possible because of the historical rootlessness of many Asians which was not lessened by either the colonial or the independent governments in Uganda. For the Africans, emigration, if not unthinkable, is very rare. Also African resignations from the civil service did not arouse suspicion or draw criticism because they helped to Africanize other fields of national life.

During the colonial period, when Asians were generally confined to the middle tier of the UCS, there was indeed a tendency among many of them (Goans being an exception) to regard government employment as a transit stage to a business venture where they would encounter fewer restrictions. However, the post-independence Africanization of commerce substantially curbed such proclivities among Asian civil servants. Hence it is reasonable to believe that the professional employees such as doctors, economists, teachers, lawyers, veterinarians, and others would not have viewed the UCS as a stepping-stone to something else, if there had been no discrimination against them and had not the 1970 austerity measures reduced its attractiveness. Their professional qualifications also conferred a certain amount of international mobility and many of them had already emigrated from Uganda by 1971-2. In other words, the behaviour of professional Asians seeking employment in Uganda was conditioned by the prevailing labour market rather than by their race.

The decline in manpower after the departure of non-citizen Asians and other expatriates from Uganda caused an acute shortage of high-level skills in many sectors throughout the 1960s.[49] This further inflated the market value of citizen Asian professionals who found private employment comparatively rewarding, just as African graduates from Makerere did. It is common knowledge in Uganda that oil companies, banks, and insurance firms were generally rated above the public service by African graduates—once Africanization had opened up these areas to them.

In late 1970 the morale of those professional and executive class Asian public servants, interviewed by the writer in Kampala and Entebbe, was extremely low because of uncertainty about their future prospects. Right up to the early 1950s, British equivocation about the Africanization of the bureaucracy had led many capable Africans to treat Protectorate employment as a springboard to chieftaincies or other more lucrative native administration posts. Similarly, the Uganda government's equivocation concerning Asians by politicians as well as senior civil servants offered very little assurance to them.

It should, however, be mentioned that in addition to *real* discrimination there was probably *alleged* as well as *imaginary* discrimination against Asians in the post-independence UCS. Certain capable and proven individuals known to the writer had been frequently overlooked for promotion or refused appointments to fill vacancies. On the other hand some citizen Asians who complained about discrimination were simply using it as a convenient excuse to disguise their incompetence or mediocrity.

At the Asian conference of 8 December 1971, Amin enumerated certain other aspects of Asian conduct in the UCS that enraged his government. He fumed at those Asian resignations caused by the government decision to transfer them from urban to rural areas. Amin rejected the reasons given by the Asians—lack of comparable educational, housing, and medical facilities—and attributed their refusal to be transferred 'to the fact that a good number of them have side businesses. . .from which they get extra huge sums of money. . .'

Transfer of civil servants has always been a thorny problem almost everywhere. In Uganda's case African civil servants have generally been unhappy about transfers, especially to areas outside their tribal territory. Besides disliking the idea of being removed from their own cultural and linguistic group, many have *shambas* (vegetable and fruit gardens) where they grow their own food. Thus to many Africans transfers had been and continue to be not only socially disruptive but also financially disadvantageous. Before the availability of *matoke* (plantain) in other parts of Uganda and East Africa, the Baganda were traditionally reluctant to work outside the plantain-growing areas. Their efficiency and morale were somewhat low if separated from Ganda diet and society for prolonged periods.

Undoubtedly, transfers were distasteful to some Asians because they were either silent partners in businesses managed by relatives or because their spouses ran small shops. But there were other important reasons. While Asians did not have *shambas* to provide them with food or supplementary incomes, they often shared their houses with parents or other family members for economic and social reasons. Ugandan towns are relatively small and they are the only places with proper educational, medical, and social amenities. Also, Asian mosques and temples were usually found only in the urban centres. Hence Ugandan towns—unlike the large, sprawling, polluted, and overcrowded industrial cities of the developed world—are eminently livable. Not surprisingly Asian civil servants, like their African colleagues,[50] resisted transfer to up-country areas.

Moreover, the Asians' equivalent of 'tribes' were the 'communities' which for historical and other reasons were concentrated in the townships. The Asians had not yet been fully dislodged from their communal cocoons and were as communally-minded as the Africans are tribally-oriented. This was another important factor that made up-country appointments unpalatable to the Asians. Since the situation was not very different among African staff, the Asian attitude to transfers needs to be seen as part of a national phenomenon and not as something peculiar to the Asian civil servants.

Lastly, the Asian community as a whole was held primarily responsible for corruption in government departments and parastatal bodies dealing with that community.[51] Corruption in these organizations, however, is to a great extent a cause of governmental failure to fill vacancies, restructure the UCS, discipline some of its senior officials, and curb their 'mercenary tendencies'.[52] During the 1960s senior public officers increasingly became indifferent to their duties and arrogant and opportunistic in dealing with the public.

According to Jacobs' review of the UCS in 1964, the main causes of inefficiency in the UCS were poor organization, improper allocation of work, staff shortages, and the unhealthy attitude of senior African staff—which regarded its salaries and privileges as inadequate. Shortage of skilled personnel and the wrong or arrogant outlook of departmental heads, among other things, slowed down the entire government machine, lowered its morale, and attracted people interested in benefits rather than careers. The effects of all this on the public was that, since normal channels failed to produce quick results, the public tried round-about ways. The civil servants, on their part, welcomed the situation for obvious reasons.[53] The picture had become grimmer by 1970. In Peter Kawesa's words, senior officials had become 'empire builders and embryonic monarchs'.[54] When dealing with such uncivil and avaricious officials, the public realized that only oiling their palms would produce satisfactory results.

The arrogance and 'master' mentality of civil servants towards the common man was also acknowledged and condemned by Abdalla-Anyuru, the Chairman of the Public Service Commission, in 1970.[55] Ordinary Africans as well as the Asians were victimized by many government officers. The plight of the Asians was well known to them. Numerous unnecessary visits, insults, and deliberate obstruction in obtaining trading or other related licences and passports would, it soon became evident, disappear if a bribe was offered. It is also likely that some African civil servants regarded the Asian community as a useful, if not legitimate, group to exploit in this way while to others the Asians had apparently become an indispensable source of extra income. When the pattern set by the 'empire builders' at the top goes un-punished, the temptation at the lower levels to follow suit becomes irresistible.

In conclusion one may ask: how will the Asian professionals regard government employment in their countries of settlement since their expulsion? For the vast majority, the countries they now live in will be their permanent homes. They will probably approach government service in two fairly predictable ways, depending somewhat on family and communal backgrounds in Uganda. The commercially motivated ones who place a premium on acquisition of wealth rather than pro-fessional careers may possibly treat it as a stepping-stone to private practice—once they have familiarized themselves with local conditions and saved enough money. The second type of Asian professional, particularly from the Goan and other communities with no firm business traditions, will tend to be career-oriented and will serve faith-fully unless real or imaginary discrimination dictates otherwise.

8

ASIANS AND POLITICS
IN LATE COLONIAL UGANDA:
SOME PERSONAL RECOLLECTIONS*

Sir Amar Maini

The recent history of East African Asians is often said to fall into merely two periods: the colonial and the post-colonial. On this view, apart from the short decolonizing phase when African politicians were pre-occupied with other matters and anyway too dependent on the Asian vote in the towns to come out openly against them, East African Asians constituted a privileged minority who were bound to suffer once British colonial rule ended. While there is some truth in this view, there are several drawbacks to conventional wisdom here, and in this chapter attention will be drawn to one particular error in it. This is its chronological naivety. For within both the colonial and the post-colonial eras in East Africa not one but several periods need to be distinguished. In this chapter we shall be concerned with one such period in Uganda of which the writer has special knowledge—the late colonial period. First, a general review of this period will be attempted. Then several aspects of it will be isolated for particular comment, before finally considering again that crucial catalyst of late colonial politics in Uganda, the Kabaka crisis of 1953–5.

During the run-up to the Second World War, Uganda was politically a very quiet place. In Kenya all was commotion. If settlers were not attacking non-settlers, one tribe would be rivalling another; if the settler and non-settler tribes happened to be silent, the Asians would be at one another's throats—Muslim struggling against Hindu, one Hindu community vying with another. By comparison Uganda seemed very quiet. Protectorate administrators were rarely attacked in public, the ascendancy of the Baganda among the African population seemed assured by the treaty which their leaders had concluded with the British in 1900, and the Asian community there was too small yet to be seriously divided by religious animosities.

* This chapter is based on several tape-recordings of Sir Amar Maini in conversation with Professor W. H. Morris-Jones, Dr Hugh Tinker, and the editor. The last has undertaken selection and presentation of material but the views expressed are those of Sir Amar Maini who has approved the final draft.

The war brought a speeding up of activity throughout the country, bringing new problems and adding new dimensions to existing ones. The Asian community inevitably felt the impact of these changes. There was considerable expansion in agricultural production, trade, and industrial development. Educating the increasing numbers of children in the community needed attention. There was the question of Asian representation on mushrooming public bodies, which in turn intensified personality conflicts between the various aspirants for office. In all these matters the community groped for elucidation, guidance, and organization in order to protect its interests. A poor class of Indians had also started to emerge in the larger towns. These, then, were some of the reasons why we revived the Indian Association at Kampala and the Central Council of Indian Associations (CCIA) at this time. Another was concern about new restrictions on immigration, concern that was to have not unimportant implications for the subsequent citizenship issue. Yet another factor was anxiety among those of us with experience of Kenya lest Muslim-Hindu animosity be replicated among Indians in Uganda as vehemently as it had shown itself in Kenya.

There were not many Asian families with businesses in both Kenya and Uganda at this time. To Indians in Kenya, Uganda was the land of blackwater fever where pioneers were to be admired more frequently than followed. To most of their counterparts in Uganda, Kenya was just a succession of railway stations linking Lake Victoria to Mombasa, the principal point of embarkation on the East African coast for India. My father was one of the relatively small group of Asian businessmen then having substantial contacts in both territories. As Punjabi Hindus we were a small community even in Nairobi, and as a boy at the local government Indian school my classmates belonged to all communities. Most Punjabis then came to East Africa in order to work as skilled artisans, law clerks, doctors, and in other professional capacities, or on the railways or in some government department. When I was a boy most substantial businesses were in the hands either of Gujerati-speaking Muslims—Ismailis, Bohras, and the like—or of members of those leading Gujerati Hindu communities in East Africa, the Oswals, the Lohanas, and the Patidars. But gradually my father built up a family interest in the construction business sufficient to support my studies at the London School of Economics and the Middle Temple, and during the inter-war years he was also persuaded by a Punjabi friend to acquire an interest in property in Uganda. That was one reason (another was my father's failing health) why in 1939 I gave up my legal practice in Nairobi in order to become a businessman in Uganda.

How I also became involved with public affairs in Uganda is not difficult to explain. In Nairobi I had been a member of both the municipal and legislative councils and had been involved with Indian political bodies like the East African Indian National Congress. Shortly after settling in Uganda I was asked to become a member of the Township Authority of Kampala and, after some time, also to write a report on it in the light of my Kenyan experience. After this the protectorate authorities promulgated a special ordinance, the Mehta family of Lugazi donated £10,000 towards the cost of new buildings and, as effective chairman by now of the township authority, I was appointed Mayor of Kampala in 1950. This office I held for five years. In 1944 the Governor also invited me to take the place of M. M. Patel, a leading doctor in Kampala and a member of the Patidar community, as one of the two Indian members of Legislative Council, but Legco in Uganda operated very differently from its counterpart in Kenya. In Uganda there were no lengthy speeches, no open confrontation with government officials. Since membership was by nomination rather than through election, the Governor was a far more powerful figure than any of his creatures in the Legislative Council. The number of advisory committees to which members belonged was thus much more important than volubility in Legco.

Gradually I started serving on many committees, boards, and bodies covering a wide spectrum of Uganda's life. On one of these committees we had to deal with applications for entry into the country under the new immigration rules. First in 1944 under defence regulations, then under ordinance four years later, immigration into Uganda was strictly controlled and the number of Indians coming into the country drastically reduced. In India this policy was unpopular but in Uganda, although most Asian bodies publicly opposed it and there were genuine fears of political motivation behind the controls, there was much to be said for it. Already there was serious over-crowding in Kampala, and a class of poor Indians had already started to emerge there. Animosity towards Indians was apparent in the riots that had erupted throughout Uganda in 1945, and there were further evidences of it in the disturbances associated with Ignatius Musazi (an important Uganda politician who was a founder-member of both the Federation of Uganda African Farmers and the Uganda National Congress) four years later. As regards implementation of immigration policy, there was no racialism about it in Uganda. Where Indians wanted to accept jobs in Uganda at this time and real vacancies existed, and satisfactory housing was shown to be available, no genuine cases are known to have been refused. In Kenya the issue became politicized, and was argued on that basis—but there was little that could be done about that in Uganda. Furthermore, an ordinance represented a considerable improvement on defence regulations: what had previously been a question of personal discretion now became a straightforward matter of law.

In India the matter was viewed differently. It was also the view of the East African Indian National Congress that these controls should be opposed, and at a very representative meeting of the East African Indian National Congress at Mombasa a resolution was passed requesting Asian members of legislatures to propose resolutions for the repeal of these immigration control regulations. Delegates from Tanganyika and Uganda also attended this meeting and, if my memory is correct, this was the last occasion when Asian political leaders from all three East African territories met together. My first act as newly-appointed member of Legco in Uganda was to support H. K. Jaffer, a prominent insurance agent at Jinja and member of the Ithnasheri community, in proposing a motion deploring government action over immigration. The motion was a flop, largely because Jaffer had been unnerved earlier by an interview with the Chief Secretary who denounced us both for 'giving in to the Kenya agitators', and this was the first time that Jaffer was publicly opposing the protectorate authorities. However, we were both assured that the British government had no desire to proceed at the expense of any one section of the community and we worked on the basis of that assurance.

The first official representative of the independent Government of India in East Africa was Apa Pant. He soon became a good friend of mine. Kenya kept him extremely busy but he had little trouble to contend with in Uganda. Indeed, the only time that Uganda really required his close attention was immediately after the Musazi riots of 1949, when Indian traders in the Bulemezi/Bombo area of Buganda were frightened and we both toured the area to reassure them. His tranquillizer was 'integration'. The precise implications of this were never wholly spelt out by him but implicit in it was the assumption that rich Indians like the Mehtas and the Madhvanis would contribute towards African advancement through timely concessions, and that the common *dukawallahs* would be prepared to reform themselves completely. It was not a very auspicious message to preach in a country where existing Indian *dukawallahs* considerably outnumbered potential Indian philanthropists.

Nevertheless, there was one area in which the advice of the new Government of India and the views of the Indian *dukawallahs* in Uganda were in harmony, and this concerned citizenship. Once India became fully independent from Britain, it became possible for Indians abroad, upon satisfying certain conditions, to acquire Indian citizenship. Pant advised Indians in East Africa not to apply for the new Indian passports but to retain the ones to which they were already entitled as British subjects or as British protected persons. In this way East African Asians would be able to demonstrate irrefutably the sincerity of their desire to 'integrate' with local colonial peoples, though whether that consideration actually proved the prime motivation in the behaviour of East African Asians in this sphere is anything but certain. What is certain is that had Apa Pant been Indian High Commissioner at the time of Uganda's independence he would have urged local Asians to replace their British passports with Ugandan ones. Instead, as is well known, most Asians in Uganda preferred to retain their British passports. However, at the time that Pant was in East Africa it must be admitted that his advice was of more theoretical than practical value. In practice there was then not much pressure on Asians nor any real necessity for them to make any change in their formal citizenship status.

By 1959, however, it was clear that the future of Asians in Uganda would be a very precarious one. Following the Musazi riots and the appointment shortly afterwards of Sir Andrew Cohen as Governor of Uganda, control of cotton ginneries increasingly passed from Asian to African hands in the form of government-sponsored cooperatives. The coffee-processing industry was also open to African participation. Already land policy was especially favourable to Africans through the great difficulties involved in alienating *mailo* land to non-Africans in Buganda and through comparable restrictions elsewhere in Uganda. In the transport business considerable efforts were being made to encourage African participation, and the Ugandan civil service had already been Africanized to a degree unknown elsewhere in British East Africa. Parastatal bodies were now being set up which effectively pre-empted the possibility of non-Africans acquiring strangleholds over areas of economic activity as yet underdeveloped, such as electricity supply, cement manufacture, tea, textiles, and tourism. Yet, paradoxically enough, Africanization in these many spheres did not lead to any appreciable diminution in popular opposition to Asians in Uganda during the late colonial period. Indeed, while it must be admitted that xenophobia is the norm rather than the exception throughout human history, opposition to Asians (particularly in Buganda) seemed to increase rather than diminish with the progressive diminution of their actual control over the Ugandan economy.

Perhaps part of the explanation for this unexpected turn of events must be sought in the unintended consequences of certain policies implemented by Sir Andrew Cohen—in particular, in the shift of popular support in Buganda that his deportation of Mutesa II prompted from cotton and trade agitators like Ignatius Musazi to cultural traditionalists like Mikaeri Kintu. But the continuing exclusiveness of so many Asians living in Uganda at this time certainly provided their African opponents with sitting targets, and among the Asians themselves only the Ismailis seemed to possess an internal chain of communal command sufficiently strong to enable poorer members of their particular community to respond to the demands of the new situation created by the Kabaka's deportation with any degree of effectiveness compared with the richer ones.

To my mind, therefore, the die was cast not at the time that Africans took over as the recognized rulers of Uganda at the time of independence, but some time before as a consequence of the Kabaka crisis of 1953–5. Nevertheless, once it became clear several years after this crisis that Africans would soon be the recognized rulers, a group of younger Asians formed the Uganda Action Group (UAG) and declared that they would identify with the African cause in a manner which was totally unprecedented in earlier Asian history in Uganda. The group did not last very long, because on the formation of the Kabaka Yekka (KY) movement and the Uganda Peoples Congress (UPC) as well as the Democratic Party (DP) it became necessary for it to dissolve. But, while it lasted, UAG was a pressure group of 'young Turks' not unlike the one that we had formed when reviving CCIA at the time of the Second World War. Then, too, there had been an unprecedented situation requiring special action—poorer Indians no longer being able to return to India because of the war, few more being allowed in and both becoming clearly unpopular with Africans. Now UAG arose to tackle the situation created by imminent African independence.

Of course, once KY and UPC got under way as well as DP, it was difficult for idealism even among younger Asians not to be tempered by realism. Electoral campaigning is costly, especially in countries where communications are poor and the candidates themselves are not especially wealthy. In Uganda, where was it better to look for finance than to local Asian traders? All that was needed could be obtained from a small number of people but in every small town in the country there were to be found Indian traders who assisted African political parties and African leaders. This was done not only by providing useful organizational know-how and assistance with transport but with canvassing expenses too. The variety of collaboration was complex. What pay-offs were expected (or received) for such assistance is difficult to say. The Asian community in Uganda never got down to any systematic discussion and analysis of the implications of independence so as to decide upon any concerted approach to it. There were a multitude of responses within the Asian community in Uganda, most of them designed to keep open as many options as possible. These resulted in certain inconsistencies of behaviour by Asians, which led in turn to inevitable charges of hypocrisy when private actions did not (and could not) match up to public, stated aspirations. Much Asian behaviour at the time was therefore confused, but—with the benefit of hindsight—it must surely be said that it was somewhat naive for UAG members and others of similar opinion to assume that, by unreservedly associating themselves with African political parties at this time, the future of Asians in Uganda would necessarily be better secured.

To be sure, it was probably also naive for me to accept further public office in East Africa at this time. Sir Frederick Crawford had promised that my resignation from the government benches in Legco would be accepted well before independence but the anti-Asian boycott of Asian shops in Buganda during 1959–60 delayed things somewhat and it was not until after the boycott that I was able to accept the speaker-ship of the East African Central Legislative Assembly in Nairobi. The assembly had been established in 1948 and I had been a member of it from the start (first in a personal capacity, later as a government minister in Uganda) and now there was an invitation from all three Governors in East Africa for me to become Speaker. Perhaps it was foolish to accept the offer but at the time the central institutions were still intact and they covered a range of activities—railways, airways, income tax, customs and excise, research services, posts and tele-graphs, etc.—that seemed to represent a considerable transfer of power by the new states of Tanganyika, Uganda, and Kenya.

As it happened, the central institutions did not get a revenue of their own until it was too late for it to be effective: settlers in Kenya blocked it through fear that their interests might be harmed, and financial secretaries in all three territories were suspicious lest civil servants in the central institutions might lord things over them. Finally, as is well known, African politicians in Uganda sabotaged the whole concept of East African federation once it became clear that there would be little in it for Ugandan politicians if the status of Buganda and other ad-ministrations entrenched in the Ugandan constitution as federal units was to continue unchanged. Service in the Central Legislative Assembly was challenging and rewarding but gradually it became very clear to me that the parochial attachments of CLA members to their individual states were such as to preclude any early blossoming of the flower of unity in East Africa.

Nevertheless, CLA was exciting because my involvement with it was not simply as an 'Asian politician'. In Uganda, it was also one of my concerns to be more than this. As an Asian serving on multifarious boards and committees there it was difficult to be much other, and throughout the Second World War it was impossible for any Indian involved in public affairs in Uganda to ignore related duties in this sphere (for example, Jaffer and I acted as arbitrators for the Indian Merchant Chamber during the war, determining what share of incoming cotton piece-goods should go to whom among the Indian trading community). But after the war Kampala Township Authority constituted a much wider political field, as also did the executive council and subsequent ministerial positions in corporations and regional communications and in commerce and industry. In the latter position the wheel almost came full circle in an attempt to set up joint partnerships between Asian and African traders retailing such basic commodities as sugar, salt, cement and corrugated iron sheets, bicycles, etc., in West Nile District. African and Asian participants were to have equal shares in a wholesale company, with the local trade development officer controlling the casting vote. Unfortunately, this particular scheme was thwarted by the delaying tactics of the Asian traders and by my resignation from the ministry.

There was also another reason why one was concerned to be more than merely an 'Asian politician' in East Africa. Asian politics there tended to gravitate to the communal level, and it was clear that anybody in Uganda belonging to so small a community as the Punjabi Hindus could hardly expect much support at any polls on purely communal grounds. Communalism was always a fact of life in Uganda, though perhaps to a lesser extent than in Kenya. We had been particularly conscious of its divisive potentialities at the time of the Second World War. But the partition of the Indian sub-continent into the successor states of India and Pakistan made things much worse. There were the inevitable disputes about money. Before partition a fund had been set up in Uganda to relieve famine in Bengal. After partition there were endless disputes over how much money had been donated to the fund by Muslims, what proportion by Hindus. Then there were other internal divisions among the Asian population of a non-communal nature. The split between the East African Indian National Congress and the Federation of Indian Chambers of Commerce was largely a split between Asian politicians in Nairobi and Asian merchants at Mombasa. It was primarily a Kenyan split but in so far as Ugandan Asians took sides it was mostly because their dealings were more with Mombasa than with Nairobi. There was also a territorial split between Asians in Kenya and Asians in Uganda, of which the Gandhi Memorial Academy became symbolic.

This was the product of a fund established to honour the memory of Mahatma Gandhi in East Africa. Since both the Madhvani and Mehta families were likely to be major contributors to this fund and both had their principal bases in Uganda, several of us in Uganda felt strongly that the resulting memorial should be sited in Uganda. The Principal of Makerere College in Kampala was approached to see whether the Gandhi Memorial Academy might be established there. The Principal listened to our proposal, but later reported back to us that there would be 'various difficulties' should we persist with the proposal; it was because of this answer of 'neither yes nor no' that the Academy was eventually established in Nairobi. Subsequently, it was said that an objection had been raised on the Makerere College Council when the proposal was first mooted there, to the effect that, should the Academy be associated with Makerere, Asians might subsequently claim special privileges at an institution originally founded with the principal intention of benefiting Africans.

This draws attention to another problem. African education in late colonial Uganda was still mostly in the hands of Christian missionaries and with few exceptions Asians did not attend the same secondary schools as Africans. As the main custodians of African education, European missionaries tended to be wary of Asian schoolchildren who competed for the same jobs in the civil service as their own pupils. This concern was shared by many British administrators. Furthermore, such rivalry was not confined to the civil service. As major vehicles too of industrial training in Uganda, Christian schools also produced Africans rivalling Asians in the artisan sphere and, especially outside Kampala, Catholic priests were popularly regarded as being antagonistic towards them for this reason alone. The Goans, being Catholics, were of course an exception to this general rule, but their community was only really numerous at Kampala and Entebbe, and elsewhere was too small to be of much consequence in this matter. Furthermore, the philanthropic assistance given to such bodies as the East African Muslim Welfare Association by Muslim Asians further seemed to incense Christian missionaries. So, given this background, it is perhaps not surprising that Makerere should have taken up such a negative position over the Gandhi Memorial Academy.

Immediately before and after independence things did change somewhat in the educational sphere. First there was more mixing between African and Asian schoolchildren with the establishment of Higher School Certificate courses at the leading Asian urban schools, then still more with the opening of School Certificate courses in these schools to African pupils. Milton Obote was genuinely non-racialist in his policies towards the Asian population of Uganda after independence, and his Trade Licensing Act was directed, not against Asian traders as such, but against those of them who were non-citizens of the country. But Obote had such huge problems to contend with in Buganda and in the armed forces that he had insufficient time to consider those papers that were put up to him through the Milton Obote Foundation on the role of the Asian minority in post-colonial Uganda. And it must be admitted that, even if Obote had enjoyed sufficient leisure to decide on positive policies towards the Asian minority population, there was such a short-fall in civil service capability in the first years of independence (a three-fold increase in work-load, combined with a 35 per cent lacuna in filling even existing positions) that it would have been virtually impossible on purely administrative grounds to implement any further schemes for joint trading partnerships between Africans and Asians of the sort that had been attempted earlier in West Nile District.

It was because of considerations such as these that there arose in late colonial Uganda the dilemma of the Asian abroad in colonial conditions in an unusually acute form. In Uganda you had a community mainly commercial, clerical, and artisan, possessing no real power of its own and existing in a country where the British government was still supreme and where British administrators still operated through a system of personal rule. These traditions did not recognize the legitimacy of public agitation. On the contrary, they stressed the duty of a minority community under British protection to obey the law. The laws with regard to sedition in East Africa were especially strict, as became clear whenever sedition cases arose with regard to African newspaper editors, and Asians were in a much weaker political position here than Africans, lacking as they did a clear territorial base. Granted those considerations and also the fact that African political consciousness had not yet really developed very much, it is hardly surprising how little was known among Asians of the political views of Africans. The resulting dilemma confronting Asians in Uganda was a recurrent one, but it was the Kabaka crisis of 1953–5 that caused it to arise in a particularly acute form.

The main details of this crisis are well known, the fullest account being D. A. Low, *Buganda in Modern History* (London, 1971). The initial decision to deport Mutesa II was conveyed to members of the Ugandan executive council by the Governor and, except for that Governor and his immediate legal and political advisers, nobody else had been consulted before the decision was made. When the Kabaka was deported, the British Colonial Secretary also announced that he would never return. Several unofficial members of Legco, African and European as well as Asian, felt strongly that as the Baganda possessed such strong clan structures and formed such a closely knit tribal community, in order to avoid further trouble it was essential to proceed to the appointment of a new Kabaka. However, the Governor's principal advisers disagreed and a chance was therefore missed. Instead agitation increased among the Baganda for the return of the Kabaka and we had the case of the bearded man, the man who wore barkcloth, and so on.

The eventual outcome was that the British government agreed that the Kabaka should return to Uganda. There were three conditions. First, the Kabaka would act constitutionally; that is, he was to rule with the advice of his ministers and in any conflict between his government and the central government it was his ministers who were to be held responsible. Secondly, the Kabaka's representatives would participate in the Legislative Council. Thirdly, the Baganda would accept the central legislative set-up which had been an emotional issue in Buganda for some time. The extent to which the Baganda adhered to—or, more correctly, did not adhere to—these conditions goes beyond the scope of this chapter, but we must take note of the impact of the Kabaka crisis as a whole upon Indo-Bugandan relations.

Immediately after Mutesa's return, the view was expressed in traditionalist circles in Buganda that the non-African community had not done anything to bring the Kabaka back. They had not participated in the bearded man agitation, they had not put on barkcloth, they had not even made public representations about the deportation to newspapers or even in letters to the Secretary of State. Since there were comparatively few Europeans in Uganda at this time in unofficial positions, the charge was directed principally at the Asian community and it developed into a political issue. It is my belief that there were certain people in Buganda who actively helped on this process, Mikaeri Kintu, *Katikiro* (the chief minister in the Kabaka's government) of the time, was one such person; deeply rooted in Baganda traditions, he clearly felt that Asian behaviour during the Kabaka crisis had demonstrated once and for all their basic incompatibility with the Baganda. Sempa, one of the Baganda ministers after Mutesa's return, said much the same sort of thing. Clearly both these men had learnt more than one lesson from the Musazi riots of 1949, and they were now harnessing popular resentments of the sort that Musazi had earlier articulated in the service of Buganda traditionalism. One inevitable side-effect of this traditionalist revival was anti-Asian animosity.

At the time one was aware that something was afoot, but it was the late Gupala Menon (who followed Apa Pant as Indian High Commissioner in Nairobi) who told me during one of his visits to Kampala that there was a tremendous amount of hostility among the Kabaka's ministers, and chiefs had stressed to him that, as a member of the executive council of the day and subsequently a central government minister, I myself had not done anything to speed the return of Mutesa. One was able to tell Indian diplomats like Menon that the role of the executive council in the matter was one of courtesy rather than one of tendering advice, and that indeed it could hardly have been otherwise. In Uganda Kabaka-British relations were solely a matter between the

Kabaka's government and the British government. However, in Buganda these legal niceties were not considered important, and non-Baganda had little control over Baganda opinion here. All that one could do was to adjust as well as possible to the situation created by Mutesa's return. It was a situation characterized by considerable coolness between the Kabaka's ministers and people like myself. Just before he left Uganda, Sir Andrew Cohen told me that he had met the Kabaka privately and been told by him that the Kabaka's regard for me was as high as ever, but that he could not vouch for his ministers.

Before Mutesa's deportation he would greet me at the Town Hall almost like one of his own chiefs, and we discussed many matters of mutual interest. One such matter was the central institutions of East Africa. Mutesa would always say that these institutions had become such an emotional matter for the Baganda that it was impossible to consider them rationally at *lukiko* (formally established as an assembly of chiefs under the 1900 Agreement with Britain, but by now at least partly democratized) level, but that Buganda's interest was best preserved by retaining the *status quo*. And the Baganda stance at this time ('We don't want the High Commission, but we don't want to change it either') did further Baganda interests. Individual Baganda benefited from employment opportunities provided by further development of the post office, and the area of Buganda around Mityana benefited considerably from the extension of the railway from Kampala to Kasese under High Commission auspices. Before Sir Andrew Cohen deported Mutesa II, it was clear that what in India was merely irksome would prove intolerable in Uganda: the native prince turning into a black white man. It was clear then that in the conservative and clannish society of Buganda Mutesa was already finding things difficult, as indeed had also his father with none of his opportunities (military service in Britain, university study at Cambridge). But what no Indian in Uganda could possibly have anticipated was that one day Mutesa would be so reconciled with his people as to make the Asian dilemma in Uganda quite frightfully acute. The Baganda were traditionally hostile to anyone but themselves, and one always wondered how friendly they really were towards one another. They struck me as the the most complicated phenomenon outside India, matching some of our Indian communities in the complexity of their intrigues and social attitudes. The Baganda were always difficult for non-Baganda to understand, but after the deportation of Mutesa their attitudes towards outsiders became positively opaque.

When Kabaka Yekka became an important political force at the very end of the colonial period in Uganda, it competed for the Asian urban vote as energetically as did the Democratic Party and the

Uganda Peoples Congress. Indians like Sugra Visram joined KY as other Asians joined other parties. There was therefore a turning to Asians for political support just before independence, but it is clear that it was a false dawn. The Baganda traditionalists had already made up their minds to harass the Indians. This to my mind is the significance of the Kabaka crisis of 1953-5 for the Asian problem in Uganda.

9

INDIA AND THE ASIANS IN EAST AFRICA

Anirudha Gupta

Three aspects of the Asian situation in East Africa are relevant to an understanding of Indian official policy towards the Asians who have settled there:

(a) *The Image of Asian Settlers:* To an average African the dress the Asians wear, the food they take, and the social customs and relations they follow, appear so strikingly similar that he sees them as a single entity and seldom notices the differences between them as individual groups or communities. Indeed the social exclusiveness maintained by the Asians in inter-racial relations and the fact that a majority of them are engaged in petty trade and commerce have only helped to perpetuate the image of Asian settlers in the host countries as a single racially distinct community interested only in making money through unscrupulous business practices.

(b) *Legal Status:* For a variety of reasons[1] a majority of Asians chose to retain their British passports. Although technically this made them aliens in the host countries, the implications of their status as British citizens did not dawn upon them until recently. Except for occasional visits to Britain and putting a part of their savings in British banks, they did not attach much importance to their British citizenship. It was not until the controversy over the 1968 immigration bill started a wave of panic among them that they took their legal status seriously. Since then the issue with non-citizen Asians in East Africa has been one of seeking escape-routes to Britain rather than of adjusting their position or role with the changing African scene.

(c) *Socio-cultural Ethnocentricism:* Notwithstanding their long stay in Africa, whether as citizen or non-citizen, the Asians in general have preserved their native—essentially Indian—tradition and culture. Not only that. They have continued to maintain their contact with their ancestral homes in India through frequent visits, marriage, and caste and kinship ties. Their tastes and habits modelled on Indian motifs, their craze for Indian cinema and music, their lavish hospitality and welcome to visitors from India, have tended to accentuate their 'Indianness' to a point which is most irritating to the Africans. Not unnaturally therefore the Africans question their bona fides, citing their apparent apathy towards African causes and problems, traditions and symbols, as proving their political disloyalty.

The cultural ethnocentrism of the Asians has made their position vulnerable in yet another respect. With the possible exception of a few Muslim sects,[2] they have come to acquire a 'dependency-complex' towards India. This is evident from the way they crave help and advice from Indian officials and visitors even on such petty issues as obtaining a licence, or sending their wards abroad for higher education, or simply in getting their in-group rivalries settled. The net result of this attitude of dependence has been an erosion of an independent Asian will and initiative in Africa.

What bearing, it may be asked, have these matters on the shaping of India's policy towards the Asians in East Africa? The question is not easy to answer. For, as will be seen from the following discussion, all these aspects, whether singly or jointly, affect in some way or other the whole gamut of India's relationship with its countrymen on the one hand and with the East African governments on the other. Thus, the fact that the Asians constitute a privileged group in the East African societies definitely conflicts with India's commitment to the African aspiration for economic advancement and racial equality. In principle, India cannot but support the measures taken by the African governments to oust the Asians from their 'dominant heights' in the economy. But does it mean that if the immigrants had comprised a poorer stratum of society, as in Ceylon and Malaysia, India's attitude towards them would have been different? Considering the fact that they were not Indian nationals, how would India have intervened on their behalf? Further, what about the basic paradox: that of the Asians preferring to remain British citizens and yet expecting (at least till the end of the 1960s) India to protect their interests? How can this paradox be explained? Can it be attributed to what we have just described as their 'dependency-complex'? Or is it the result of some ambivalence in India's own stand in regard to their problems?

Answers to these and such other questions have been attempted in this chapter. The discussion is presented in three parts. Part I examines at length the essential features of India's association with her nationals settled in East Africa during the nationalist as well as post-independence periods. Keeping this background in view, an attempt has been made in Part II to provide an understanding of the obligations the Asians expected India to fulfil, the role the latter wanted them to perform, and what followed in consequence. Part III is devoted to an analysis of the factors which influenced India's reaction to the Asian crises in Kenya and Uganda. The two related issues examined here are whether these crises affected India's relations with the African countries and to what extent the Asians considered the Indian attitude satisfactory from their own point of view. Finally the main points of the discussion are summarized.

I

The historical associations between the Indian nationalists and the Indian settlers in East Africa are considered in the chapter by Hugh Tinker. Here I shall confine myself to noting only such of those relations which have had a bearing on the shaping of India's official attitude towards these particular settlers.

The fact that these particular Indians left the security of their ancestral home to make a living in foreign lands, often against severe odds, evoked in India a sentimental and romantic image of them. Their self-reliance, adventurous spirit, and rigid adherence to Indian traditions and customs were a matter of pride for the Indian nationalist leaders. As Nehru once said: 'Wherever in this wide world there goes an Indian, there also goes a bit of India with him.'[3]

Politically, Gandhi's epic struggle in South Africa to secure a just and equal status for the Indian community in a European-dominated territory influenced a good deal of the nationalist attitude in India. The similarities between the South African and East African situations induced the Indian leaders to extend a wide measure of support to the Indian communities in East Africa even though there was a certain divergence of views among the Indian nationalists on other matters. Thus, whereas the Indian Liberals felt that if Indians and Europeans in East Africa enjoyed an equal position it would secure for India an equal status in the British Empire, the leaders of the Indian National Congress held that unless India became completely independent from British control there could be no justice for Indians in any British dependency.[4] The latter therefore advised the Indian settlers in East Africa to organize themselves on the model of the Indian Congress, cooperate with the aspirations of the local people, and contribute their mite to the struggle for Indian independence.

At the instance of Nehru, around the close of the Second World War Indian nationalist opinion was imbued with the image of a resurgent Asia working hand-in-hand with a resurgent Africa; the two strands of resurgence being anti-imperialism and anti-racialism. In fashioning such a broad view, it was hardly necessary to define very carefully the position of Indian communities in different parts of the world. The point was that in the East African territories, where Indians constituted both a privileged minority and a separate racial group, a struggle against racial and imperial domination was bound to take a course which would have affected their interests adversely. Although this did not become apparent immediately, when it did there was a divergence of opinion among the Indian nationalists on the subject. Those who were inspired by the image of a greater India with a part of its surplus population settled in different parts of the world were thus in favour of supporting and protecting the interests of Indian communities abroad. They argued that this would be advantageous to India in the long run.[5] This was a view which leaders like Nehru and his followers considered as a form of imperialism in reverse. They argued that the new relationship between the ex-colonial peoples should be founded on national and racial equality without caring for the special rights of the Indian communities abroad.

The first clear directive in this regard was given by the All-India Congress Committee in September 1953 in a resolution which supported the just struggle of Africans against 'the domination of one race over others'.[6] The resolution noted with gratification the growing co-operation between Africans and Indians but at the same time added a note of caution: 'Indians abroad [should] demand no official privileges at the expense of the country in which they live. In Africa the interest of the Africans must be paramount and it is the duty of the Indians there to cooperate with them and help them to the best of their ability.'[7]

In the early 1950s this policy was reiterated more vigorously by the Government of India. It was by then becoming clear that one of the roles India wanted to play in international affairs was to champion the cause of the oppressed people under colonial and racial domination. Under the circumstances it would have been inconsistent on India's part to call for the protection of certain groups of people in Africa merely because of their being Indian in origin. At the same time there were indications that India wanted to make use of the Indian settlers in East Africa as a means of supporting the African nationalist interests. It was with this end in view that India's official representatives were asked to educate the Indian settlers about the basic aims and implications of Indian policy.[8]

Initially the Asians accepted the advice of the Indian government to take up British citizenship which gave them equal status with the Africans.[9] Technically this enabled them to join the African movement for political independence and for a brief period it appeared as though the two communities would forge a common platform against the European settlers. The outbreak of the Mau Mau violence in Kenya, however, impressed on India that inter-racial strife might take a course similar to that of South Africa unless Africans abjured violence in principle and the colonial government took steps to restrain the local Europeans. Thus, commenting on the declaration of emergency following the Mau Mau uprising, the Government of India made it clear that 'while they unreservedly condemn violence, repression alone offers no solution and. . .efforts should be made to deal with the root causes of the outbreak of violence by the Kikuyu tribe, and for the removal of their just grievances and numerous disabilities.'[10]

Whether or not India wanted the Asian community to exert a softening influence on the militant elements among the African nationalists is a matter on which we know little but the fact that it encouraged greater Asian participation in nationalist politics caused great misapprehensions among the Europeans. In the long run this proved most damaging to Asian-European relations in East Africa. Fraternization with the African nationalists, on the other hand, did not help very much to boost the Asian image in the eyes of local Africans. Instead, the latter wanted to make sure that the withdrawal of European power from East Africa should not be taken by the Asians as an opportunity to entrench their own position. This was a point which India too was anxious to emphasize, probably with a view to allaying African fears, and therefore it insisted that Asians must surrender all privileges and identify themselves with the local inhabitants. Thus, in 1953, Nehru went as far as to declare:

We have rather gone out of our way to tell our people in Africa. . .that they can expect no help from us, no protection from us, if they seek any special rights in Africa which are not in the interest of Africans. . .[We have told them] we shall help you naturally, we are interested in protecting your dignity or interest, but not if you go at all against the people of Africa, because you are their guests; and if they do not want you, out you will have to go, bag and baggage.[11]

This statement created a good deal of misunderstanding among both Asians and Africans. The insistence that Asians should not go against the Africans, being so vaguely worded, was interpreted by the latter in various ways depending on their predilections. The Asians also were not clear as to what Nehru meant by describing them as 'guests'. Was he visualizing that the Africans after gaining independence would force them out from their adopted lands? If so, how was the advice relevant to the Asians?[12]

Thus, by the time independence came to East Africa, Indian official attitudes on matters concerning the Asians left a large number of questions unanswered. Neither Nehru nor his government stated what exactly would be India's stand if the Indian minority were discriminated against or victimized by the African majority, nor whether it would take any responsibility for the Indian settlers even if they opted for African citizenship. All these questions remained buried under the obsessive concern for integrating the Indian settlers with the local Africans.

It is pertinent to ask here what the term 'integration' implied, the more so since neither the African nor the Indian leaders cared to define it. Broadly, the term has a legal as well as a socio-cultural connotation. In the legal sense, what India meant was that the Asians should accept local citizenship. Implied in this advice there was perhaps the expectation that the Indian settlers would accept, as in the colonial era, India's leadership on matters of vital importance to them. If so, it did not apparently take into account the far-reaching changes that have since transformed the East African scene. By 1962, as a result of the British Immigration Act, Indian settlers had opted for British citizenship for three important reasons: (i) the abolition of the dual citizenship system under the Indian Constitution; (ii) the uncertainties caused by the process of decolonization in Africa; (iii) the assurance given to them by the British government that they would have free entry to Britain.[13]

Until their right of entry to Britain came to be questioned in 1967–8, there was no immediate inducement for the Asians to choose East African citizenship. And by the time the choice had to be made it was too late to get African citizenship. At any rate the East African governments were not interested in giving citizenship to a large number of Asians.[14]

Notwithstanding these circumstances, the Government of India instructed its missions in East Africa to persuade the Asians to surrender their British passports and accept local citizenship. The arguments advanced in favour of this move seem to have been as follows: (a) by becoming citizens Asians could play a constructive role in African society; (b) by surrendering their British passports, they would appeal to African sentiment by showing that they were anti-imperialist; and (c) that in fact there would still be no difficulty in their returning to India whenever they wished. During the two years' period of grace when applications for citizenship were entertained by African governments, Indian diplomats made an intensive effort to mobilize the Asian community in favour of this move. These efforts did not, however, make much headway as the Asians were not convinced that by becoming African citizens they would fare any better. Also, since a number of applications for citizenship were not accepted, the Asians argued that it was not entirely in their power to obtain African citizenship.

As for the socio-cultural connotation, this only helped to create further misunderstandings. The Asian settlers argued that integration would involve not only surrendering their tradition and customs, but also giving their daughters in marriage to local Africans. If, on the other hand, integration meant only acceptance of African leadership, the Asians pointed out that this was precisely what they were doing. As a matter of fact, being a minority, all that they were anxious about was that they be left alone to pursue their economic activities. In the economic sphere, also, there was difficulty. The pattern on which most Asian business was conducted made it difficult to co-opt Africans as partners in business ventures. Excepting a few prosperous Asian families with large investments in industrial and commercial undertakings, it was not easy for the Asian *lah* either to employ Africans or to make them shareholders in their family enterprises. Given time it was probable that a number of relatively prosperous Asians might have accepted Africans as partners—if only to help adjust their position to growing African expectations. But even this would only have remained at best a remote possibility, as most African politicians usually doubted the motives behind such gestures. A Kenya politician once said that he would view such an offer of a business partnership as nothing more than a stage performance.[15] Similarly, social intermixing by Asians was dubbed as an excuse to meet Africans on a 'cocktail party' basis. On the whole it was made clear by African rulers, especially in Kenya and Uganda, that Asians were unwanted 'guests'. Faced with such overt antagonism from all sides, the Asians had no alternative but to withdraw into their traditional social grooves, accentuate their exclusiveness, and in general abstain from all public affairs. In short, they became even more insular than before.

Why, then it may be asked, did the Asians not try to return to either India or Britain once they found that they had no prospects in Africa? An answer to this must be sought in the divergent economic interests of the different segments of the Asian communiity. Those with substantial investments in commerce and industry obviously had no inducement to leave Africa. They felt themselves more secure in view of their close contacts with African politicians.[16] The two richest families in Uganda—Madhvani and Mehta—who contributed enormous sums for the development of the Ugandan economy thus dismissed the idea that they could ever be dispensed with by the Ugandans.

Next to this group were the professionals—doctors, lawyers, solicitors, etc.—who pursued their vocations independently of the first category. They were not directly affected by the programme of Africanization. They also knew that they could emigrate elsewhere whenever the local situation appeared desperate to them. A third group of Asians included the *dukawallahs*, white collar workers, lower-grade clerks, mechanics, craftsmen, and so on. Although these people were directly affected by Africanization, they were not willing to migrate to Britain or India because of their uncertain social and economic future there.

In general the Asians belonging to all these categories feared that if

they settled in Britain their children would degenerate by their association with a permissive society. As for India, there was no question of
going back and getting trapped in the vicious grip of poverty, filth,
and unemployment. Associated with this perhaps there was also an
underlying submissiveness to fate—a characteristic typical of the Hindu
mind. As an old Gujerati in Kenya told me: 'We Indians are like leeches
which cling to an animal's hide in a pond and fall out only when they
are dead.' Even as early as 1965–6 Asians in East Africa had come to
realize that their days there were numbered. But they were willing to
wait and see how fate shaped their destiny.

To sum up thus far, the inability of the Asians to accept Indian
advice in regard to both citizenship and integration widened the gulf
between them. By and large certain stereotypes came to be formulated
on both sides. In India an impression grew up, mainly through the
medium of the press and the articulation of Indian officials, that East
African Asians were not interested in improving their lot and that they
had none but themselves to blame for this. It also came to be believed
that Asians there had without exception amassed immense wealth and
that they therefore constituted a privileged and exploiting element in
African society. Their failure to take up East African citizenship was
also interpreted as proof of their pro-British leanings. If the Africans
called the Asians 'imperialist agents', there were many in India who
thought that they were both anti-Indian and anti-African.

The Asian community in East Africa also began to nurse many
grievances against India. They pointed out that by advising them, first,
to take up British citizenship, and then to surrender it in favour of
African citizenship, the Indian government was only trying to confuse
them.[17] They started questioning the wisdom of every visiting digni-
tary from India preaching to them the virtues of inter-racial integration. There was a point in this objection, as sermons of this kind only
encouraged the Africans to make further demands on them. The
Asians also felt that in its anxiety to cultivate African goodwill India
was not averse to condoning the injustices being committed against
them by African governments. As an Asian leader said: 'India should
exercise greater pressure on African nationalist leaders to observe non-
violence and adopt the ideals of peaceful existence. It should say this
openly and should also indicate that moral support should be withdrawn if the African nationalist leaders did not follow the fundamentals
of civilized humanity.'[18]

II

Despite the growing estrangement between India and the Asians in
East Africa, the latter continued to hope that India would not altogether

abandon them. On its part India too found it difficult to sever its associations with the Asians even though it was aware that such associations would complicate its relations with the independent East African countries. The discussion which follows is concerned with analysing the factors responsible for limiting India's diplomatic options and thus making it difficult for it either to disengage itself from commitment to the Asians or to act more resolutely on their behalf.

During the initial years following independence in East Africa, the Asians were confronted with a situation in which neither the host countries nor Britain were willing to accept their responsibilities. The Africans considered them not only aliens but also an irritating obstacle to their economic advancement. Hence the various measures initiated under the programmes of Africanization were directly aimed at removing the Asians from commerce, services, and other sectors. The British attitude was equally unhelpful. Initially, as we have noted in the preceding section, the Asians themselves were not keen to involve Britain in their affairs. In the later years, as public opinion in Britain hardened against the large-scale entry of coloured immigrants, it became fixed policy with British diplomatic representatives in East Africa to avoid mixing with the Asians. Under the circumstances, the Asians sought redress through Indian officials. But this created new complications. Since the Asians were not Indian nationals, the Indian officials had no legal standing to act on their behalf. Nor could they refuse to meet them as it would have constituted a denial of the traditional sentimental bonds which held the Asians so closely to India. But the fact that Indian officials were found keeping constant company with the Asians gave rise to the view that India was somehow responsible for shouldering their burdens. This view found expression in the utterances of African politicians and administrators both private and public. Thus, in 1966, on the occasion of the presentation of a chair by India to the Speaker of the Kenyan Senate, member after member rose to ventilate their grievances against the Asian community calling upon India to instruct them to mend their ways. As Senator Gikunju put it:

I would like the Government of India to advise Indians who are here to change their characters. Before we achieved independence Indians used to make Africans feel subordinates and they belittled Africans and we hope that these Indians who are spoiling good relations. . .should be warned strongly so that this relationship can continue satisfactorily. . .These people, these Indians who still have the old mentality should be warned by the representatives of the Indian government here and also be warned by their relatives at home.[19]

If only India had wanted it, it could have stopped dabbling any more in the affairs of the local Asians. But, for very substantial reasons, India did not want to close its options by severing all ties with the Asian settlers in East Africa. In the first place, functioning within a democratic set-up, it was not possible for the Government of India to ignore such pressures as were exerted through the press and parliament by elements who had close associations with their countrymen in Africa. Secondly, there was an underlying assumption that in times of crisis the Asians could be relied on to render useful services to India. Thus, during India's dispute with China and Pakistan, India welcomed contributions from the Asians in East Africa to help boost its defence efforts. When asked about this, Prime Minister Nehru was reported as having said to a foreign journalist that Indians overseas had a dual loyalty, one to their country of adoption and the other to their country of origin.[20] This remark caused a good deal of controversy among Asians in East Africa.[21] Yet it was generally assumed that Indians settled abroad should not do anything which would harm India's interest. Thus, when Asian businessmen were found to be selling Chinese-made goods, it was deplored as an act of disloyalty to India. Similarly, the failure of Asians to mix socially with Africans was criticized more on the ground that it created the wrong impression about India and its culture than from the point of view of its harmful effect on the interests of the Asians themselves.

Around the middle of the 1960s, however, there were indications of an attempt on India's part to fit the Asians within the broad framework of its policy goals in Africa. In view of the apparent isolation and lack of support from the non-aligned countries during its armed clashes with China and Pakistan, India came to recognize that its relations with these countries needed to be built on more positive grounds than periodic assertions of anti-racial and anti-colonial solidarity. For the first time serious thought was given to whether the presence of Indian settlers in Africa could not be more constructively used to further India's national interest. In East Africa especially India took the initiative to persuade prosperous Asians to invest their resources in industrial projects and to help promote Africa's economic development. India itself also made a modest beginning in this direction by extending economic and technical assistance to a group of African countries. In 1966 India started negotiating with Kenya to build an industrial estate with Indian, Asian, and Kenyan collaboration. 'The long term objective of cooperation', it was defined, 'was to seek the integration of the Indian community, numbering about 150,000, in the economic life of Kenya, thus fortifying the foundations of a multi-racial society.'[22]

The success of the programme, however, depended on a number of imponderables, viz. (i) the extent to which Africans were willing to trust Asians; (ii) the level of Asian participation itself, and (iii) the British stand on the future of the Asian non-citizens. None of these factors was under India's direct control. The new laws and regulations which came into force undermined the Asian will to make further investments in Africa. By 1967 the Kenyan government enacted new licensing and immigration laws to replace Asian businessmen by Africans. In Uganda, and to a limited extent in Tanzania, pressures were also mounting against the Asians.[23] It was precisely at this time that the controversy over Asian entry into Britain took a seriously political turn. Caught up by these developments and faced with the impending British legislation on immigration, the Asians in East Africa panicked and the exodus from Kenya began.

Thus, by the close of 1968, the issue before the Asians, in spite of India's efforts, no longer remained one of readjusting their position in African society but of finding the quickest and cheapest means of escape from there. As Justin O'Brien has remarked:

Race relations in East Africa suffered as a result because the occasion vividly demonstrated the Asian sense of insecurity...British-East African relations suffered also because it created misgivings in the minds of the East African Governments about the credibility of British obligations towards its citizens in East Africa. And it introduced in the U.K. the new dimension of race in calculations of who should enter in Britain. Things have never been the same again since the 1968 Act.[24]

III

At the height of the Kenyan crisis India took certain initiatives which, though well intended, proved hardly beneficial to the Asian community. In March 1968, the Indian government imposed visa regulations with a view to controlling the movement of Asians from Kenya to India. Obviously, the step was taken to put pressure on Britain to accept its responsibilities towards its own citizens.[25] But it aroused such intense feelings and misgivings among the Asians that the regulations had to be replaced by a new arrangement, reached between the Indian and the UK governments, under which the Asians were allowed to come to India on condition that the British High Commissions in East Africa endorsed their passports guaranteeing their right to enter Britain.

While these efforts were in progress India's Minister for External Affairs announced that the government would try to intercede with the Kenyan government to relax its pressures on the Asians. Following this, Mr Bali Ram Bhagat, State Minister for External Affairs, was instructed to meet the Kenyan President after attending the independence celebrations in Mauritius. Though the objectives of Mr Bhagat's mission were not officially spelt out, it appears that he went to Kenya in order (a) to instil confidence among the Kenyan Asians; (b) to persuade the Kenyan government to relax its Kenyanization policy so as to provide 'some breathing spell to the people of Indian origin to resettle themselves',[26] and (c) to obtain Kenya's support against British immigration policy.

These objectives were not only confusing, their implications were also not clearly thought out. If the Indian government wanted to instil confidence among the Asians it should have announced the concrete steps it had in mind to bring this about. As for persuading the Kenyan government, references to its policy of Africanization laid India open to the charge that it was interfering in Kenya's internal affairs. Added to this, the Bhagat mission was undertaken despite the advice given against it by the Indian High Commissioner in Nairobi.[27] In the end, Mr Bhagat failed to meet the Kenyan President and no one came to receive him or to see him off at the airport on behalf of the Kenyan government. Obviously, this cavalier treatment hurt India's pride. In the Indian parliament, opposition members denounced the Kenyan behaviour as 'an insult to India'. One of them even sarcastically asked whether it was for the opposition to remind a government which did not know when it was insulted.[28] Faced with these criticisms, the Government of India eagerly looked for a scapegoat. The manner in which the Indian press and parliament magnified British influence in Kenya provided the much-needed opportunity. Some sources even intimated that it was due to British pressures that Mr Bhagat failed to meet President Kenyatta.[29] Once more the demand was made in parliament that India should quit the Commonwealth and nationalize British firms. It was easy for government to pick up the cue. Mr Bhagat made vague references to a certain unspecified country which, he said, was interested in seeing 'that his mission to Kenya was frustrated'.[30]

Conceding that British influence in Kenya was substantial, it is still difficult to see how India expected to rally Kenya's support against British immigration policy. The contradiction became all the more marked because of the divergence in the Indian and Kenyan approaches. For whereas the Indian government opposed the immigration bill on the ground that it would unsettle the Asians in East Africa, the Kenyan government wanted Britain to take back the Asians because they were no longer welcome in Kenya.

To sum up, the Asian exodus from Kenya underscored three important lessons for India. First, India learnt that African governments were not amenable to outside persuasion or intercession on behalf of non-citizen Asians. Instead, they considered such moves as undue interference in their internal affairs. Second, although the African and Indian governments felt strongly that the responsibility for British Asians

rested solely on Britain, there was a substantial difference in their attitudes towards the Asians. Third, the historical limitations within which
the Asians functioned now became obvious to India. As an Indian
diplomat put it: 'The story of the Asians in East Africa resembles
closely a Greek tragedy, the denouement of which is already known to
the spectators.'[31]

Coming three years later, the expulsion of Asians from Uganda
should not have surprised India but for the unusual animosity which
General Amin showed towards a community of different colour. His
intemperate statements and outbursts of violence left no room to doubt
his racialist attitudes. Also the fact that at one time he expressed his
desire to expel all the 23,000 Asians who held Ugandan citizenship
woke up India to the grim reality that his regime was not even willing
to honour the legal contract enshrined in the Ugandan Constitution.
Meanwhile reports of atrocities committed by Ugandan soldiers on
helpless Asian families caused great concern in India. What shocked
Indian opinion most was that, as in the case of Zanzibar where some
Asian girls were forced to marry Africans, General Amin wanted
forcibly to marry an Asian widow![32]

The developments in Uganda left no scope for Indian intercession on
behalf of the Asians. On the contrary, India was taken aback when
Amin accused it of planning to invade his country with the help of
British and Tanzanian troops. At the same time India was equally,
though pleasantly, surprised to find Mr Heath's government revising
earlier British policies and boldly announcing its decision to honour
its responsibilities towards the expelled Asians from Uganda. In its task
of resettling the refugees, the UK government also called for help from
other countries, particularly the Commonwealth nations. Speaking on
television on 31 August 1972, the British Foreign Secretary, Sir Alec
Douglas-Home, declared that his government was getting in touch
with other governments to give refuge to Asians. But, he admitted, 'in
the last resort, if homes elsewhere in the world cannot be found for
them, we must take these unlucky people in'.[33]

Following this declaration, India closely cooperated with British
efforts to resettle the Asians. The visa regulations which were imposed
soon after General Amin's ninety days' notice were lifted. The Indian
High Commission in Kampala was instructed to grant entry visas to all
British Asians willing to renounce their British citizenship and become
permanent Indian citizens.[34] This signified that once the British government acknowledged its moral obligation towards the Asians, India was
willing to absorb the entire refugee population from Uganda if it
opted for Indian citizenship. That this offer was not readily taken up
by the Asians showed that whatever misfortune and humiliation they

may have met with in foreign lands did not prove sufficiently compelling for them to return to India.

In this chapter we have endeavoured to show how certain historical factors continued to involve India in the problems of a group of people for whom it bore no legal responsibility. To a large extent this involvement was a consequence of both humanitarian and selfish considerations. Although, diplomatically, India did not consider using the Asian settlers in East Africa as a channel to expand its influence in Africa—a possibility which local European settlers had feared most in the early 1950s—it did make attempts to organize them in support of the African demand for racial equality and self-government. After the Africans achieved independence, India hoped to persuade the Asians to play a role which not only improved their own position but also promoted Indian relations with the African governments. But this only led to a chain of misunderstandings. While the Asians thought that India would help them more in times of crisis, the latter made such claims on their loyalties as could not be easily fulfilled. The result was a growing estrangement between the two.

In reviewing India's attitudes, many Asians pointed out to me that their community would have fared better had India entered into treaties with the East African governments safeguarding their interests. There were others who held the view that a tougher stand on India's part would have discouraged the Africans from discriminating against them. Both arguments appear to be based on unrealistic premises. For one thing, India had no *locus standi* to act as the guardian of the British Asians. For another, how could India have persuaded the African rulers to make agreements protecting the position of an alien minority endowed with a colonial legacy and representing an impediment to African advancement? Any such assurance by African leaders would simply have robbed them of their political base.

Had the Asians held Indian citizenship, the situation might have been different. In that case it was possible that they would, like the Indian settlers in Burma and Ceylon, have returned to India at a much earlier date. At any rate it would have saved the British from taking painful decisions about a people who were not wanted in Britain. Here, it may be emphasized that, whatever passport the Asians held, it had never been India's policy to debar their entry if they wanted to resettle in India. In fact, the Government of India issued special regulations and some state governments provided extra inducements for the Asians to resettle in India with their savings and assets. Despite such offers the majority of East African Asians have refused to return to India. Perhaps this had something to do with the social composition of Asians in East

Africa. The older generation who went to Africa with a view to improving their material prospects had already been replaced by another generation who, having enjoyed a standard of living far superior to that in India, were no longer keen to return. It is they who have proved—and are today—most determined to make their entry into Britain.

10

ECONOMIC ASPECTS OF THE EXPULSION OF ASIANS FROM UGANDA[1]

M. A. Tribe

When President Amin called together leaders of the Asian community in Uganda in December 1971 for a meeting at the International Conference Centre he emphasized Asian trading malpractices and capital outflow.[2] Within the context of Uganda many, if not all, of these 'Asian malpractices' may have been entirely consistent with the economic objectives of the community and the circumstances within which they found themselves. Again, many aspects of behaviour which were criticized were hardly surprising, so that one could readily imagine that Africans or Europeans would behave similarly in like circumstances. There was, however, something more than pure racialism behind the expulsion, and in this chapter an attempt will be made to assess some of the economic aspects surrounding the event.

A major problem which immediately arises is that of separating effects of the expulsion from effects of the many other happenings around the time of the expulsion. These range from government financial problems before the Amin coup, particularly relating to the financing of the Nile Hotel, the International Conference Centre, and the Entebbe runway; the confusion surrounding the implementation of the 'Move to the Left', especially the partial nationalization measures embodied in the Nakivubo pronouncements; the concern over what might be regarded as the somewhat mediocre performance of the economy as a whole; the heavy military expenditure both before and after the coup, together with considerable disruption of the public service and the economy as a whole owing to extensive levels of uncertainty; and events such as the expulsion of the Israelis and the 'nationalization' of a large number of foreign-owned firms.[3]

At the time of the 1969 population census the reported citizenship status of the Asian community was 36,593 British, 8,890 Indians, 253 Pakistanis, and 25,657 Ugandans, a total of 71,393.[4] Assuming that those Ugandan Asians stripped of their citizenship would be treated as non-Ugandans for emigration purposes, and making allowance for net emigration between 1969 and 1972, I have assumed that approximately 8,000 households were expelled. The important point in this regard was that under the exchange control regulations non-citizens leaving Uganda permanently had fairly generous capital transfer allowances. These were drastically reduced for the period of the expulsion so that all those expelled were treated alike regardless of citizenship and were essentially expropriated.[5]

Throughout the discussion it should be borne in mind that the most fundamental fact about the Ugandan economy is that it is based on a peasant smallholding system of agriculture. Thus we may safely surmise that 80 per cent of the population relies mainly on own-produced foodstuffs and shelter. In addition all cotton and almost all coffee, which in a processed form together account for about 75 to 80 per cent of exports outside East Africa, are produced by peasant farmers, as are virtually all locally produced foodstuffs (with the important exception of sugar). The basic standard of living of a large part of the population is therefore somewhat independent of the 'modern' sector of the economy, and in addition a continued inflow of imports depends on export revenue, which in turn depends on peasant production, and the maintenance of a relatively efficient system of marketing, processing, and transportation.

This chapter will start by discussing some aspects of the Ugandan economy as a background to the events of 1972, will then discuss some of the most salient elements of the Asian position in the economy, before moving on to consider the economic effects of their expulsion.

Economic development cannot be seen as a unilinear or unidirectional process. Least of all should it be seen as necessarily coinciding with the value judgements of any particular observer or participant. I shall therefore attempt as objectively as possible to view the Asian involvement in, and rude disengagement from, the economy as a chapter in the development of Uganda.

THE UGANDA ECONOMY[6]

At the time of the coup in January 1971 there was considerable concern about the state of the economy, quite independently of any problems associated with Obote's 'Move to the Left'. In the financial year 1970–1 the budget deficit increased substantially, largely owing to the commitment to the International Conference Centre, the Nile Hotel, and the redevelopment of Entebbe Airport. A substantial part of this deficit was financed by advances from the Bank of Uganda, representing a large increase in the domestic money supply, much of which went into expenditure on imports and was therefore reflected in the adverse movement of the balance of payments. Table 1 shows the means of financing government expenditure, indicating the importance of borrowing from the Bank of Uganda and of contractor finance.

TABLE I. Financing of Government Expenditure 1969–70 and 1970–1

	1969–70	1970–1	% Change
	(Shs million)		
Total revenue	1,083.8	1,288.0	+18.8
Total expenditure	1,497.2	2,032.4	+35.7
Deficit to be financed	−413.4	−744.4	+80.1
Financing	413.4	744.4	+80.1
Foreign	160.1	357.2	+123.1
of which contractor finance	(50.3)	(159.9)	
Domestic	253.3	387.2	+52.9
other than banking system	(107.0)	(70.0)	
Commercial banks	(130.1)	(46.0)	
Bank of Uganda	(16.2)	(271.2)	
of which ways and means advances	(−5.0)	(110.3)	

Source: Bank of Uganda, *Annual Report 1970–1*, p. 38.

Between October and December 1970 domestic credit increased by Shs 265.2 million of which central government took Shs 175.7 million, and foreign assets fell by Shs 124.9 million.[7] This compares with equivalent figures of Shs 135.0 million, Shs 82.4 million, and an increase in foreign assets of Shs 110.4 million[8] in the same quarter of 1969.[9] The Minister of Finance referred to concern over this in his Budget Speech of June 1971, drawing attention to the Conference Centre, the Airport, and their relation to the balance of payments.[10] Military expenditure added to the expansionary nature of credit policy on behalf of government, and put further strain on the balance of payments:

The most noticeable change from previous years is the large increase in expenditure on defence in both the recurrent and development budgets. Military spending in the development budget jumped from Shs 51 million to Shs 160 million and currently absorbs 27 per cent of the total development budget. In the recurrent budget expenditure on defence is expected to rise 50 per cent above its approved estimate in 1970/71 from Shs 96 to Shs 145 million. (We note that the actual expenditure in 1969/70 was Shs 122 million and it is likely that actual expenditure in 1970/71 was greater than the Shs 96 million allocated.)[11]

We have seen that the concern in relation to public finance was linked closely to the question of the balance of foreign payments. Table II shows the net figures for 1969 and 1970. A number of interesting points arise from this data but we are concerned with only a few of these. We first note that the negative net monetary movement figures represent balance of payments surpluses of Shs 70 million in 1969 and Shs 31 million in 1970. However, in 1970 a positive item of Shs 38 million was incorporated on account of Special Drawing Rights (on

TABLE II. Balance of Payments (net) Estimates for 1969 and 1970
(Shs million)

	1969 (revised)	1970 (provisional)
Goods and services	− 27.1	184.6
Merchandise	(150.1)	(402.0)
Factor income	(− 125.6)	(− 107.4)
Other current a/c items	(− 51.6)	(− 110.0)
Transfer payments	− 16.7	− 38.6
Private	(− 34.7)	(− 49.6)
Official	(18.0)	(11.0)
Capital account	113.8	− 153.7
Private★	(− 46.0)	(− 259.6)†
Official	(170.2)	(105.9)
SDR allocation	—	38.4
Net monetary movement	− 70.0	− 30.7

Source: Bank of Uganda, *Annual Report 1970–1*, Table 25, p. 90.
★ Includes errors and omissions.
† There is some doubt about the meaning of this figure, and reference is made to this in the text.

the International Monetary Fund) allocations. This turns a surplus of Shs 31 million into a deficit of Shs 7 million, in direct comparison with the previous year. The next important point to note is the turn round from a deficit on goods and services account of Shs 27 million in 1969 to a surplus of Shs 185 million in 1970, owing entirely to an improvement on merchandise account of Shs 252 million. This improvement was commented on in the Quarterly Bulletin of the Bank of Uganda:

This performance derived principally from an exceptional increase in coffee earnings, mainly connected with the rise in the international prices, and in those from cotton, as a result of an increase of about 50 per cent in the volume of exports made possible by the record 1969/70 cotton crop, coupled with the concomitant slackening of merchandise imports, which on an adjusted basis increased by only 3 per cent. The latter was the outcome of a realisation of stocks and a decline in private fixed capital formation, due mainly to the uncertainties prevailing in the private sector during 1970.[12]

The third point then relates to the capital account, where there was an apparent deterioration of Shs 268 million between 1969 and 1970. Of this Shs 100 million can be accounted for by the inflow of funds following the local incorporation of the commercial banks in 1969 (reducing the 'surplus' on capital account of that year to Shs 14 million, and the change from 1969 to 1970 to Shs 168 million).[13] The deterioration on private capital account (including errors and omissions) was Shs 114 million. Of this Shs 55 million represents a reduction of capital inflow and Shs 59 million is then left as an increase on the debit items.[14] If Elliot's speculation relating to the failure of the customs authorities at Entebbe Airport to record air-freighted imports in respect of the International Conference Centre and the Nile Hotel is correct, then the reduction in foreign assets and increase in government credit in the fourth quarter of 1970 lead us to conclude that a large part of this Shs 59 million extra debit is probably due to the under-recording of imports rather than to an increase in private capital outflow.[15] Part of the additional debit is also due to payments on suppliers' credit/contractor finance arrangements which are included in this account but were not separately reported in the published data.[16]

The published net private capital outflow data cannot therefore be used as an indicator of the increase in capital outflow between 1969 and 1970. Given the various methods used in capital export, including over-invoicing of imports and under-invoicing of exports, false declaration of factor incomes such as profits and rents, and improper use of personal transfers, it is very difficult to distinguish the true private capital outflow within the balance of payments as published. There is certainly evidence of a deteriorating balance of payments which in 1969 was covered by the inflow of Shs 100 million at the time of the local incorporation of the banks, and in 1970 was exacerbated by additional government expenditure on imports. Had it not been for the 'windfall' gain through a favourable cotton crop and favourable world prices in 1970 a serious payments crisis would have arisen at the end of the year, assuming that the Conference Centre and Nile Hotel construction was an unalterable political decision. Despite this conclusion there can be no doubt that there was considerable private capital outflow from Uganda in this period. Further discussion of this will follow.

We do have separate data on the purchases of Bank of Uganda notes from the other East African central banks from 1968 and this may be seen in Table III. The data in Table III gives grounds for suspecting that the increased outflow was due initially to immigration and trade licence legislation in 1968–9, and then to the publication of the Common Man's Charter in late 1969 and the Nakivubo Pronouncements of 1 May 1970 relating to the partial nationalization of a large number of foreign and Asian-owned firms.[17] Given increased restrictions, and also increased uncertainty in Uganda, incentives to export funds to Kenya were great, notwithstanding the fact that the exchange control regulations for transfers outside East Africa were essentially the same in all three East African countries. The introduction of exchange control

TABLE III. Net Flow of Notes between Bank of Uganda and
Other East African Central Banks (Shs 000s)

	Net purchases from Central Bank of Kenya	Net purchases from Bank of Tanzania	Total net purchases
1968	21,866	961	22,327
1969	37,381	7,385	44,766
1970 January	8,717	1,579	10,296
February	9,402	575	9,977
March	6,158	1,819	7,977
April	9,067	852	9,919
May	13,545	2,705	16,250
June	18	1,394	1,412
January–June total	46,907	8,924	55,831

Source: Republic of Uganda: *Statistical Abstract 1970* (Entebbe, 1971), Table UL8, p. 62.

within East Africa in May–June 1970 after the Nakivubo Pronouncements clearly had the desired effect on this element in the balance of payments, although it involved quite considerable hardship for Kenyan workers in Uganda wishing to take or send money home.

The data in the Table, however, exclude commercial bank transactions and in this respect would not include the transfer of bank balances of East Africa-based firms to Kenya or Tanzania. In addition to capital outflow engendered by the Asian community and by East African firms, there would be capital export by foreign companies wishing to reduce their commitments in Uganda following the Nakivubo Pronouncements, and also, one may surmise, by Ugandan politicians and businessmen concerned about their uncertain future. The black market exchange rate for the Uganda shilling in Switzerland gave some indication of the increasing pressure through 1970 and 1971 to get funds out of Uganda, although this represents only part of the black market, and presumably not only capital export by the Asian community.[18]

The World Bank Mission of 1960–1 had referred to non-African capital export in the region of Shs 100 million per annum from the mid-1950s for which 'the most likely explanation stems from the fact that investment opportunities in Uganda are limited for the non-African community because of their inability to acquire land'.[19] This emphasis on land may be misplaced but the report at least records a fairly early recognition, and estimates, of private capital outflow (albeit legal at this time). Before 1964 there was, of course, no exchange control on the movement of funds from East Africa within the sterling area and it was only in 1970 that exchange control was introduced on the movement of funds within East Africa. It should perhaps be noted that British exchange control regulations were changed in 1972, making export of funds from Britain considerably more difficult except for current account items.[20] Prior to these changes Britain was an attractive holding ground for Asian capital funds since they could be fairly easily moved elsewhere, whereas funds in India could not be moved. This is one of the reasons why Britain would probably have received a large proportion of the capital outflow from Uganda.

In addition to familiar practices such as over-pricing of imports and under-pricing of exports, one area which was important for capital outflow was the tourist industry. A high proportion of tour firms were Asian owned and either worked within the package tour system or ran charter flights. In either case it was relatively simple to receive payment in foreign currency in Europe or North America for flights and local costs, which were then paid for in Uganda shillings without the con-comitant foreign exchange inflow occurring. Although Bank of Uganda regulations were tightened on this practice, the complete eradication of this type of capital export was difficult to achieve. The notorious 'Nkunze Island Incident', involving a British diplomat and some Asian residents in Uganda, uncovered part of this system of capital export in 1970.[21]

The data in Table IV relate to imports from outside East Africa of commodities which may broadly be termed 'investment goods'. This

TABLE IV. Uganda Imports of 'Investment Goods' from outside East Africa
(Shs million)

	1967*	1968	1969	1970	1971	1972
Machinery (including agricultural machinery)	153	170	178	167	285	262
Transport equipment	141	134	146	124	249	83
Iron and steel	18	15	50	56	72	34
Other metals and metal products	52	62	70	59	108	65
Total imports from outside East Africa	827	876	911	865	1,362	813

Sources: Standard Bank, *Standard Bank Review*, June 1968, May 1970, June 1971, July 1972, and July 1973. East African Community, *Annual Trade Report 1972* (Mombasa, 1973), summary Table 1.

* The comparability of the component items for 1967 with the other years is uncertain.

shows no substantial change in the structure of these imports over the period 1967 to 1970 but there are significant changes in 1971 and 1972. Imports of machinery rose substantially to a level of about Shs 100 million higher in 1971 and 1972 than in the previous years, that is a jump of 60 per cent in value terms. Transport equipment imports doubled between 1970 and 1971, then fell back in 1972 to a level below that of 1969, and similar changes occurred in iron and steel and other metals and metal product imports.

It is rather difficult to interpret these data, particularly in the context of excess capacity in several industries which, together with market size problems, was tending to restrict private investment incentives, slowing down capital formation.[22] Unfortunately official statistics on gross capital formation for recent years are not available but Table V

TABLE V. Gross Capital Formation, monetary sector
(current prices, Shs million)

	1964	1965	1966	1967	1968	1969 (estimate)
Construction	268	356	324	397	442	492
Plant and machinery	205	274	281	361	310	349
Transport equipment	124	120	130	121	114	130
Total	597	750	735	879	866	971

Source: Republic of Uganda, *Background to the Budget 1970/71* (Entebbe, 1970), Table 4.1, p. 22.

shows an upward trend in investment at current prices (i.e. not adjusting for price increases) in both construction and in plant and machinery through to 1969. The uncertainties surrounding the introduction of the Common Man's Charter and the Nakivubo Pronouncements in 1969 and 1970 would have started to work through to private investment by 1971. Since a very large proportion of private investment was undertaken by Asian businessmen, the uncertainties relating to the future of their businesses in Uganda brought about by the changes in the immigration law would also have had an effect. The expulsion of the Asians would not have affected 1972 imports very considerably since virtually all of them would have been ordered before President Amin's August announcement. Two factors in particular probably account for much of the rise in 1971 and 1972. These are an increase in military equipment imports subsumed within the general import data, and over-invoicing of much investment equipment which was imported as pressures became even stronger for the Asian community to get capital out of Uganda. Indeed, it is possible that much of the equipment imports might have been ordered specifically as a means of capital export through over-pricing.

I have attempted to show that in relation to government finance and to the balance of payments there was cause for grave concern well before the end of 1970, or for that matter the middle of 1972. Two issues which had created perhaps more political heat than any others were those of the Asian predominance in retail trade and in responsibility for capital outflow. In the case of the former there has been considerable trouble in Buganda during the trade boycott of Asian-owned shops in 1959. The boycott, together with uncertainty related to impending independence, had led to an increase in capital outflow.[23] Much of the resentment about Asians came from what were considered to be 'unfair trading practices', which were enumerated in President Amin's December 1971 speech as well as in other places.[24] Here I want to put these two issues in the context of the Uganda economy.

The method of Africanization of trade pursued in Uganda has been discussed at some length in the second edition of *Portrait of a Minority*[25] and by Parson.[26] In summary, this method consisted of advances of credit and advice to African traders in the first instance, followed by a more rigorous system of trade licensing and state control through the National Trading Corporation. The trade licensing arose out of the 1969 Trade Licensing Act which 'allowed the government to prohibit non-citizens from trading in specified areas and in specified items'.[27] This Act, together with the uncertainty over the status of many 'citizen' Asians (owing to lack of clarity over renunciation of previous citizenship, not completing the processing of a large proportion of citizenship applications, and since in many cases Uganda citizenship had been taken by only one or two members of a family as a means of obtaining licences and free education),[28] the impact of the British Commonwealth Immigration Act of 1968, and the Ugandan Immigration Act of 1969 tightening up regulations on work-permits and residence permits for non-citizens, had the effect of shortening the time horizon of non-citizens, particularly Asians, in relation to their expected stay in Uganda.

The system of transfer of trade to Africans was essentially conservative, as Ghai and Parson both point out, inasmuch as the private ownership system was not changed even if the racial characteristics were. Even wholesale trade was not substantially encroached upon by the National Trading Corporation, which tended to grant commissions to agents to fulfil its distributional functions. Parson shows that in many cases Asian traders continued operating much as before at the wholesale level, using African distributors as 'fronts'.[29] By the beginning of 1972 'the Asian community as a group still dominated, financially, the commercial sector of the economy. Almost no headway had been made in the area of changing the structure of Asian business activity to admit more African participation in ownership or management. This aspect of economic life could and probably did intensify the frustration felt by budding African businessmen.'[30]

During this period the prices of food and manufactures had been rising quite sharply, having a large impact on the cost of living. Food prices, particularly for low-income groups, had tended to fluctuate quite considerably, depending on variable weather conditions,[31] but had started to rise from 1968 without showing any signs of falling back to their former level. This may be seen from Table VI. This rising trend in Kampala food prices was almost certainly due to a combination of the rapid increase in the urban population, structural problems on the supply side,[32] and a 'ratchet effect' through irreversible price increases in times of shortage.

Despite the fact that a number of commentators referred to the food price problem, there was little attention to the non-food items in the indices.[33] The price increases for clothing and household goods are substantial for middle- and low-income groups but not for high-income groups. This is confirmed by more detailed data on particular commodities published in the *Statistical Abstract*.[34] One factor which could account for part of these price increases was the introduction of sales tax in the middle of 1968. Between the second and third quarters of 1968 the cost of living indices for all three income groups rose by approximately 6 per cent. In the higher-income index the increase came in food (6 per cent) and drink and tobacco (21 per cent); in the middle-income index the increases were more evenly distributed, the main areas being drink and tobacco (19 per cent) and personal medicines and household (12 per cent); in the lower-income index increases were recorded in drink and tobacco (10 per cent), household goods (50 per cent), and clothing (43 per cent). Given the rates at which sales tax was introduced, the latter two increases cannot have been due only to this factor. Table VII demonstrates that for the lower- and middle-income groups the price of clothing continued to rise quite rapidly after 1968, as did food. This implies that from 1968 onwards the increase in the cost of living index was at a substantially higher rate than previously, and the source of these increases was in foodstuffs and essential manufactures. Clearly the supply factors affecting these two groups are different.

It is, of course, possible that the basis for the collection of the data changed in the groups where the large price increases were recorded. This type of statistical quirk has, on occasion, occurred previously. There are however some other explanations. First, for clothing and household goods greater protection through licensing led to substitution of high-price local products for imports. Second, the introduction of sales tax (and some other minor tax changes) and the increase in sea

TABLE VI. Cost of Living Indices (excluding rent), Kampala (January 1961 = 100)

High-income Index (average Shs 27,000 per annum in 1963)

	Weight	1966	1967	1968	1969	1970	1971	2nd quarter 1972
Food	25.4	115	116	120	134	139	148	149
Drink and tobacco	7.0	132	137	155	170	170	171	178
Transport	34.9	132	136	145	151	153	157	163
Household	11.6	115	116	121	124	127	127	135
Clothing and footwear	7.2	127	131	133	138	144	147	149
Pharmaceutical and personal	2.2	116	118	125	137	145	160	160
Domestic servants	7.5	130	130	140	141	147	152	152
Entertainment and miscellaneous	4.2	112	115	127	139	143	148	157
Total	100.0	124	126	134	142	146	151	153

Middle-income Index (average Shs 11,000 per annum in 1963)

	Weight	1966	1967	1968	1969	1970	1971	2nd quarter 1972
Food	41.7	120	127	120	130	146	175	168
Drink and tobacco	16.5	137	141	153	163	162	161	172
Labour	3.8	159	172	192	194	193	188	188
Transport	8.3	103	103	105	112	112	114	116
Fuel	4.3	132	118	104	119	118	111	110
Personal medicines and household	13.6	116	121	133	140	144	157	162
Clothing	10.6	126	129	131	139	151	157	162
Miscellaneous	1.2	113	113	117	129	129	129	129
Total	100.0	123	128	129	139	146	161	161

Lower-income Index (average Shs 1,800 per annum in 1963)

	Weight	1966	1967	1968	1969	1970	1971	2nd quarter 1972
Food	70.0	119	127	118	129	146	182	173
Drink and tobacco	11.0	117	117	124	133	126	121	120
Fuel and soap	8.0	129	116	106	120	122	118	119
Household goods	2.0	106	109	138	181	179	173	176
Clothing	9.0	109	108	131	168	180	180	181
Total	100.0	119	123	119	133	146	169	163

Sources: Bank of Uganda, *Quarterly Bulletin*, vol. iii, no 2 (March 1971), Table 41, p. 96. Republic of Uganda, *Quarterly Economic and Statistical Bulletin*, June 1972 (Entebbe, 1972).

TABLE VII. Price Increases (per cent) 1968–71

	Increase 2nd–3rd quarters 1968	Increase 3rd quarter 1968 to 2nd quarter 1972
High-income Index		
Food	6	20
Drink and tobacco	21	5
Transport	0	8
Household	− 1	9
Clothing and footwear	0	8
Pharmaceutical and personal	0	17
Domestic servants	1	8
Entertainment and miscellaneous	0	16
Total	6	10
Middle-income Index		
Food	2	35
Drink and tobacco	19	3
Labour	3	− 3
Transport	0	12
Fuel	4	1
Personal medicines and household	12	15
Clothing	3	23
Miscellaneous	0	14
Total	6	20
Lower-income Index		
Food	0	46
Drink and tobacco	10	− 6
Fuel and soap	1	9
Household goods	50	5
Clothing	43	18
Total	6	31

Sources: Calculated from Republic of Uganda, *Statistical Abstract, 1970* (Entebbe, (1971), Table UO1 (a), b) and (c). Republic of Uganda, *Quarterly Economic and Statistical Bulletin June 1972* (Entebbe, 1972).

freight rates as a result of the closure of the Suez Canal created conditions which were favourable for the raising of prices of manufactured goods. Third, the National Trading Corporation and other government policies in general were increasing trading costs to Asians in particular. This might include elements of bribery in relation to licences, which would be seen as a cost to traders. Fourth, and fundamentally, the United Kingdom Immigration Act of 1968 (with the Kenyan Immigration and Trade Licensing Acts of 1967),[35] and the expectation (fulfilled in 1969) of Ugandan Immigration and Trade Licensing Acts, produced particular types of business pressures. Inasmuch as they reduced the time horizon of many Asian resident businessmen's operations in East Africa we would expect pressures for an increase in the rate of profit in Asian industrial and commercial activities, and an increase in capital outflow, in order to provide for an economic base subsequent to emigration. More careful analysis might allow some identification of the relative importance of these factors but any such separation would be precarious. Clearly the market conditions were such as to make the raising of prices a practical possibility. Clearly, also, there was something of a vicious circle in operation so that pressure against the Asian community led to reactions which in turn led to further anti-Asian pressure.

Evidence that Asian businessmen were becoming more nervous because of changes in immigration/emigration law in the United Kingdom and East Africa comes from two other factors. First, businessmen had been reducing their stocks in order to retain as little non-liquid commitment to Uganda as possible.[36] Second, both large and small businessmen were depending increasingly on credit from commercial banks to finance their operations, rather than on their own funds.[37] To the extent that their own capital was still involved in trade this was frequently based abroad in order to facilitate payments for imports in conditions of increasing administrative delays in Uganda.

There were, then, at the time of the coup in 1971 and still at the time of the announcement of the expulsion, quite a number of serious economic issues which gave cause for disquiet. The structure of government finance showed signs of being almost out of control, the balance of payments was extremely delicate so that additional capital outflow could not be accommodated, the uncertainties to which the Asian community in particular, but also the economy as a whole, were subjected made the investment climate rather unclear, and there was a substantial and continuing increase in the cost of living. This gives only part of the totality of the state of the economy but should be sufficient to indicate that the economy was not in a very healthy condition. Some of the difficulties appear to have been inherent within the structure of the economy, and some were the direct result of political factors and actions both within and outside Uganda.

THE ASIAN POSITION IN THE ECONOMY
(a) *Employment, Income, and Ownership*

Having discussed some of the then current problems of the Uganda economy I want now to turn to the question of the Asian position in the economy. It is possible to obtain an impression of the significance of the 'Asian community'[38] in the skill structure and industrial structure from the data in Tables VIII, IX, and X. Table VIII relates to the racial composition of high-level manpower at the time of the 1967 survey. The survey shows the great importance of Europeans and Asians in top

TABLE VIII. High-level Manpower in Uganda, 1967

Occupation Group	Ugandans	Non-Ugandans Asians and Africans	Europeans and others
Top management	779		
Junior management	3,150		
Professional	926	988	1,696
Medical doctors	181	201	162
Accountants	77	89	52
School teachers	195	415	881
Technical	5,636	1,031	1,176
School teachers	1,547	506	453
Artisans	7,154	1,912	349
Foremen	825	287	143
Fitters	707	411	83
Motor mechanics	903	215	7
Electrical fitters	383	150	3
Engine operators	70	103	17
Skilled Office Workers	8,342	1,507	250
Personal secretaries	335	241	175
Book-keepers	975	391	24
Clerks	5,651	699	44
Others	14,515	410	26

Source: Republic of Uganda, *High Level Manpower Survey 1967* (Entebbe, 1969), Appendix I.

Note: The second column refers to both Asian and African non-Ugandans. Table IX shows that there were a large number of non-Ugandan Africans in the enumerated labour force in 1969. The largest proportion of these may be found in relatively unskilled work in agriculture and industry, and not among high- or middle-level manpower. The second column therefore refers largely to non-Ugandan Asians. In addition a fairly large number of Ugandan citizens in these categories were Ugandan citizen Asians, but how many we cannot tell from the published data. This table therefore *understates* the importance of Asians in the high-level manpower category if we do not allow for the fact that many of those in the first column were citizen Asians.

management and professional occupations, and the key position of Asians in junior management, technical, and artisan categories. It is clear from the Table that there were a number of specific skills where the ratio of Asians to Africans shows a particular dependence on Asians. Examples are medical doctors, accountants, and school teachers at the professional level, electrical fitters and engine operators at the artisan level, and personal secretaries and book-keepers at the skilled office-worker level. This level of Asian skills has to be seen in relation to an overall shortage of skills in the country. Those skills which depended on education and/or training had, in general, been acquired as a result of the ability of Asian families to pay for education privately because of their relatively high-income level; there had been considerable Asian expenditure on education after the Second World War in particular.[39] Another factor which is not adequately shown in the Table is the level of experience of those surveyed. Asian personnel in all occupations covered by the survey would, on average, be older and therefore more experienced, and implicitly more proficient than the average Ugandan African. In addition some key personnel in various professions were Asians who would be hard to replace, an example being the high incidence of Asians as finance and establishment officers in the public service. The implications of these phenomena will be discussed later in this chapter.

Table IX shows the racial structure of the enumerated labour force.

TABLE IX. Number of Enumerated Employees by Race*

	Africans	Ugandan Africans†	Non-Ugandan Africans†	Asians	Europeans
1964	211,419	154,600	56,800	9,385	3,163
1965	227,489	171,600	55,900	9,182	3,319
1966	231,296	174,700	56,600	10,583	3,573
1967	241,497	182,200	59,300	11,099	3,760
1968	266,800	206,754	60,046	11,212	3,760
1969	280,526	224,542	55,984	10,986	3,457

Source: Uganda Government, *Enumeration of Employees* (Entebbe, annual).
   * Those enumerated exclude domestic servants and employees of peasant farmers. It includes 'every known firm employing one or more persons for a cash wage or an agreed salary', but 'for all years the undercoverage within small firms might be quite considerable' (1969 report, p. 1).
   † Available only to nearest 1,000 prior to 1968.

The enumeration excludes domestic servants and employees of peasant farmers, and has an 'undercoverage within small firms [which] might be quite considerable'.[40] Many Asian enterprises, especially in the retail trade, were small, and there was considerable self-employment. The figure for Asians employed in commerce in 1966, however, is fairly consistent with the equivalent in the Census of Distribution carried out in the same year.[41] The increase in the number of Asian employees between 1964 and 1968 is presumably accounted for by changes in the coverage of the enumeration (e.g. more employees falling within the criteria used). Within the context of the total working

age population of Uganda, Asians were obviously of still less significance in terms of numbers (say, 11,000 out of 2 million adult males
aged 15–49).[42]
    Table x shows the industrial composition of the 'Asian and other non-

TABLE X. Industrial Composition of Enumerated Employees by Race, 1969

	Total employees	Of which Asian and 'other Non-African'		
		Public	Private*	Total
Agriculture	53,359	11	463	474
Cotton ginning	5,588	—†	95	95
Coffee curing	5,579	—†	193	193
Forestry, fishing and hunting	2,897	5	11	16
Mining and quarrying	6,268	—	26	26
Manufacture and food products	13,144	—†	804	804
Miscellaneous manufacturing	29,823	9	2,360	2,369
Construction	42,352	126	694	820
Commerce	14,773	7	3,121	3,128
Transport and communication	11,826	69	308	377
Government (admin. and misc.)	18,299	263	—	263
Local government	21,301	45	—	45
Education and medical services	53,571	905	782	1,687
Miscellaneous services	16,189	98	591	689
Total	294,969	1,538	9,448	10,986

Source: Republic of Uganda, *Enumeration of Employees 1969* (Entebbe, 1971),
Appendices XIII and XIV.
    * Uganda government statistical practice includes the parastatal and cooperative
sectors in the 'private' rather than the 'public' sector.
    † No separate categories included.

African' (i.e. non-African and non-European) enumerated employees.
    The concentration of Asians in manufacturing and commerce is
notable, as is the overwhelming 'private' sector orientation (but see the
first note to the Table). The notable exception to this is in education and
medical services but even there about 47 per cent were employed in the
private sector, compared with 60 per cent of African employees. The
high proportion of African employees in education and health activities, in the public and private sectors, is due to the inclusion of non-
teaching and non-medical staff. From Table VIII we can see that the
Asian proportion of teaching and medical staff is very high.
    Table XI shows the average wage of enumerated employees by race,
indicating very clearly the position of Asians in an income category
between Africans and Europeans. Wage income, however, does not
represent by any means the totality of income distribution. Most
Africans, for example, receive income not from wages but as a return

TABLE XI. Average Wage of Enumerated Employees by Race, 1969
(Uganda Shillings per annum)

	Private industry	Public service	Total
Africans			
Males	2,806	3,486	3,078
Females	3,627	4,474	3,912
European			
Males	43,968	31,984*	38,936
Females	17,280	20,107	18,303
Asians and other non-African			
Males	16,284	20,153	16,706
Females	11,643	14,154	12,425

Source: Republic of Uganda, *Enumeration of Employees 1969* (Entebbe, 1971).
  * This figure represents the average salary paid locally. Most European expatriates were paid an additional allowance in their own country.

for work on peasant agricultural smallholdings in addition to their non-marketed output. In 1969 the value of coffee and cotton alone to African growers was Shs 700 million, compared with a total wage bill of Shs 1,150 million and a monetary national income of Shs 5,000 million.[43] On the other hand, within the high average income received by Asians in Uganda, there was a fairly wide distribution. While the highest-income Asians received considerably more than any European employee, the lowest-income Asians had been perceived as a problem for many years.[44] In the 1950s we find references to Asian groups in Kampala's so-called 'slum areas'[45] and a special report appeared in 1950 on Asian overcrowding in Kampala (even here Asians of low-income groups were taken as those of an average income of approximately Shs 550 per month, against a minimum wage for African employees at this time of Shs 33 per month).[46] Reference to 'low-income' Asians is, then, relative to high-income Asians rather than to low-income Africans.

Table XII shows the ownership structure of wholesale trade by race, illustrating the predominance of Asian ownership whether measured in terms of enterprises or receipts. The large average size of the European-owned enterprises is apparent from the comparison of percentages of enterprises and of receipts. Even this European predominance, however, occurs largely as the result of the control of the petroleum and equipment wholesale trades, largely of course at the import level. By comparison Asian predominance is apparent throughout the range of products with the exception of these two groups. Unfortunately, similar data on the ownership structure of other industrial groupings

TABLE XII. Breakdown of Receipts by Ownership of Enterprise and Kind of Business, Wholesale Trade (percentage of total receipts)*

Kind of business	African	Asian	European	Other
Groceries, provisions, confectionery, drinks	5	95	—	—
Agriculture products	3	83	13	1
Clothing, footwear and textiles	1	95	3	1
Machinery, industrial equipment and supplies	—	19	81	—
Electrical goods	—	97	3	—
Petroleum products	—	—	100	—
Timber	—	100	—	—
Building materials and hardware	—	100	—	—
Chemicals, oils, drugs and related products	1	99	—	—
Glass, china, earthenware, rustic ware, cutlery and hosiery	5	95	—	—
Paper, stationery and books	49	51	—	—
Bicycles and spares	—	100	—	—
Metals and other metal products	—	81	19	—
Other goods and materials	—	100	—	—
General wholesalers	7	66	26	1
Total	4.6	73.6	21.5	0.3
Number of enterprises	54	448	44	3
% of total enterprises	9.8	81.6	8.0	0.6

Source: Republic of Uganda, *Census of Distribution 1966, part 1* (Entebbe, 1967), p. 33, Table A.11, and p. 11, Table 9.

* The survey of wholesale trade was carried out on a complete enumeration basis.

are not available, although the Asian-owned portion of industrial, transport, and service sectors was also considerable.[47]

From the data presented above we can see that the Asian position in the high-level manpower stock in the economy was very significant, that on average the level of income of the Asian community fell between that of Europeans and Africans, that they held a very privileged income position in relation to the African population, and that they owned most of the wholesale trading firms as well as a large segment of the retail trade sector, industry, and other commerce. I now want to turn to the evolution of the wealth structure in the economy.

(b) *Wealth and Accumulation*

Superficially we might attribute the development of this substantial Asian role in the economy to sociological traits of East African Asians in trade, for example, allowing the building up of a surplus for accumulation in other activities. In part this attribution would no doubt be correct, and this might be generalized in terms of a small, highly skilled, alien, ascriptive group.[48] This characterization, however, while superficially attractive and partially true, would be far from a completely accurate description. Rather, it will be argued that the role of the Asian community in the structure of the economy was largely developed as a result of specific measures of the colonial government. In general this argument will support the points made at the beginning of President Amin's December 1971 speech to the Asian community.[49] Asian involvement in trade resulted from the absence of local African experience in import and export trade and internal marketing, and the general lack of interest of Europeans in direct involvement in these activities. Parson has summarized the system as it developed from an early period:

A three tiered system thus developed based mainly on race whereby Europeans occupied the best posts in government and the economy, Indians were in middle level and service positions and occupied a strategic role in trade (the most lucrative lines of wholesale and to a lesser extent retail trade plus a crucial role in cotton ginning and produce marketing), with Africans occupying the roles of primary producer, low level civil servant and, increasingly, petty retailer and hawker.[50]

In recent years there was to some extent a process at work in Uganda similar to that noted by Kilby in his study of industrialization in Nigeria.[51] This is the tendency for business groups, such as the Asians in Uganda, when threatened, to retreat from visibly prominent to less prominent activities. There was some movement of Asian traders from small town retail trade into the larger urban areas which was exacerbated by the Buganda trade boycott. This was partly accounted for by a market development of the type where African traders took over more trade partly owing to the lower profit margin they were prepared to work for in the socio-economic circumstances. There was also a tendency for Asian traders to move back into specialization in wholesale trade, which is less noticeable to the public than retail trade, and to invest in manufacturing and/or assembly activities. This latter movement into manufacturing from a base in trade was quite important in 'middle-scale' industry.[52] Many of these product markets were naturally protected, and an initial stimulus came in the 1939–45 war when this factor was particularly important.[53] Some investors were able to negotiate in one way or another fairly heavy protection through higher tariffs, or more likely through import licences, requiring much more collaboration with government. An additional factor was that of changes in regulations and/or institutional pressure in the sense of the take-over of cotton ginning and crop marketing by cooperatives, or the take-over of retail trade by African traders in the main towns by government action.

Trade was, then, an important base for the development of Asian wealth in Uganda. Here, however, I want to take two areas in particular which illustrate very clearly the crucial reliance for wealth accumulation on specific policies of the colonial government. In some cases these policies may have been consciously related to wealth accumulation but it seems more likely that many of the points made below were important side effects of policies which had a certain inner logic and momentum from some other unrelated starting-points. These two areas are the development of the cotton ginning industry and the determination of the producers' sugar price. My argument is that these two were very important in the control of the level and disposition of a large part of the economic surplus[54] generated in Uganda. This control extends to the level and disposition of capital accumulation, capital export, and luxury consumption, and depended very considerably on the policy of the colonial government.

Cotton ginning was an important element in Asian economic activity, and cotton was the major export crop of Uganda, coffee becoming more important only after 1955. Ginning capacity expanded rapidly after 1914 when there were 20 ginneries, so that there were 42 in 1919, 100 in 1921, and 192 in 1929.[55] In 1925 there were 125 ginneries of which 100 were Asian-owned.[56] The increased competition led to strains between growers and ginners and among ginners, and the 1929 Commission of Inquiry introduced a considerable amount of government control into the industry, which was further extended after 1939 and which was to remain until the take-over by the cooperative movement in the 1960s.[57] This control tended to protect the interests of the ginners rather than the growers, and a comprehensive price formula included a ginning margin. Thus a system of zoning guaranteed a share of the crop to each ginnery; later a ginning margin was introduced, assuring an income for each pound of lint produced, and these together determined the level of profits. Secondly, the gradual take-over of the industry by the cooperative movement from the early 1950s allowed for the excessive compensation of private ginners based on the capitalization of high profits. Although the Asian predominance in cotton ginning developed in the 1920s, it was in the 1950s that the main economic windfalls came.

The only published material on the economic implications of the 'Lint Price Formula' appears to be in the *Report of the Committee of Inquiry into the Affairs of all Cooperative Unions in Uganda*, a committee chaired by Shafiq Arain. It is worthwhile quoting from this report at some length:

By means of the ginning pools they [the ginners] were protected from competition, and by virtue of the price formula they were guaranteed fixed minimum profits, above which most of them were able to obtain very much more, by one way or another...

...The effect of this restriction was that ginneries have an inflated value, on account of the buying rights that went with them...The Lint price formula which was worked out every year by the Lint Cotton Price Fixing Committee, was based on fairly generous estimates under no less than 59 heads, calculated on average ginnery costs under any of which the more efficient ginner might be expected to effect savings. In particular the outturn figure based on private ginners' figures alone used to be as low as 29 per cent lint cotton with 3 per cent allowance for wastage, and 68 per cent outturn of cotton seed. Actual figures only became apparent when cooperative ginneries started working and it soon became obvious that the correct figure for wastage should be between 1.2 per cent and 1.5 per cent...cotton seed outturn 66.5 per cent and lint outturn 32 per cent. When it is appreciated that a difference of as little as 1.5 per cent on the lint outturn is capable of doubling the profits per bale made by the ginner the incentive and scope for falsification of returns, either by overdeclaring deliveries of seed to oil mills (often the property of the ginner himself) or by overdeclaring purchases of raw cotton, can be realised...Super profits, therefore, appear to have been made by the private ginners, mainly at the expense of the struggling cooperatives who were not only saddled with vast loan repayments, plus interest rates, on mainly antique ginneries, but whose members being so keen, invariably succeeded in collecting more than the amounts fixed under the pool agreements, thus involving the union in costly penalties in payments to the pools.[58]

Even the income tax authorities found it impossible to obtain a 'True and disinterested statement of the cotton ginning industry from the private business sector' and 'had to rely upon "reasonable" voluntary declarations from ginners whose books were indecipherable'.[59] In the period after the cooperatives started to take over a much larger proportion of the industry, the ginning margin was reduced quite considerably (on average from 46.6 to 31.8 cents/lb. lint between 1961–2 and 1965–6) at the same time as the cooperatives were having to repay government loans for the purchase of ginneries.[60] This reduction apparently led to a number of ginneries operating at a loss on the 1965–6 crop. The purchase of ginneries was undertaken at considerably inflated prices, partly because of the factors outlined by the Arain Committee but also possibly as a result of either incompetence or collaboration on the part of those negotiating on behalf of the cooperatives.

In April 1963, within six months of independence, the government announced a new policy with regard to the ginning industry:

In order to stop the paying of what was described as exorbitant compensation, the Government had decided against either compulsory purchase or nationalisation of private ginneries. Instead growers' cooperatives would be provided with funds and could make their decisions whether to purchase an existing ginnery or construct a new one. . .Examples were quoted of the prices that were paid under the compulsory purchase scheme that had been introduced ten years before. One ginnery at Tororo had been purchased at £116,223 when it was estimated that a new one should not have cost more than £40,000. . .Two ginneries in Buganda were also quoted as examples of extravagant prices paid for old ginneries, on top of which it cost more than £20,000 to carry out necessary repairs and to rehabilitate these ginneries in order to make them run properly.[61]

The Committee of Inquiry found that:

through our visits to cotton unions we were time and time again forcibly struck by the indifferent quality and poor selection of personnel in positions of key responsibility particularly ginnery managers, whose entire previous experience maybe ranged from a few years as teachers to some years as a hospital dresser, or general storeman. Only where ginnery managers who had been previously employed in that capacity, or as fitters in private ginneries, and these, of course, were inevitably Asian, had been retained or re-engaged by unions, was any fund of experience encountered, and in the majority of these cases the ginnery concerned was clearly running more smoothly as a result.[62]

The latter aspect of the take-over of the ginneries is one that we shall have to return to at a later stage of the discussion. At this point we are more concerned with the Committee's judgement on the issues of pricing and compensation. Some elements of the Committee's report are not satisfactory in supporting their contentions in their entirety. This may not be entirely surprising, given Shafiq Arain's membership of the Uganda Action Group. This more radical Asian political grouping challenged the 'old guard' leadership during the independence negotiations and this would imply a tendency to be against the cotton ginning interests.[63] There is, however, sufficient material to support the view that private ginners, predominantly Asian, received considerable profits through the pricing formula over a long period and that the compensation for compulsory take-overs, in being based on that formula, was very generous indeed, particularly in the early stages of the take-over.

A second area of similar, and probably greater, significance was the formula used for setting the producers' sugar price. Sugar was produced in Uganda by two major firms until late in the 1960s when one other joined. The most important of these was the Madhvani group, the other being the Mehta group.[64] Both of these were able, over a long period, considerably to diversify their economic interests (sometimes in direct collaboration with the Uganda Development Corporation), firstly within Uganda, then in East Africa, and finally internationally.

Their pattern of development follows quite closely that outlined by Meir Merhav in his seminal work on industrialization in small countries.[65] The producers' sugar price seems originally to have been based on an import parity price related to the negotiated Commonwealth Sugar Agreement London price.[66] The price formula was such as to allow a very large profit margin, such that a considerable part of the capital accumulation of the sugar-producing family enterprises was financed by this means. In addition many of the investments were in activities which were either statutorily or naturally protected from foreign or local competition.

The World Bank Mission to Uganda in 1960–1 commented on the sugar price:

> The mission believes that there should be changes in the system of fixing the price of sugar in Uganda. The price paid to millers is based on the Commonwealth Sugar Agreement price of raw sugar landed in the United Kingdom from which is subtracted the cost of moving sugar to the coast from the plantations in Uganda, and the cost of pre-war ocean freight to the United Kingdom. . .While no sugar is refined in Uganda (either on the basis of method of production or on the nature and quantity of impurities involved) the base price to millers includes. . .a refining margin of Shs 110 a ton. The millers thus receive a wholly unwarranted windfall on this account which, in conjunction with the method of price-fixing, gives them a high price for their unrefined mill-white product. The consequences of the method of price-fixing are twofold: the price of sugar to the consumers is high and there is no incentive to refine or improve the quality of mill-white sugar.[67]

If this description of the formula was correct then, with local production of sugar in the 1960s at about 120,000 tons per annum, the additional profits on account of the refining margin would be about Shs 13,200,000 each year shared between Madhvani and Mehta in proportion to their share of sugar production. This represented something marginally over 10 per cent of the revenue from sugar production of the two producers.[68] To this must be added an amount arising from the use of a pre-Second World War ocean freight rate in deducting transport costs from the Commonwealth Sugar Agreement UK landed price. The deduction of the 1939 rate from the current UK sugar price implies a higher Uganda producer price than would be the case if current freight rates were used.

It is unclear, however, whether the World Bank Mission had correctly reported the price formula. Charles Frank, in his study of the East African Sugar Industry, implies that the 'refining margin' was added to allow for conversion of the London raw sugar price to a Uganda mill-white price;[69] and therefore did not notionally allow for completely refining the sugar as the World Bank Report implies.

Frank considered that the sugar price was somewhat generous, pointing out the outdated nature of the freight deduction. In addition a comprehensive investigation of the sugar industry in East Africa was carried out in 1959 by Dr K. Douwes Dekker and this recommended substantial reductions in the producers' sugar price. Apparently these reductions were never fully implemented.[70] A further source is the 1963 report of the International Sugar Council where the Uganda producer price is reported as the 'Commonwealth Sugar Agreement negotiated price adjusted for f.o.r. [free on rail] Mombasa, less Shs 67/20 per long ton'.[71] This description implies that the internal producer price in Uganda was something approaching an import parity price. Finally, Booker Brothers McConnell commissioned a report in 1953 on a possible new sugar project in which a guaranteed price was proposed of approximately £45 per ton ex-factory which would compare with the then current price of £43 10s. per ton paid to Uganda producers. They noted that 'it is recognised that a Base Guaranteed Price computed so as to be equitable to a new industry might, if applied to production from sugar estates established at pre-war prices, provide these existing producers with a disproportionately high level of profit'.[72] Thus, although it has not been possible completely to clarify the sugar price formula owing to conflicting evidence, there would appear to be general agreement that the price was sufficiently high to give considerably more than comfortable profits, thus allowing a comparison with the case of cotton ginning.

Apart from these sugar plantations and a few, mainly European-owned, tea plantations, there was no land alienation in Uganda on a basis similar to that in Kenya or even Tanzania. Out of 74,748 square miles of land in Uganda, 530 square miles were alienated to non-Africans.[73] The laws of Uganda had been quite explicit from early in the colonial period in severely restricting the alienation of land to any non-Ugandans, be they Asians or Europeans.[74] This meant, among other things, that bank loans or trade credit could not be advanced by non-Ugandans or non-Ugandan institutions (such as banks or other firms) using African-owned land as collateral. A large part of trade credit to rural Africans was advanced against future deliveries of crops to Asian traders.[75] The take-over of crop-marketing by cooperatives, and the movement of Asians out of rural trade, steadily reduced any prospect of such land alienation. The system of leasing off land in towns and the system of wealth accumulation, however, meant that very considerable areas of towns in Uganda were on long leases to Asians, and an even higher proportion of property was owned by Asians.[76] The pressure for rent control in towns had been from two directions,[77] from African traders renting property from Asians and from unpropertied Asians renting residential and commercial property from propertied Asians.[78] The fact that Asian ownership was dominant in urban real estate is of great practical and theoretical interest. For example, suppose that demand for office space increases, as it did after independence, then new offices will be erected at current building costs, and if rented will be rented at current market prices (largely determined by the government). With increasing demand for offices we would expect that rents would rise for existing buildings, and private owners would receive income not for the services they were performing as economic actors but owing to the expanding activity around them. In this sense, then, property owners receive a 'pure economic rent' in the classical economist's sense, the rent being a part of the nation's economic surplus. The fact that property owners receive this income is of considerable social and political, as well as economic, significance, and with the structure of ownership this implied fairly considerable property incomes to some Asian families. In fact, a fairly large part of the compensation for the take-over of ginneries had been invested in urban real estate.

Elsewhere I have referred to the system of the fixing of housing rents at the higher income end of the market.[79] This made it clear that the government, after independence, exerted little pressure to reduce rents paid for houses rented from the private market, because of the vested interests of the Ugandan African elite, If, in fact, many of the larger African landlords are senior public servants or ministers, then market conditions are likely to be such as to keep the level of rents high. We have then some kind of alliance between the African and Asian elite vested interests which would keep rents relatively high in order to control part of the disposition of the economic surplus. The political conditions for rent control do not exist in these circumstances.

One interesting development within the few years before the expulsion was in the construction industry. From 1966 onwards a fairly high proportion of public and parastatal construction projects were undertaken under a system known as 'contractor finance'. The financial arrangements surrounding these were of doubtful probity and adversely affected the design and cost of the projects.[80] The extent of profitable sub-contracting, however, allowed a number of Asian construction firms to obtain relatively high profits and to invest in equipment (sometimes second-hand), thus tendering for projects requiring more equipment-intensive techniques and competing to some extent with the established European firms.[81] This aspect of development shows how market structures may change by roundabout means, but space is insufficient to expand on this point here.[82]

From this range of examples it is possible to see that in a number of ways the Asian community wielded considerable economic power in Uganda, and in a sufficiently flexible way as to adapt after independence so as to become possibly even more powerful than before.

THE EFFECTS OF THE EXPULSION

In assessing the economic effects of the expulsion the first major problem is the extent to which any such effects are predictable. Two specific questions relate to the availability and reliability of data before and after the expulsion, and to the accuracy with which predictions may be made about the behaviour of the socio-economic system in Uganda. My own feeling is that in interpreting the expulsion the importance of the Asians as retail traders should be de-emphasized, or at least assessed very carefully. A large proportion of the export trade and of internal trade in non-industrial commodities was already handled by Africans, or by the public sector with contracted expatriates (for example, the Coffee and Lint Marketing Boards). To the extent that the number of retail traders was reduced this may eliminate much competition and reduce the aggregate level of experience of such traders. We might therefore expect trading costs to increase as a proportion of turnover owing to decreased efficiency, together with a less satisfactory service to consumers owing to delays in deliveries and inadequate stock control. There might also be higher profit margins because of the elimination of some competition. In any event we would expect retail margins and prices to increase, thus furthering the inflationary conditions in the economy. We have seen above that the Asian involvement in wholesale trade was comparatively more important than in retail trade. To the extent that the wholesale trade was linked to imports of consumer goods demanded to a large extent by the Asian community there is little problem. Given the time-lags between orders and deliveries of imports and the consequent importance of stock control, however, 'essential' imports of consumer goods and producer materials would be likely to suffer and would be likely to create a range of economic problems. The loss of the Asian experience in the wholesale sector is probably relatively greater than that at the retail level, although in towns outside Kampala the two were to some extent intermingled.

A second area where much emphasis tends to be laid is in the question of professionals such as lawyers, accountants, doctors, and teachers. From the 1967 data in Table VIII we can see that Asian teachers represented an important part of the supply at secondary level (classed as professionals), although not nearly as important as Europeans (respectively about 400 non-Ugandans of Asian and African origin who would be mainly Asians, nearly 900 Europeans, and about 200 Ugandans of whom a few would be Asian in origin). At other levels (classed as 'technical' in the manpower survey) Ugandans outnumbered Asians and Europeans together by 1.5 to 1.0. The expulsion would have hit the secondary schools, especially in urban areas, very severely indeed, but primary schools less so, and, together with the removal of British and other expatriate teachers, would have seriously disrupted the educational system.

A point made by Jill Wells in 1968 relates to the extent to which, for example, an expulsion such as that in Uganda considerably reduced the market for the very services of many of the people expelled:

. . .the demand for such personnel will undoubtedly change in composition— if not in total volume—as a result of the exodus of a large number of highly educated, wealthy and sophisticated people. . .it makes little sense to talk of the urgent need to expand the supply of doctors, architects etc., when approximately 74 per cent of the services of such personnel are at present catering for the needs of some 1 per cent of the population. . .[83]

Notwithstanding possible doubts on the accuracy of figures such as '74 per cent', we may suggest that in the case of lawyers and architects this factor may go some way to outweighing the negative aspects of the expulsion, so that the scarcity of supply, and lack of effective demand, for such services from the bulk of the population is merely emphasized. In the case of doctors the factor is still relevant, but clearly to a smaller extent. This type of argument will recur in relation to the discussion of industrial market structures.

The question of technical skills is one which has been given little emphasis in the published discussions of the Amin regime.[84] In some senses teaching, accounting, and management functions may be regarded as technical. If we limit the extent of the definition to those largely in the artisan category of Table 1, however, we find that non-Ugandans supplied a fairly substantial proportion of the groups itemized under this category. Most of these non-Ugandans would have been Asians, although here the number of Kenyans, for example, would be greater than elsewhere. Two issues are raised in relation to these data. First, how does the skill structure relate to the industrial structure? For example, the Arain Committee on Cooperatives remarked that cotton ginneries where the fund of Asian technical skills had been maintained operated more smoothly than others. This industry is crucial for a considerable part of peasant farmer income in the east and north of Uganda, and for a large proportion of export earnings. The transport industry is of course very important for the continued working of the internal marketing system, which includes foodstuffs as well as export crops. Asians were also very important at the supervisory level in the construction industry.

The second issue is then related to the first. This is that the manpower survey report gives no information on the structure of experience and proficiency of skills in groups such as fitters or motor mechanics. In many cases the utility of technical skills is considerably affected by length of experience and the degree to which improvisation with spare parts/repairs is possible. Most Africans in the groups in this category would have considerably less experience, and therefore in all likelihood considerably less capacity for improvisation, than their Asian counterparts. To the extent that Africans have been more formally trained than Asians this in itself may militate against improvisation. The important question in relation to this is, then, the extent to which it was possible after the expulsion to substitute African skilled workers for Asian skilled workers at a time when the stock of African skills may not have been sufficient. There would be two possible effects of lower levels of skills being substituted in, for example, factory machinery or transport equipment maintenance: more frequent repair and greater time with the machinery lying idle; more frequent need for replacement. Both these effects would lead to less efficient working and higher costs, as had already been observed at the time of the hasty introduction of mechanized farming in the 1960s.[85] This might be particularly important in sectors such as cotton ginning (crucial for exports), internal marketing (particularly transport), and the production of mass consumption goods such as cooking oil, sugar, soap, textiles, etc., as well as the construction industry. A likely guess is that this loss of efficiency would occur for at least something in the region of five years from the expulsion.

It is probably not the case that a substantial proportion of local industrial production was dependent on Asian demand. Many of the manufactures locally produced, such as those listed in the previous paragraph, together with beer, spirits, cigarettes, timber, cement, etc., depended on markets much more widely based than that represented by the one community. The basic structure of demand would therefore seem likely to make these industries still viable if they can be operated without previously employed Asian skills. Thus the changes in demand consequent on the expulsion which was remarked on in relation to professional services is not replicated in the demand for most locally produced commodities. The changes in the structure of demand, however, would probably have cut the demand for consumer goods imports (particularly consumer durables) considerably, which even increased demand by members of the armed forces and other African high-income groups could not replace. There might then be some favourable effect on the balance of trade as a result of the expulsion, which may be offset by imports of commodities previously locally produced which become scarce owing to disruption of production or other problems.

Perhaps the most important effect on the Ugandan economy as a result of the expulsion relates to the balance of payments in general and capital outflow in particular. We have seen how events over the period from about 1965 to 1966 led to additional pressure for Asians to increase their capital exports by legal and illegal means. Suppose that the Uganda government had attempted to find ways of keeping this capital finance in the country. Initially this would have the effect of increasing the already rather liquid position of the commercial banks[86] and of the financial system as a whole. This was clearly in the minds of the various interests proposing the setting up of a Ugandan Stock Exchange. If the investment incentives were deficient owing to the market structure in the industrial and services sectors, there would have been additional investment in property, additional purchases of consumer goods imports, or capital outflow. Imports could be restricted, and property investment increasingly required business connections with influential Africans in order to obtain land, and would merely have increased land prices. Suppose, however, that the government had been successful in encouraging additional investment in immovable property (equipment and buildings). With the gradual emigration of non-citizen Asians (leaving aside the vexed citizenship issue) the encashment and transfer of these assets would be subject to exchange control regulations. There is then some element of contradiction in any policy designed to retain funds in the country in the short period, if in the long run the capital is going to be expatriated. This is, then, a special case of the general contradiction of foreign private investment where profits are reinvested locally. The Asians' economic position was then one of building up assets in Uganda, with the inevitable counterpart of wishing to expatriate as many of these assets as possible either before or after emigration, and probably preferably before. This was a perfectly logical position for the Asian community to take in the circumstances, and the Asians therefore maintained the 'openness' of the economy in many respects.

In the case of the European farmers in Kenya the resettlement of the former White Highlands was carried out by a system of land purchase financed by British government loans to the Kenya government, which were then re-lent to African farmers. Thus the foreign exchange cost of the export of capital by the European farmers was borne by Kenya but the short-term financing was undertaken by the British government.[87] A similar operation was undertaken in the early 1960s when the building societies experienced a substantial withdrawal of deposits and funds were exported at the time of the Kenya independence negotiations.[88] In East Africa there was therefore a very firm precedent for external loans to undertake the short-run financing of capital export on the part of European emigrants who were largely British. This system of assisted export of funds, together with the maintenance of asset values, might be considered of doubtful morality in terms of its effects on the East African economies. Since, however, a large proportion of the Asians expelled from Uganda were British citizens, the British government displayed a perhaps remarkable degree of inconsistency in not offering a similar 'baling-out' operation in 1972 in Uganda. The fact that British Asians arrived in their country of citizenship without having been compensated in any way for the loss of assets in Uganda is, in the circumstances, probably at least as much due to the British as to the Ugandan government, given the extremely delicate state of Uganda's balance of payments and foreign exchange reserves.

Exchange control with the sterling area had been introduced in 1964, and with Kenya and Tanzania in 1970. Parts of the regulations refer to the combined value of funds and movable property which may be taken abroad at the time of permanent emigration. These parts were clearly instrumental in relation to the permanent emigration of Asians, and had been progressively tightened up in all three East African countries in order to maintain their foreign exchange position. Let us assume that at the time of the expulsion the standard exchange control regulations had applied to the approximately 8,000 households expelled. In 1969 the foreign exchange allowance for people emigrating from Uganda had been reduced from Shs 100,000 to Shs 50,000 and subsequent annual allowances reduced from Shs 40,000 to Shs 20,000, with the balance of assets transferable five years after emigration. This change in regulations came after the introduction of the entry permit system of immigration to Britain for British citizens of Asian origin, so that emigration was to some extent predictable, and at about the same time as the introduction of the new trade licensing and work permit systems for non-citizens. If we assume that on average households would have been capable of utilizing the initial allowance of Shs 50,000 to the full, then the total amount of foreign exchange required to undertake the expulsion of 8,000 households would have been Shs 400 million in the first instance, and would have been outside the capacity of the balance of payments or foreign exchange reserves. Even with the substantially reduced emigration allowance that was given to most households,[89] the foreign reserves fell by Shs 179 million (a fall of 47.4 per cent) between September and December 1972, although in the same period of 1972 there was an increase of Shs 35.5 million.[90]

Some of the short-term effects of the expulsion were obviously going to be reflected in the government's financial position, or would be reported in the Budget Speech. In the Budget Speech of June 1973 the then Acting Minister of Finance, Planning, and Economic Development, referring to the previous year, mentioned 'shortages of certain commodities due to either inavailability of raw materials required in the industries in which they are produced or because there has been lack of spare parts for machineries used in these industries'.[91] There were declines in the output of a number of industries, leading to a reduction in demand for electricity from manufacturing establishments. Imports from outside East Africa fell from Shs 1,362 million in 1971 to Shs 813 million in 1972 (see Table IV above), a drop of 40 per cent, while exports outside East Africa rose by 11 per cent from Shs 1,670 million in 1971 to Shs 1,850 million in 1972, giving an external trade surplus of Shs 1,040 million. After adjusting this external trade surplus to get figures for the value of exports and imports at the Uganda border (rather than at Mombasa, where most of the trade is recorded by the East African Customs and Excise), and allowing for a deficit on East African trade of Shs 190 million, the adjusted trade surplus apparently comes out at Shs 480 million. Taken with a total balance of payments surplus on current account of Shs 90 million, this implies a non-merchandise deficit of approximately Shs 390 million, which is high compared with the figures, for example, in Table II, largely owing to the travel and other current costs of the expelled Asians. The capital account on the balance of payments had a deficit of Shs 90 million, including an estimated private capital outflow of Shs 240 million. The Minister stated that 'a big portion of this capital flight was in the form of merchandise imports ordered and already paid for by the departing non-citizens and which were never received into this country, as well as export proceeds which were never repatriated'. The Minister concluded the section on the balance of payments: 'Mainly as a result of the sizeable private capital flight and the large foreign exchange disbursements on passenger fares, emigration treatment and freight charges on personal effects of departing non-citizens an overall surplus of only Shs 35.5 million was recorded in the country's balance of payments.' Given the current account surplus and capital account deficit of approximately Shs 90 million each, this balance of payments surplus must be due to the allocation of further IMF Special Drawing Rights which were incorporated into the balance of payments as in previous years. From this we can see that in the short period the expulsion did have a fairly large unfavourable effect on the balance of payments which was barely covered by the reduction of imports owing to a reduction in 'commercial activity' and to a 'government decision to restrict imports' which had led to a large trade surplus.

In terms of government finance the expulsion, and associated economic happenings, had a possibly even more drastic effect. Estimated government recurrent expenditure for 1972–3 had been Shs 1,430 million, and the actual out-turn was Shs 1,429. The estimated recurrent revenue had, however, been Shs 1,525 million, which compares with an actual out-turn of Shs 1,006, giving a recurrent deficit of Shs 423 million compared with the estimated surplus of Shs 95 million in the 1972–3 budget. The revenue shortfall amounted to almost 30 per cent

TABLE XIII. Government Revenue Estimates and Collections as of April 1973 for Financial Year 1972–3* (Shs million)

	Estimate 1972–3	Collections to end April 1973	Revised Estimate 1972–3
Customs duty	255	150	180
Sales tax	316	177	n.a.
Income tax	350	212	250
Total recurrent revenue	1,525	n.a.	1,006

Source: Budget Speech 1973–4, *Voice of Uganda*, 15 June 1973.
* The financial year runs from July to June.

of the estimate, and was spread fairly uniformly over the major sources of revenue, with the exception of export taxes. Customs duties clearly fall when import value is reduced considerably, and, given the disruption of local commercial activity and the importance of the Asian community in relation to both personal income tax and company tax, the falls in sales tax and income tax revenue were also to be expected. The budget estimate of recurrent revenue for 1973–4 of Shs 1,241 million represents, then, a possibly optimistic view of the new revenue situation following the expulsion.

The expulsion may therefore be seen as having a range of effects on the economy, only some of which have been discussed here. Nevertheless, the effects on trade (particularly wholesale), the skill structure (particularly the professions and technical expertise), government finance, and the balance of payments are probably the most important. Of these the balance of payments is perhaps the most salient. Given the essentially expropriatory nature of the expulsion, the immediate effect was largely to increase current outgoings (travel, etc.), the capital outflow apparently not being substantially increased. In the longer period the capital outflow may be expected to be reduced for we may assume that African elite and European capital outflow together will remain approximately at the same level as before in total. If then the level of exports, particularly of cotton and coffee which together accounted for approximately 75 per cent of exports outside East Africa, can be approximately maintained, the balance of foreign payments is likely to benefit from the expulsion in the long period. This must give an indication of the economic rationale of the expulsion since the previous situation of lack of clarity of the Asian position in Uganda had the effect of increasing considerably the incentives for capital export. Nevertheless, apart from the expropriatory element in relation to the effects on the balance of payments, the overall effects on the economy as a whole must be very largely speculative, particularly in the context of the other factors affecting the economy which were outlined in the introductory section.[92]

CONCLUSION

This conclusion first summarizes the discussion in the context of the structure of the Ugandan economy, then relates the expulsion to other recent developments in the Ugandan political economy, and, finally, compares the 'Asian' position in Kenya and Tanzania with that in Uganda.

It is fairly clear that the expulsion, together with what amounted to expropriation, was a radical political break from previous policies towards the Asian community. In the short term a number of economic problems have arisen, ranging from a decline in manufacturing output, further balance of payments problems at the time of the expulsion, public finance shortfalls on the revenue side, manpower shortages, and further impetus to increases in the cost of living. Many of these problems existed before the expulsion, albeit in a less severe form. The expulsion changed the ownership characteristics of the enterprises which were taken over. Depending on the efficiency with which the enterprises are operated after the take-over, there will be a change in the sources of savings and capital accumulation. To the extent that the enterprises lose efficiency there may be a lower potential level of savings. To the extent that the external orientation of the Asian community led to capital outflow, however, the expulsion may have increased potential domestic savings. Certainly the expulsion has changed Uganda's relations with the outside world in a number of significant ways. Of these the capital flow question is probably the most important since it is unlikely that the African elite groups and remaining foreign firms will achieve levels of capital outflow commensurate with those before the expulsion.

The skill structure of the labour force was seen to have changed rather abruptly at the time of the expulsion, so that the vacuum created in, for example, education and technical skills could not possibly be filled in the short term. Despite the importance of the Asian community in the skill structure of the labour force, the income distribution in the country as a whole was little changed by the expulsion. The bulk of the population remain as rural-based peasant farmers, and the higher-income African groups remain. Some African employees of Asian households and businesses would have become unemployed but in relation to the economy as a whole this would not be of major significance. The removal of part of the higher-income end of the income and wealth distribution through the expulsion does not seem likely to have had a significant redistributive effect from high- to low-income receivers. The demand for local products, both agricultural and industrial, seems unlikely to fall very substantially. Nevertheless, the removal of the consumption patterns of the Asian community, the loss of import trade expertise, together with import restrictions, are likely to reduce the demand for imported consumer goods fairly substantially.

The main economic effects of the expulsion in a somewhat longer period appear to be the reduction in foreign exchange demand for purposes of capital outflow and import of consumer goods, and the loss of important groups of skills which is likely to lead to a reduction in the operating efficiency of large parts of the economy. If these are in fact the main effects, then we may ask whether the favourable effects could have been achieved in some other way or whether these effects were the major objectives of the expulsion. This requires some view of the political economy of the situation rather than of the purely economic.

In the first year after the 1971 coup President Amin, together with his advisers, managed to establish power with the implicit support of a wide range of economic and political interest groups which had been alienated by Obote. Most important among these was Buganda, where the upheaval of 1965-7 left strong political animosity. The exercise of returning the Kabaka's body from London for burial was crucial in relation to this. In addition, it was from among the Baganda that a large proportion of the more successful businessmen and public servants with substantial business interests came, who were most likely to have their economic interests challenged by any 'Move to the Left'. The *mailo* (freehold) land tenure system in Buganda had been challenged both explicitly and implicitly by Obote, and this factor threatened both large and small landholders. These vested interests were, to a greater or lesser extent, replicated outside Buganda. By appearing to ally himself with these diverse economic and political interests Amin gathered quite a considerable amount of support. Nevertheless, Obote's handling of the 'Move to the Left', including the lack of any form of leadership code (largely owing to the diversity of *his* support groups), mishandling of the negotiation of the partial nationalization of the banks and oil companies, the interminable delay in working out the details of the national service scheme, together with the lack of any grassroot base for the Uganda Peoples Congress, had alienated any 'left' wing support groups. Amin's attack on Obote's pamphlets (referring to the Common Man's Charter and other documents of the 'Move to the Left') could be interpreted as an attack from either the left or the right.[93]

The effects of the balance of payments difficulties became clearer after the middle of 1971 and severe import restrictions were introduced at the end of that year.[94] By this time the permanent effects on food prices of the dry period at the end of 1970 and the beginning of 1971 were also clear. Shortages of processed foodstuffs, locally produced and imported (sugar, cooking oil, and butter, for example), were more frequent. Whatever might have been the major political motivations, the Tanzanian confrontation and the expulsion of the Israelis represented hardly any respite to the dissatisfactions building up among the majority of non-military urban dwellers of all income groups.

Earlier in this chapter I have illustrated the position of the Asian community in the Ugandan economy. It is clear that the development of its very powerful economic position in terms of access to opportunities for wealth accumulation, skills, and income for consumption purposes, was built up during Uganda's colonial period. Much of the economic power depended on specific policies of the colonial government. After independence the power of the largest and most influential Asian businessmen became greater, while the smaller businessmen and the salariat were subjected to greater uncertainties and challenges to their positions through the various elements of the Africanization programmes. This difference between the treatment of the various groups reflects the relative difficulties of, and relative political pressures for, the replacement of Asian by African skills, using the gradualistic policies of President Obote—policies to a large extent determined by the British Commonwealth Immigration Act of 1968. The permit system written into this Act restricted entry of British citizens into Britain, and could therefore be seen as forcing a degree of gradualism which was acceptable neither to the Uganda government nor to British Asians resident in Uganda who wished to enter Britain. The British permit system arguably reduced capital outflow in the short period, owing to the lower level of emigration that probably occurred compared with what it might otherwise have been. Owing to the delay, however, British Asians were able to continue working while waiting to emigrate and the volume of capital outflow might have increased as they made efforts to get more money out. On the other hand, those who were not able to continue working because of changes in Ugandan Immigration regulations would have their stock of past savings reduced, and therefore the capital transfer on emigration would also have been reduced.

The Asian expulsion may then be seen as fulfilling a wide range of objectives, both short and long term. In the short term it drew attention away from the current economic and political problems, and allowed the Asian community to be used as scapegoats in this respect. It created the possibility of Africans taking over seemingly prosperous businesses. According to some sources, the army in particular were given opportunities of looting, or at least purchasing, many consumer durables at very low prices, and much of the 'auctioning' of Asian assets was biased in favour of particular groups within the army.[95] It removed a considerable source of capital outflow, unlikely to be replaced by any other group in society in terms of numbers involved, sums involved, or in terms of the objectives of capital export. In the longer period, the expulsion removed a major externally oriented group in society and, together with other 'nationalist' measures such as the take-over of foreign firms and the reduction in the number of expatriates, reduced considerably that element in the structure of the economy which had been inherited from the colonial government. While itself containing elements of racialism, the expulsion certainly further revealed the discrimination between coloured and white British citizens embodied in the British Commonwealth Immigration Act of 1968.

A very brief comparison with the policy towards the Asian communities in Kenya and Tanzania can be instructive in an overall view. In Kenya the European community was, of course, more dominant in all respects than it had ever been in Uganda. The political and economic transfer of power was very much from Europeans to Africans at the time of independence.[96] In addition, in the period after the end of the Emergency African peasant farmer incomes had risen buoyantly following the removal of restrictions on the range of agricultural products Africans could produce, for example high-grade cattle, coffee, and pyrethrum, which were the critical aspects of the Swynnerton Plan, and later the land transfer in the former White Highlands. Moreover, the larger European and Asian communities in Kenya (with the more uneven income distribution this implied) and the existence of the East African Common Market made Kenya an attractive place for industrial investment, so that the manufacturing sector had a fairly high growth rate. Within the context of an expanding economic system it was possible for transfers of economic power to be made with greater flexibility than was the case in Uganda.

In Tanzania, particularly after the Arusha Declaration of 1967, the 'Asian problem' became considerably subsumed within the objective of restructuring the economy on the basis of the Declaration. This restructuring was not without its own major problems. It did, however, mean that, for example, the take-over of wholesale trade was undertaken in a substantially different way from that followed in Kenya and

Uganda, where privately owned firms were the main instruments of the take-over. Perhaps the most notable policy measure with relation to the Asian community was that of the nationalization of buildings where properties of more than Shs 100,000 value were taken over, with compensation, irrespective of the race of the owners, although Asians predominated as property owners, as in Uganda.[97]

This comparison, brief and selective as it is, illustrates two significant differences between the Uganda case and those of Kenya and Tanzania. First, in Uganda post-independence politics had been dominated by the Buganda issue, and the economy had been somewhat stagnant and economic policy rather unadventurous up to the time of the 'Move to the Left'. In this case stagnation implies growth dependent on pre-existing policies and structures (cotton and coffee, miscellaneous manufacturing) rather than on new departures. This contrasts with the growth stimuli in Kenyan agriculture and manufacturing. Second, there was the racial competitiveness of Africanization policies in Uganda and in Kenya compared with more attention to structural changes in the economy which occurred in Tanzania. Given the relative lack of economic dynamism, and the element of racial competitiveness, it is perhaps not surprising that the expulsion of Asians occurred in Uganda. It is, however, likely that the over-riding factor making the expulsion feasible was the military nature of the Amin regime.

Whether post-expulsion Uganda can give greater welfare to Ugandans is an imponderable, particularly given the rationale of the military government. Ultimately, for example, there could be some new kind of external dependence brought about through the coalition of various interests. In that event, however, it seems unlikely that Ugandans would regard the Asian expulsion as the central cause of their new dependence.

THE NUBIANS: THEIR PERCEIVED
STRATIFICATION SYSTEM AND ITS RELATION
TO THE ASIAN ISSUE[1]

Dennis Pain

In considering the relative status of the Nubians vis-à-vis the Asians, I shall concentrate more on the former, in inverse proportion to the amount of common knowledge about the two groups that exists in England, and perhaps in direct proportion to the amount of power that they have wielded in the second Republic of Uganda. Of course there are widespread misconceptions about both, such as the myth of an 'Asian community' in East Africa. But to claim that the Asians came seventy years ago as railway labourers is like claiming, with more justification, that the Nubians came a hundred years ago as slave-traders. Both views are current in Uganda, and both are based on a selection of the facts.

NUBIAN ORIGINS[2]

The description 'Nubian' derives from the area of the Nile north of modern Khartoum, where 600 years ago there existed two Christian kingdoms of Dongola, one of which was known as Nubia. In the fourteenth century the Arabs overthrew the Nubian kingdom and there followed throughout the area a steady process of Afro-Arab racial integration and assimilation of Islamic culture with strong non-Islamic and traditional elements. But Arab expansion never extended below the tenth parallel until the development of slave-trading in the eighteenth century. Throughout the nineteenth century, for much of which Sudan was under Egyptian control, slave-trading expanded. By 1860 the slavers were operating as far south as the present Ugandan border and to the west into what is now the Central African Republic and north-west Zaire. By 1872 they had had devastating effect on Acholi and the present Madi, Lugbara, and Kakwa of Uganda. The largest trader in the southern area had 2,500 'Arabs' in his pay, and altogether there were at least 20,000 such slavers operating in the whole province. At the end of the 1870s, Gessi estimated, from the capture of slaves and documents, that 80,000 to 100,000 slaves were being taken from the area annually. This had been going on for several decades, in spite of the Khedive's desire to stop the trade and his use of such men as Baker, Gordon, and others. In fact the pressure they put on the slave-trade, especially when Gordon closed the Nile to traffic, is seen as a major cause of several rebellions which culminated in the successful rising of the Mahdi.

Almost all the men involved were Nubians, especially of the Danagla-Ja'aliyyin groups on the Nile at Dongola and further south. They founded trading stations at various points on the White Nile and were the main inhabitants of Khartoum itself. Although the Nubians in their original areas had managed to maintain an independent language, the Nubians of the diaspora spoke a hybrid urban dialect of Arabic. They were all Muslims of the dominant Sunni orthodox sect and the Maliki rite. Though syncretic in practice, they were often fanatical Muslims, and, apart from the politico-economic climate, there was a frequent religious theme of Mahdism present with various claimants. Mohammed Ahmed was a Dongolawi (pl. Danagla) and most of his followers initially were the Danagla-Ja'aliyyin, and his Khalifa was a Ja'aliyyin.

The very same men are referred to in the literature variously as Sudanese, Danagla, Nubians (or Nubis), Khartoumers, and 'Arabs'. In the literature on Uganda in the early part of this century they were referred to as Sudanese or Nubians. I shall follow the modern usage of 'Nubian', as 'Sudanese' is ambiguous owing to the refugees from the ravages of southern Sudan since independence until 1972. I think this also accords with their own usage since Ugandan independence, for obvious reasons.

Those same men who worked as traders also worked for the government in various capacities. It is frequent to find mention of Nubians switching their allegiance from slave-trading to government service and then to the Mahdi, and vice versa. They were a powerful, if disorganized, military presence and had a lasting effect on the political structure of the southern Sudan peoples. They would ally themselves with one chief against his neighbours and set up puppet chiefs in other areas. Moreover they accumulated large numbers of slaves, servants, and hangers-on. Some of these were freed slaves who were armed and joined in slave-trading, adopting the culture of the Nubians and ultimately calling themselves Nubians. Though they had made allies with the Bari, it seems that the greatest number of accretions came from the smaller and weaker groups to the west—the Moru, Mittu, Monbuttu, Azande, etc. In a separate and later movement many Nigerians came to the Sudan and some of these joined the Nubians and are today to be found among them in Uganda. Indeed Emin found some among them in the 1880s. The Nubians also joined forces with the Makaraka—later seen as part of the Azande—from whom Emin was later to recruit many soldiers to join his Nubians as part of his policy of self-sufficiency, especially when he was later cut off by the Mahdists and deserted by many of his troops.

It is not possible in such a short chapter to give more sociological details. Besides trading in slaves, and ivory to a lesser extent, and being a powerful military force, they made use of their knowledge of Koranic medicines. Their influence in the spread of Islam was negligible except in terms of the accretion of personnel. When Emin reluctantly left with Stanley and a few of his Egyptian clerks and men and their entourages, there were probably left with Selim Bey on the west of Lake Albert about 200 men and a total population of 2,000. The rebel Fadl-al-Mulla had about 14,000 persons, some of whom later rejoined Selim Bey, and others went to the Makaraka country to the west. Apart from these 16,000 'Nubian' men, women, and children, there must have been at least as many of the earlier rebels and traders. For the next few years they continued to live off the country by force of arms in their traditional manner.

THE UGANDA PROTECTORATE

In 1890 Lugard arrived with a handful of seventy 'Sudanese', recruited through Egypt, as did the Germans for German East Africa, later reinforced by another such group, including Swahilis. In the fighting that shortly took place between Buganda and Bunyoro, and the Christians and the Muslims, Lugard felt insecure. The Nubians had a reputation for fighting from Baker and Emin, so Lugard decided to seek out Selim Bey and recruit some of his men. Four years later, some of Fadl-al-Mulla's men also came to Uganda hoping to join up with the British. Altogether over 18,000 men, women, and children were brought from the west of Lake Albert to Uganda. Initially only about 2,500 were enlisted, mostly with their own arms and ammunition. But from 1893, when there was a minor rebellion and Selim Bey was deported and others dismissed, to 1897, when the major mutiny occurred, there was continual unrest among the Nubians.

Five years later, Johnston, Special Commissioner of Uganda, commented:

From the time, however, that the [Nubians] were introduced into the future Protectorate trouble with them began. Themselves mostly ex-slaves, they had all the cruelty and unscrupulousness of the Nubian slave-traders, whose name, principles and religion they had inherited. Placed in Toro under the late Mr de Winton, they were supposed nominally to support the power of the king, Kasagama, who had been appointed to rule that country by Lugard; but their ravages, robberies, and rapes were more terrible even than the misdeeds of

Kabarega's warriors. After the greater part of them and their locust-like wives and followers were removed from Toro and placed under better control [in Buganda], they rendered very efficient service in fighting the Banyoro and the rebel Baganda in the years which followed Lugard's departure, and included the work of the first railway survey. . .The ease with which the brave and steady [Nubians] encountered and defeated large bodies of Banyoro, Baganda and Bahima inspired them with a great contempt for the pagan or Christian natives of the Protectorate. They were fanatical Mohammedans; they secretly despised the white man as an unbeliever, and they hankered continually after the founding of the Muhammadan kingdoms of their own in these fertile, easily conquered countries. Occasionally, their officers were not as well chosen as Major Cunningham and the late Major Thruston, who at any rate were able to converse with their men in Egyptian Arabic. Englishmen of no great experience of actual warfare, and of no knowledge of Arabic, were occasionally placed in command of these [Nubians], of whose intrigues they remained in absolute ignorance (through the linguistic barrier), and whose loyalty and affection they failed to secure by adopting a harsh and unsympathetic demeanour towards them.[3]

Apart from operations against the kingdoms, the Nubians were used in the east in parts of modern Kenya, and in Lango and Acholi, where their presence caused a cool reaction to British rule, culminating in their disarming of the Acholi. The Belgians had appointed many of them as 'Wakils' in their administration, and the British continued to appoint them as chiefs in many counties of West Nile when they took over the administration of that area. Johnston recognized Lugard's need for a force recruited outside in order to maintain his position. But the Khedive of Egypt disowned these Nubians in 1892 and the only solution seemed to be to settle them in colonies throughout Uganda. Wherever a station was founded, a colony of Nubians would settle around as small-time traders and cultivators. Some of them were used as police or reservists, and settled accordingly. When the Uganda Rifles were constituted in 1895, the Nubians formed its basis in spite of opposition from the London War Office. However, the importance of recruiting local Ugandan soldiery was realized, and a policy of steady replacement of the Nubians was officially adopted.[4]

THE INTRODUCTION OF ASIANS

At the turn of the century a strong fort had been built at the top of Nakasero Hill, opposite the earlier Lugard fort on Kampala Hill, and in the vicinity there was 'fast springing up. . .a town of Indian traders and a large [Nubian] settlement'.[5] Apart from their short-term presence as railway labourers and troops, the Indian presence was primarily felt in the commercial sphere, as it had been for the previous fifty years nearer the coast. Early Indian traders had been responsible for the recruitment of Indian labourers. In the commercial sphere they were encouraged by Johnston, within his terms as Special Commissioner. They undercut the German traders and operated in places where the Germans would hesitate to penetrate. Johnston writes that, 'Within the terms of my Special Commission, Indian traders advanced their posts from Kampala (Mengo) to Toro and the vicinity of the Congo Free State, to five places in Bunyoro, and all the posts at which Europeans and native soldiers were established in the Nile Province, besides opening bazaars at all the stations in the Eastern half of the Protectorate.'[6] There is no hint in Johnston's writing at this stage of Nubian traders.[7]

One result of the 1897 mutiny was the introduction of Sikh troops to improve discipline. In the General Report of the Uganda Protectorate for the year ending March 1903, we find that the Nubians, with 736 men, comprised half the total in the 4th and 5th Battalions. In the 5th Battalion there were 400 rank and file Sikhs and Punjabi Muslims. Economy was said to warrant a reduction in the Indians but the Nubians, though excellent soldiers when on service, 'come of a stock whose traditions it would not be altogether safe to ignore'. In the same year it was said that good furniture was being made locally in Kampala and Entebbe by Indian carpenters. During the year a 'considerable number of Indian traders came to the Protectorate, and [had] taken the retail trade from the hands of the Arabs and Swahilis who were at one time the traders of the Protectorate'.[8]

During the following year the number of Swahilis in the army was increasing but the number of Baganda was decreasing. To the single company of the former and the half company of the latter, there were five and a half companies of Nubians. It was said that the Baganda proved not to be satisfactory soldiers, but that the number of volunteers was practically unlimited, and they were found to be good in the police where they formed the majority. The Swahilis enlisted readily but there was difficulty in obtaining recruits for the Nubian companies. 'No 6 Company, which [had] a large following, supplied its own recruits. Other companies, especially those in the Nile Province, obtained their recruits from the neighbouring tribes, who [were] very similar to themselves.' This latter comment is like the later one concerning 'Sudanese' and Lendu—'a tribe akin to the "Sudanese"'—in the police.[9] It should be remembered that many Nubians could claim descent from Lendu, from the days when Selim Bey stayed in their land to the west of Lake Albert. Nine years later it was pointed out that 'the majority of troops were enlisted under the name of "Sudanese", a heading which, however, covers a number of tribes and individuals of mixed descent'.[10] By then the Baganda had largely taken over from the

Indians as artisans, carpenters, blacksmiths, and masons. The Nubian
officers had continually resented the Sikhs at Bombo and in 1913 the
last of the Indians left, to be replaced by Baganda. By 1917 there were
2,843 Indian males and 705 females in Uganda and two years later the
number had fallen fractionally.

By 1935 there were few Nubians still serving in the KAR, although
it seems that there was still a hang-over from the past in that they were
considered the more eligible for rank. By then the bulk of the soldiery
was drawn from the Nilotic groups, particularly the Acholi. The
Nubians remained a composite group, especially through intermarriage,
often with Baganda. In the 1931 Uganda census a language analysis
revealed only 5,528 Nubi speakers, some indication of the low ebb of
their status in Uganda, but probably not of their numbers. There were
13,000 Indians at the time. In the 1959 census, although there were over
23,000 Sudanese, the Nubians had effectively been defined out of
existence by the terms of the census enumeration. Some may have been
recorded as Sudanese and others by their district of birth. They were
to be found scattered throughout the country, especially in the small
trading centres and in areas around the old barracks. Thus their major
concentration was probably at Bombo, near Kampala, and many lived
around Arua in West Nile, with a large community in Gulu. But there
were others in most towns, and in such places as Ntungamo in Ankole.
Many were becoming petty traders.

LEGAL STATUS

Like the Asians, Nubians were given a privileged position in the
judicial process of the Uganda Protectorate under the British. When
various township Native Courts were established in 1923 and in 1932,
a Nubian headman or the headman of the Nubian village of the particular town was appointed as one of the three or so members of the court
in Kumi, Lira, Masindi, Hoima, Gulu, and Kitgum. In various other
smaller townships in the north and east they were represented, but in
Mbale, with its large Swahili community, the Swahili headman was one
of the two members of the court.

In the Buganda Courts Ordinance of 1940, 'native' included a Swahili along with those whose tribe was a tribe of various neighbouring
territories but excluded certain categories of Nubians. In 1935 the
legal status of Nubians had been somewhat ambiguous. For the Native
Courts in Buganda dealt with cases in which a native of the Protectorate
was involved, where 'Native of the Protectorate' includes any native of
any tribe on the confines of the Protectorate, who has been resident in
the Protectorate for a period of at least one year, and also includes
any Sudanese or Nubian, without any restriction as to period of resi-

dence. But 'civil and criminal cases in which the accused, the complainant or any of the parties, are regularly employed in government service or are Sudanese or Nubians. . .shall be tried by British Courts, under and subject to the provisions of the Courts Ordinance'. However there was a proviso that 'the Native Courts shall have concurrent jurisdiction without the reference aforesaid in cases relating to Poll Tax or Gun Tax or Sleeping Sickness or the registration of bicycles, where the accused is a native of the Protectorate, other than a Sudanese or Nubian'. Thus for some time a Nubian could insist on not being tried by a Buganda Native Court.

A Proclamation of June 1940 clarified the ambiguity by excluding from the jurisdiction of the Native Courts in Buganda 'a Nubian who (i) has proved that he is a descendant of the Armed Forces of Emin Pasha and his predecessors; or (ii) has earned exemption from taxation by virtue of service to the Crown, and has been registered as such by the District Commissioner'. But this special position for such a broad category of Nubians was drastically altered when, less than a month later, the Proclamation was revoked and a new one introduced which allowed exclusion from the Buganda Native Courts only if both requirements (i) and (ii) were fulfilled.

From 1925 until 1940 there was a Bombo Special Native Court which had jurisdiction over Nubians and Sudanese residing within ten miles of the Cantonment of Bombo. As with other Native Courts there were various limitations on the cases to be heard by it, and it dealt with all cases relating to marriages contracted under or in accordance with Nubian custom. One member of the court was always the Nubian Kadi (Islamic judge), and the chairman and other members were either current or retired Nubian officers of the KAR. There was an appeal to the court of the cantonment magistrate of Bombo. Under a law of 1908 a cantonment could be declared for any area surrounding a KAR quarter. With the ending of the Bombo Special Native Court, from the beginning of 1940, the Adjutant of the 7th (Uganda Territorial) Battalion, the KAR, was appointed to be an additional district magistrate of the second class and an additional district judge of the third class for the Cantonment of Bombo. But it appears that an informal Nubian system with unofficial Kadis may have continued. The integration of the courts in 1965 certainly removed all privileged legal status for various categories, until Amin reinstituted the Kadi system for Muslim law in 1972, with a Chief Kadi, Regional Kadis, and District Kadis, though without formal legal and constitutional recognition.

MODERN DEVELOPMENTS

A major cause of Nubian alienation from the developing patterns of advancement in Uganda was their lack of interest in education. Their factionalism made the provision of schools by the government difficult, and after the war one of the aims of placing the first Acholi district administration school at Pece in Gulu was to encourage the Nubians to send their children there. By the 1960s the Nubian leaders were adopting a different attitude, and in Gulu each faction built its own primary school. But to this day they remain a by-word for low education. The Asians, on the other hand, had placed considerable emphasis on education.

It is useful to distinguish between what might be called 'full' Nubians and 'marginal' Nubians. At the core of the 'full' Nubians are those who claim direct descent from the Danagla-Ja'aliyyin of the area of the old kingdom of Nubia. But any person whose father, at least, had attached himself fully to the Nubian group and way of life, and who no longer lays claim to any one particular ethnic origin, may be considered a 'full' Nubian. Such a Nubian will be a member of an extensive kinship network with members in various towns and trading centres throughout Uganda and perhaps elsewhere. To quote from an unpublished paper on one Nubian community, 'the Nubians, then, are a "powerful" ethnic group, with reasonably open membership conditions. Their present constitution is a direct consequence of their peculiar historical background, without any discontinuities in its development. As one of the custodians of a world religious system, with their knowledge of medicine and charms and the supernatural, and their military tradition and activity in trade, all spread over a century of involvement in the area around the upper Nile, they are obviously seen as "powerful"—supernaturally, politically and economically—by many groups and individuals. Clearly those who are cut off from their home in a small and rather powerless group, and who lack the modern "power" of education, are the most likely to be drawn to some sort of attachment to and identification with the Nubians. The basic kit that they need is to speak Nubi, become a Muslim, and not to be integrated into another community, and the Nubian world lies at their feet, with glimpses through the mist to the peaks of Uganda society.'[11] A 'marginal' Nubian is one who is not fully identified as a Nubian, and may not even possess all requisite attributes, but chooses to identify with them in many situations—probably for most of the time while in town—while keeping open options for reidentifying with his original ethnic group.[12]

It seems likely that the Nubians found themselves in an ambivalent position with respect to the Asians. Somewhat restricted in the army and excluded from leadership in an education-oriented society, they became poor images of the Asian trader, who at the same time was seen as a bar to their further advance. Many Nubians, along with other ex-servicemen, must have invested their gratuities in trade, which many Africans entered after 1944, because the supply of some goods, for example cotton piece-goods, by the government at fixed prices and profits encouraged Africans to start with low risk. The 1955 government report on 'The Advancement of Africans in Trade' stated that African traders then controlled about £10 million of trade each year, and that three-quarters of the traders were Africans, although few were in towns and this number really represented many petty traders. These traded mostly in 'bread and butter' lines, such as kerosene, salt, sugar, etc., which have low profit margins. These traders were said to imitate the Asian bazaar approach, which resulted in competition on prices rather than variety. In 1950 Girling could write that 'In Acholi District the Nubians are mostly small traders; they operate on the margins of the Indians' influence.'[13] With the withdrawal of the Asians into the towns during the late 1960s, and especially as a result of the 1969 Citizen Trading Act, the Nubians increased their control of those margins.

Like the Asians the Nubians disapprove of 'work' in the sense that, it is claimed, most Africans in Uganda would refer to 'manual labour which dirties the hands'. When a Nubian talks of going back to farming, he will usually clarify this as meaning organizing employed labour on his land to do the work for him. Perhaps they are not alone in emulating Asians and Europeans in this. More recently the educated Ugandan traders provided further threats to the perceived avenues to success and prosperity open to Nubians. This is somewhat symbolized in the issue about butchers, a matter close to the heart of Muslims. In 1972 the new Muslim Supreme Council received demands that all butchers should pay a licence fee to the Council, in an attempt to Islamize the trade. The proliferation of 'Pork Butchers' around Kampala is perhaps regarded as a statement that the butcher is not a Muslim rather than the fact that he sells pork, though the latter is popular among non-Muslims.

But the earlier, rather lengthy evidence that I have been producing is designed to show the basis, however time-distorted, for the current myth among Nubians that under the British they held all the top posts, from which they have been steadily removed by the Obote regime and to which they intend, according to a Nubian in early 1972, to return. Similarly, one is told that there are old Nubians who will refuse to eat with anyone who speaks against the British, for they are seen as co-operators in the colonial process.

Not all Nubians, however, are sympathetic to these political aspirations, and one Nubian leader was not interested in the top post of the Muslim Supreme Council because 'he wanted nothing to do with this Nubi business'. But more and more what I would call 'potential Nubians' from the Sudan have been recruited into the Uganda army in large numbers. Others have been entering as traders, and in vastly in creased numbers since the Asian exodus, as was pointed out to me by a Nubian in 1972.

AFRICANIZATION V. UGANDANIZATION

A major problem in Uganda since independence has been the distinction between Africanization and Ugandanization. Ramage, in October 1960, had been asked to advise on means of 'localization' of the EAC civil service, and the 'localization not Africanization' policy had received currency at the 1959 Conference in London on African civil services. The policy of Africanization rather than localization was first formulated in Tanganyika and then in Uganda. The Udoji *Report of the Africanisation Committee* for the EACSO in 1963 commented that localization, which perpetuated Europeans and Asians at the top of the service while giving preference to Africans in recruitment, did not satisfy the impatient African civil servant, nor the ambitious politician. From the Public Service Commission Regulations, they took what they termed an authoritative definition of the term 'African':

'African means a person of African race domiciled within the Territories and includes an Arab who was born, and is domiciled, in the Territories and any person either of whose parents is, or if deceased was, an African within the meaning of this definition, who is domiciled within the Territories' i.e. There are two qualifications: one of race; the other of domicile. It includes a mulatto and an 'Afro-Asian' domiciled within the territories, but excludes an African domiciled in either Central or West Africa. It also excludes a local European or Asian domiciled in the territories.[14]

Obote always carefully used the word 'Ugandanization', to the point of irritating his opponents but was in practice more ambiguous. His government's statement, just before independence, said that 'the Government has decided that the word Africanization is no longer suitable for the present purposes of the Government; and much loose thinking could be avoided if everyone was sure exactly what the phrase meant. For example, it is not clear whether Africanization includes persons of African extraction who come from territories other than Uganda; nor has it been made clear in the past whether it includes Asians, and indeed Europeans, who have been born and brought up in Uganda, and propose to make a career in the Civil Service in Uganda. The Government has therefore decided that in future the term "Ugan-

danization" should be used in the context of appointing and promoting
people of local origin to posts in the Civil Service.'[15] The statement
went on to say that the conception of 'Ugandan' must be clearly tied
to the conception of Uganda citizenship, which would be possible after
suitable citizenship legislation had been enacted.[16]

In 1968, however, there was constituted a Committee on *Africanization* of Commerce and Industry. Early on they reported that 'several
members of the public complained about the use of the term "Africanization" rather than "Ugandanization" in the Committee's terms of
reference, saying that this was discriminatory. They pointed out that
this was against the principle of Human Rights as advocated by the
U.N. and suggested that the Committee should recommend Ugandanization of the private and public sectors, whereby all Ugandan citizens
could have equal rights regardless of their racial origin.'[17] And the
following heading in their report was: 'Implementation of Africanization (or Ugandanization)'. But the government's memorandum on
their report refers to 'Africanization' and various such adjectives thirty-
three times; to 'Ugandan Africans' and 'Ugandans of African descent'
five times; and to 'Ugandans' and their converse 'non-Ugandans' and
'non-citizens' only ten times. The Application for a Trading Licence
form, resulting from the 1969 Act, requires shareholders to be categor-
ized as Ugandans, as Ugandan Africans, and as non-Ugandans. But do
the Nubians fall into two of these or only one of these categories?
Over three years later, on the same form, the applicant still had to state
the percentage of shares or capital held by Ugandan citizens on 1
January 1969, if the company had been incorporated or registered in
Uganda on or before that date.

This is all understandable in the light of the constitution introduced
by Obote in September 1967, which had several clauses inserted with
specific immediate circumstances and objectives in mind. Thus section
20 of chapter II on 'The Protection of Fundamental Rights and Freedoms of the Individual' has the primary clause that 'no law shall make
any provision that is discriminatory either of itself or in its effect' where
'discriminatory' means affording different treatment to different persons
'attributable wholly or mainly to their respective descriptions by race
. . .colour. . .', but this clause 'shall not apply to any law so far as that
law makes provision. . .for the employment of a proportion of African
citizens of Uganda in any trade, business, profession, or occupation'.
In this particular sentence, ' "African" means a person who is a member
of an indigenous African tribe or community of Uganda or a body
corporate or unincorporate entirely composed of such persons.'[18] Thus
Obote was consciously building into his new Constitution the possibility of discriminatory legislation and action, not only against the

Asian non-citizens but against Asian Ugandan citizens and also, by his definition of 'African' in this context, against, for example, Kenyan Luos and Nubians. Such action was taken against Kenyan Luos in 1969.

Tandon, in relation to the Asians, saw some justification in a process of Africanization of the economy, parallel to the idea of differential development for hitherto less developed districts, but pointed out the need for a time limit to be set, else the Asians would become disillusioned.[19]

For the forthcoming elections of 1971, Obote had considered allowing non-Ugandan Africans, and in particular Sudanese, to vote. But it was still not always made clear what was the process of acquiring citizenship for Africans: for instance, for the Kakwa or Rwandan refugee, or migrant labourer, or settled farmer, as opposed to one from the Kakwa County in West Nile District or from the Banyarwandan County of Bufumbira in Kigezi District.[20] Kenya has fully accepted the Nubians, and the MP for Nairobi is from the Nairobi Nubian community.

Obote's speech at the opening of parliament on 20 April 1970 attempted to clarify these issues of citizenship.

Honourable Members must be aware of the three categories of non-Ugandan residents. First, we have the non-Ugandans who are also non-Africans; second, immigrant Africans from neighbouring countries who have settled in Uganda, and, third, refugees from neighbouring States. Starting with the third category, Government policy is that refugees must go back to their own countries. . .As for the second category, that is, those who claim to be immigrant settlers, the Immigration Act 1969, does apply to them and they should endeavour to fulfil the provisions of that law. Regarding the non-Ugandans who are also non-Africans, the majority of whom are British citizens of Asian origin, a comprehensive exercise is now being undertaken. . .For the moment I wish to emphasize that as far as Uganda is concerned, these people are not Uganda citizens and are not entitled to remain in our country at their own will or because they cannot be admitted into any other country. They have never shown any commitment to the cause of Uganda or even to Africa. Their interest is to make money, which money they exported to various capitals of the world on the eve of our Independence. They are, however, human beings and much as they have shown every sign of being rootless in Uganda, we would like their departure not to cause either them or others dear to them, or even ourselves, any human affliction. Government, when the two exercises are completed, will arrange for a systematic manner through which these persons are to disengage themselves from their hold on and continued residence in our country.[21]

Amin has been less ambiguous than Obote and openly proclaims that 'Black Africans', which would clearly include Nubians, though occasionally 'black Ugandans', which might not so blatantly include them, should take over businesses. Certainly the Nubians have received more than their share of the top businesses throughout Uganda, often at the direct expense of Ugandans. But there is some ambiguity over his attitude to Arabs. The Nubians are, of course, closely linked with North African Arabs but perhaps opposed to the Muscat and Omani Arabs whose connection is with the Coast Swahilis of the Shafi'i rite.

The Nubians fit neither the facile racial analysis of African/Asian/European, so popular in African newspapers and to some extent here, nor that based on ethnic allegiance, so popular in the Western press and skilfully used by Amin himself. Without a land base they just do not exist!

STRATIFICATION

In terms of perceived stratification systems seen from the relative point of view of different groups in the society, one of the best indices is the attitude to intermarriage between the groups and strata. We know that little, if any, intermarriage took place between the various major sectors of Asians, such as Ismailis, Hindus, Sikhs, and Goans. There was balanced competition between these groups, which may be seen structurally as vertically divided components of the society. There has been a negligible number of European-Asian marriages in either direction in East Africa. The Asians saw themselves as structurally equivalent to the Europeans. I do not wish here to discuss the obviously important feature of cultural exclusiveness and conservatism maintained by this particular alien trading group. With regard to the Africans, the Asians saw themselves as structurally superior. With the prevalence of hypergamy in almost all horizontally divided societies, including India itself, it is not surprising to find that out of a number of African-Asian marriages, I know only of Asian men marrying Africans.

When Amin began his tirades on Asian exclusiveness and the need for intermarriage, he was clear that he meant African men marrying Asian women. When he denied the existence of Afro-Asian marriages, he knew as well as anyone else of the existence of the one-way marriages. The Asians immediately took his point, and only this week on television here a young Asian girl referred to Amin's desire for Asian girls to marry Africans. Indeed, quite a few Asian girls were captured for this purpose in a way reminiscent of the equivalent status conflict in Zanzibar between the Afro-Shirazis and the Arabs. Now the Nubians themselves keep a similar close control over their women, and I know of no Nubian women marrying out, but plenty of cases of Nubian men taking wives from other groups. As with some of the Asians, these often became second, or 'outside' wives.

Where politics are concentrated in the hands of men, statements concerning other groups permitting or prohibiting the men of one's own group marrying girls from the other groups may best be interpreted as political statements of superiority and inferiority.[22] In a situation of conflict, marriages and sexual relationships across the boundary in the 'wrong' direction can be dangerous, as can be seen even from the attitude of the Provisional IRA in Northern Ireland to Catholic girls who do this. In times of peace, those of mixed parentage become 'bridges'. But their position is always ambiguous, and in time of confrontation their position is insecure and they may be seen as dangerous by both sides because of their bond with the other side. An Afro-European, whose looks were misleading, was stopped one day during the Asian exodus in the streets of Kampala and congratulated because the soldier thought he was an Arab, and a few days later he was told by another soldier to stop walking and to start looking busy because, 'as an Asian', he should be packing and leaving in a hurry. It is not surprising, therefore, that many of those who left Uganda on the last day of the expulsion were those who had married across the racial boundary or were themselves Afro-Asians, some of whom hardly appeared Asian.

Until independence almost all European-African marriages were of European men to African women, partly reflecting the low number of single European women in government employment, but more recently there have been as many in both directions. It is significant that the attitude of the army to European men with African wives has been markedly more hostile than to African men with European wives.

Since independence the stratification system in Uganda has been very much one of vertical divisions, with prestige and status based to a large extent on education. In one sense it was more 'open', but the criteria became achievement-based rather than ascription-based, and those who had failed to obtain education found themselves deprived. The Nubians, as a group, were so deprived and still perceived the stratification system in horizontal terms, based on ascription at birth. It is true that Nubian ethnic status could be, to some extent, 'achieved', usually by those cut off from their home in a small and rather powerless group and lacking the modern 'power' of education, as I have already argued.

Perceiving themselves as co-colonizers with the British, seventy or so years ago, yet finding their only possible advance blocked by Asian traders whom they saw, ironically, as inferior, the Nubians not surprisingly found themselves frustrated. On the other hand, most Ugandans tend to regard them as providing the base of the stratification system. When a group perceives a status system differently from its perception by the society as a whole, they are likely to try to change that status system to fit their perception of it and, given the power to do this, conflict is almost bound to occur. In achieving their current position in Uganda, the Nubians have established in reality, for the time being, their perceived horizontal stratification system.

IMPLICATIONS

A state with a horizontal stratification system is likely to have a less stable and permanent incorporation of alien groups than one in which the divisions are vertical. Conflict between the strata is to be expected. It is not surprising, therefore, that the socialism of Tanzania had provided the best incorporation of Asians to be found in East Africa, and that the opposite is to be found under Amin's ideology in Uganda. Uganda under Obote and present-day Kenya provide examples somewhere between these extremes.

I have chosen to concentrate on the Nubians because of their clear position in relation to the Ugandan Asians. They are concentrated in the urban periphery and trading centres throughout the country and, with low education, find employment as petty traders, labourers, and soldiers. But they are representative of a wider urban group. Besides the 'full' and 'marginal' Nubians, as I have described them, there are the 'potential' Nubians. Like these, there is a vast body of urban dwellers who, though they might never attach themselves in any way to the Nubians, nevertheless portray the same socio-economic background. The urban population of Uganda grew at about 10 per cent per annum from 1959 to 1969, when the urban population stood at over 600,000.

Many of those who now fill the towns and the dense areas of housing springing up in and around them are, at the least, under-employed. With an ever-increasing flow of educated school leavers— Uganda's School Certificate classes have increased at 20 per cent per annum for the decade 1960–70—the uneducated and primary school leavers find themselves increasingly thwarted in an economy whose growth is not commensurate.[23] Surrounded by affluence, the seeds of discontent are sown in a soil of relative deprivation. It is such persons, especially if led by a more cohesive community with similar qualifications and aspirations, who will support a move such as Amin's expulsion of all Asians, however self-defeating such a policy may be for them in the long-run with consequent unemployment. But the urban malcontent is essentially faced with the apparent problem of the short-run, and the millenarian promises of Utopia and distribution of largesse are a tempting prospect.[24]

It may not even need a focus in an urbanized community such as the Nubians or Swahilis for such pressures by the urbanites to be felt at the level of government power and decision-making. With the concentration of all government activity in the towns and a highly centralized administrative system, it should be remembered that government in many African states, as elsewhere, is government by the urbanites—the original 'citizens'.

12

SOME LEGAL ASPECTS OF THE EXPULSION

James S. Read

Just over ten years elapsed between the first imposition of controls on Commonwealth immigration to the United Kingdom—by the Commonwealth Immigrants Act 1962 (passed in the year of Uganda's independence)—and President Amin's announcement of the expulsion of British Asians from Uganda, on 4 August 1972. During those years immigration and the connected issues of race relations were constant themes in domestic British politics, not unrelated to the dismantling of the colonial empire—a process which reached its peak, in terms of the number of territories granted independence, at the same time. The position of the Asians in East Africa was an important element in the debates and policies which characterized that period and, in the United Kingdom as well as in East Africa, legislation sharply reflected the currents of political discussion and decision.

THE BACKGROUND IN UGANDA

Of Uganda's total Asian population of 74,308 in 1969[1] (approximately 0.73 per cent of the total population of 9,548,847), Uganda citizens formed more than a third (26,657, of whom more than 11,000 were aged under 15 years) and British Asians almost a half (36,593), the only other numerically significant categories being Indian citizens (8,890) and Kenyans (1,768). The total Asian community in Uganda had in fact more than doubled between each of the previous censal years—from some 5,000 in 1921 to 14,150 (1931), 35,215 (1948) and 71,933 in 1959. A relevant feature of the situation in 1972 was the relatively large size of Uganda's total immigrant population, non-citizens forming in 1969 over 5 per cent of the total population (546,396 out of 9,548,847).[2] Non-citizen Asians formed less than 9 per cent (48,651) of this immigrant community, the overwhelming bulk of which consisted of African immigrants from Kenya and Tanzania and refugees from other neighbouring African states (numbering at least 175,000) whom Uganda had accepted in recent years and a number of whom had been settled in that country.

During the colonial period the inhabitants of the Uganda Protectorate were not, of course, as such British subjects: they fell into the anomalous category of 'British protected persons' (except for the few who acquired British citizenship by naturalization or enjoyed that status by right of birth in British India). The position was different in Kenya where, following the annexation as a colony in 1920, the majority of inhabitants—including all those born there after that date— were automatically 'citizens of the UK and Colonies' by birth, under the terms of the British Nationality Act 1948 (although those born in 'the coastal strip' which, after 1920, formed the Kenya Protectorate, were, of course, British protected persons).

At the independence of Uganda, citizenship provisions were inevitably complex although most Asian residents were offered, in effect, alternatives: if they did not choose to become citizens of Uganda, they retained their status as British protected persons or UK citizens (as the case might be) and continued to be entitled to UK passports.[3] However, this general statement must be qualified in several ways. Firstly, second- and third-generation British Asians automatically became Uganda citizens (i.e., any UK citizen or British protected person born in Uganda, if at least one of his parents had also been born there; moreover, the child of such a person, wherever born, was also a citizen of Uganda automatically). Secondly, every person, whatever his race, born in Uganda on or after independence day (9 October 1962) acquired Uganda citizenship by birth although this rule was modified five years later (see below). Thirdly, the option of Uganda citizenship as of right for others was not available for those who had some other citizenship—e.g. of India, Pakistan, or Tanzania—but only for UK citizens and British protected persons who had been born in Uganda; fourthly, such persons could claim Uganda citizenship as of right only if they applied for it within two years of independence. After some early hesitation there was a rush of applications for citizenship as the specified period ran out—in 1964, 24,212 applications were made in all, 5,953 and 9,589 in the months of September and October respectively. By the end of 1964 it was officially reported that the total number of citizens registered (apparently since independence) was 7,448, of whom 99 per cent were Asians. It was also reported that every citizenship application was accompanied by an application for a passport 'since Asians prefer having valid passports although they may not be contemplating travelling in the near future'.[4] Fifthly, the constitution prohibited dual citizenship except for a year at the attainment of the age of majority after which the Uganda citizenship would be lost unless the other citizenship had been renounced.

The provisions outlined above were embodied in the constitution of Uganda which came into force at independence, and this also empowered the parliament of Uganda to enact legislation providing for the deprivation of citizenship acquired by registration, even in the case of a person to whom the constitution gave a definite right to registration as a citizen. Such legislation was in fact enacted in 1962: it provided for deprivation of citizenship not only where the registration had been obtained by fraud but also where a citizen has availed himself in another country of rights open only to citizens of that country, and more far-reaching still was the provision for automatic loss of status if the registered citizen did not, within three months of registration, renounce any other citizenship held at the same time and take the oath of allegiance.[5] Discretionary registration—the right to apply for registration as a citizen, the grant of which lay in the discretion of the responsible minister—was available for any citizen of a Commonwealth state or of certain designated African states or any British protected person who had been ordinarily resident in Uganda for five years and satisfied certain normal conditions.

Under the short-lived constitution of 1966 the basic citizenship rules continued, although there was, of course, no longer a right to automatic registration of citizenship for British residents as such, the time limit for such applications having expired. It was the Republic of Uganda Constitution of 1967 which introduced a major qualification of the general rule of citizenship by birth for all those born in Uganda since independence: anyone born in Uganda after it came into force on 8 September 1967 acquired citizenship by birth only if one of his or her parents or grandparents is or was a citizen of Uganda. This was a significant change in the rules affecting non-citizen Asian residents and no doubt its importance was fully appreciated by them, coming as it did in the year in which Kenya had adopted the legislation (the Immigration Act and Trade Licensing Act)[6] which is generally considered to have precipitated the increasing exodus to the UK of late 1967, which in turn prompted the enactment of the Commonwealth Immigrants Act 1968 in the UK. Ironically, that Act adopted a similar formula to that in the new Uganda constitution, to define those who were to be entitled as of right to entry into the UK.

THE LEGISLATIVE BACKGROUND IN THE UNITED KINGDOM

Even after the acceptance of separate nationalities within the Commonwealth (by the British Nationality Act 1948)[7] the principle of completely free entry and immigration to the United Kingdom for all 'British subjects' or 'Commonwealth citizens' had been preserved until the Commonwealth Immigrants Act 1962[8] imposed controls on the entry of all Commonwealth citizens (and British protected persons) except UK citizens born in the UK or holding UK passports issued by the UK government. Controls therefore applied to the citizens of all Commonwealth states except the UK, and to UK citizens who held passports issued outside the UK by a colonial government (for example, including UK citizens holding passports issued by the government of Kenya Colony).[9] The controls applied at all times to British protected persons, but after independence of a former dependency UK citizens resident there could obtain their passports not from the new government of what was now an independent Commonwealth state but from the office of the High Commissioner who represented the UK government itself. Thus it happened that UK citizens in, for example, East African states, having been before independence subject to the controls imposed by the UK legislation, became, after independence, free of such controls—for their passports were now issued by the UK government.

This was the situation which provoked the hasty and embarrassed response of the UK government and parliament to the apparently growing exodus from Kenya in 1967, with the introduction, by the Commonwealth Immigrants Act 1968,[10] of an additional condition for free entry into the UK: not only did the UK citizen have to hold a UK passport issued by the UK government, but now, in addition, he, or at least one of his parents or grandparents, must have been born, naturalized, registered, or adopted in the UK, otherwise the immigration controls were applicable to him. This was the Act which provoked much heart-searching and controversy and an acrimonious debate in the House of Commons,[11] the argument turning in part at least on divergences of opinion as to the precise nature of the implications of the right given to Asians in East Africa to retain their British status after independence. The bill was taken through all its stages in one sitting of the House of Lords—the longest sitting this century.[12] Whether or not there was at the time of independence in Uganda or Kenya any explicit or implied promise of free entry to the UK for locally resident UK citizens, there is in any event a clear obligation in international law which has a similar effect to such a promise and which was reiterated at the time of the Uganda exodus by the then Foreign Secretary, Sir Alec Douglas-Home: 'Under international law a State has a duty to accept those of its nationals who have nowhere else to go. . .'[13] Nevertheless the Act of 1968 had already introduced the international novelty of restrictions on the admission to the UK of her own citizens, within a narrow legal definition, and some seeds of President Amin's action undoubtedly lie therein. Moreover the obligation at international law accepted by Sir Alec could not prevail over the express terms of UK legislation—not, at any rate, in UK courts[14] although international tribunals such as the European Court of Human Rights might take a different view: in 1970 the European Commission on Human Rights held admissible thirty-one applications by Asians from East Africa in this context.[15]

It was, of course, argued in support of the Act that it was not intended indefinitely to exclude the UK citizens in question, but merely to phase their entry over a period of years to avoid social and other problems within the UK. This hope, however, was jeopardized by the failure of the UK government to reach an understanding with the then Uganda government, during negotiations in 1970, as to acceptable conditions and a suitable rate of absorption.[16] A criticism of the Act, at the time of its enactment, was that it represented time dearly bought and was likely to be seen, in East Africa, as a provocation and a challenge. The consequent rejection by the UK of hundreds of her own citizens[17] and their consequent experience of being 'shuttle-cocked' around the world, surely indicated that some ultimate confrontation with the East African states would be hard to avoid. Eleven British Asians deported from London Airport rated only a short paragraph in London newspapers; the same group arriving back at Entebbe Airport may well have been a significant catalyst in the formulation of President Amin's expulsion policy announced a few days later.

Meanwhile there had, since the 1968 Act, occurred a further change in the immigration laws of the UK of even greater general significance: the enactment of the Immigration Act 1971.[18] This replaced the previous Acts, including that of 1968, and established a unified body of law for all immigrants, whether Commonwealth citizens, UK citizens or aliens—although the different categories are by no means subject to the same rules. The Act redefines those who are entitled to enter the UK free of immigration controls, introducing the new concept of 'patrials' who have the 'right of abode' in the UK. This concept will—albeit never explicitly—have the effect in general of making a distinction between categories of UK citizens and Commonwealth citizens on ethnic or racial criteria. Under the terms of the Act a UK citizen is not a 'patrial' unless he, his parent or grandparent was a UK citizen by birth, adoption, registration or naturalization in the UK; a citizen of any independent Commonwealth state is, however, also a 'patrial' under the Act if his parent was a UK citizen by birth in the UK and, furthermore, in January 1973, as a concession following a parliamentary defeat over the original Immigration Rules under the Act in November 1972, the UK government in effect overruled the earlier parliamentary deletion of 'the grand-father clause' from the Immigration Bill in 1971 and reinserted it in the new Rules, extending the 'patrial' concept to Commonwealth citizens who can show that one grandparent was born in the UK.[19] The effect of the Act and the Rules made thereunder is therefore to extend to several million Commonwealth citizens at a stroke the unrestricted right of entry to the UK; they can, of course, be distinguished from the thousands of UK citizens of Asian descent in East Africa who have no such right by the facts that they have no pressing need or desire to emigrate to the UK and that they are likely to be almost entirely of European descent.[20]

The 1971 Act makes other important changes in British law. Work vouchers issued to Commonwealth citizens no longer confer an automatic right to settle in the UK but only a right to admission for a specified job for a limited period—normally twelve months—which may be extended at the discretion of the Home Office.[21] Britain's entry into the European Communities necessitated provisions for the free admission to the UK, from 1 January 1973, of nationals of partner states, to work and reside. Under the relevant Rules almost 200 million European aliens now have the right of unrestricted entry not merely to take but even to seek work in the UK. In consequence the entry channels at Heathrow Airport are now marked respectively 'Commonwealth citizens' and 'UK citizens and EEC nationals'. The Rules starkly demonstrate the contrast:

An EEC national who wishes to enter the United Kingdom in order to take or seek employment, set up in business or work as a self-employed person is to be admitted without a work permit or other prior consent.[22]

Where the passenger is a citizen of the United Kingdom and Colonies holding a United Kingdom passport, and presents a special voucher issued to him by a British Government representative overseas (or an entry certificate in lieu), he is to be admitted for settlement, as are his dependants if they have obtained entry certificates for that purpose and satisfy the requirements of paragraph 39; but such a passenger who comes for settlement without a special voucher or entry certificate is to be refused leave to enter.[23]

Moreover the EEC national may freely be accompanied, or later joined, by his 'dependants', defined as his wife, children under 21, older dependent children, dependent parents and grandparents; if he enters employment or establishes himself in business by the end of six months he is entitled to a residence permit for five years, and after four years of employment or business the time limit will be removed. These rights of free entry to the UK extend to those citizens of France—numbering over a million—who are the inhabitants of the four overseas departments of Martinique, Guadeloupe, French Guiana, and Reunion[24] but the reciprocal right of entry into European states is not available for the UK citizen of Asian descent in East Africa.[25]

There are still many hundreds of UK citizens in East Africa (some of them no doubt illegally and, their residence permits having expired, having been in prison) and elsewhere who may well wish that they were rather 'EEC nationals' with the free right of entry to the only country to which they can strictly claim to belong. Yet for them the prospect of admission to the country of their nationality has, perversely, receded even further for, with the introduction of the new Rules, the then UK government changed its stance of willingly accepting its obligations to its citizens expelled from Uganda to one of announcing (January 1973) that this reception could not be repeated: the then Home Secretary telling parliament that 'to have a similar burden thrust upon us again would impose unacceptable strains and stresses on our society. . .'[26] Is it surprising that this statement should have been castigated in Kenya as a provocative 'interference in Kenya's sovereign discretion', 'tantamount to blackmail'?[27] Thus are sown the seeds of future crises.

UGANDA: THE PRESSURES INCREASE

The Asian community in Uganda had been much affected by legislative measures introduced by President Obote's government in 1969. The Trade (Licensing) Act,[28] which came into force at the end of that year, was intended to facilitate the Ugandanization of wholesale and retail trade. It was not explicitly based on racial categories, distinguishing only between citizens and non-citizens: the latter were prohibited from trading except in areas of cities, municipalities, and towns specifically declared to be 'general business areas' by ministerial order, and they were also prohibited from trading in a larger number of specified trading centres. Although Kampala, Jinja, Mbale, Masaka, and other main towns were specified as 'general business areas', in some of them (not Kampala) the main streets were excluded from such specifications, thus closing them to non-citizen traders.[29] Further, non-citizens were banned from trading anywhere in 'specified goods' unless specially licensed to do so; some 34 items were specified for this purpose including beer, soft drinks, cigarettes, hoes, batteries, passenger motor vehicles, soap, fishing nets, and certain basic foodstuffs such as rice, maize flour, and ghee.[30] The burden of proving citizenship rested, in any case of reasonable doubt, on the person concerned; a company or firm was regarded as a citizen if more than 50 per cent of the share capital or partnership property was held by or on behalf of citizens.

The new Immigration Act 1969 also increased the pressures on non-citizen Asians to leave Uganda: it came into force on 1 May 1970 and was avowedly intended to promote 'Ugandanisation of posts in both the public and private sectors'.[31] It nullified all existing immigration permits and introduced a new system of documentation for all non-citizens resident in Uganda; a register of foreigners was also introduced. An entry permit would be issued only if the Immigration Board was satisfied that it was for purposes of benefit to Uganda and not prejudicial to the inhabitants generally. Such a permit could be valid for a maximum of five years in the first instance and would be renewable once only for a further three years. (The former 'certificates of permanent residence' had been cancelled, as from 1965, by previous legislation.)[32] The Immigration Act authorized the imposition of heavy fines (up to Shs 20,000) and imprisonment (up to two years) for engaging in any employment, occupation, trade, business, or profession without a permit.

A further tightening of the screw occurred with legislation of May 1970. The Companies (Government and Public Bodies Participation) Act, No 3 of 1970, transferred to the government 60 per cent of the shares in 84 scheduled companies, including manufacturing enterprises, banks, etc. It also stipulated that, with effect from 6 May 1970, 'no person other than the Government or other public body authorised by the Minister shall import goods of any description. . .' and any existing licences for import- or export-restricted goods were cancelled. The Export and Import Corporation Act, No 4 of 1970, set up a new body from 29 May, with the sole right to export or import goods of any description for the purposes of trade. As a result of these measures, wholesalers and retailers in Uganda would be entirely dependent on the Corporation for their supplies (although it could authorize others to export or import, but only with the Minister's prior approval).

The pressures were therefore increasing—on the Asians to leave Uganda and on the UK to admit her passport holders from there. The British government negotiated with President Obote's government but no agreed solution had been reached when, in January 1971, General Amin came to power. The respite from the pressures was short-lived. In May 1971 the British government announced that, as a result of what the Secretary of State termed a 'common point of view' arrived at after discussions with East African governments—especially that of Kenya—it would double the number of entry vouchers (to 3,000) available for UK passport holders in East Africa, and a further special quota of 1,500 vouchers was allocated for the last half of 1971.[33] (A compensating reduction of 2,000 was made in the number of work vouchers available for Commonwealth citizens.) These figures refer to voucher-holders and do not, of course, include the numbers of dependants entering with them. In fact the net balance of UK passport holders entering the UK in 1971 totalled 15,853 as against 11,007 in 1970.[34] A special census of Asians was held in Uganda on 17 October 1971 when nationality documents were examined; at his meeting with Asian representatives on 8 December 1971 President Amin stated that

12,000 applications for citizenship had been cancelled but could be resubmitted on the basis of new conditions.

THE EXPULSION

The expulsion legislation refers expressly to the racial factor; it is terse, simply amending the Immigration Act 1969 by cancelling as from 9 August 1972 every entry permit or certificate of residence issued under that Act 'to any person who is of Asian origin, extraction or descent and who is a subject or citizen' of one of the four scheduled countries (UK, India, Pakistan and Bangladesh).[35] The form of this amendment had the result that other Asians, e.g. those who were the citizens of no country, were not affected. To include such stateless persons a further amendment was introduced on 25 October 1972, which added the cancellation of the entry permit of 'any other person who is of Indian, Pakistani or Bangla Desh origin, extraction or descent' [sic],[36] a difficult formula—does it, for example, include a person of mixed descent? In accordance with Uganda government policy as corrected from an earlier announcement, the expulsion did not strictly apply to Asian citizens of Uganda, who were in any event not subject to the Immigration Act, but the process of positive verification of citizenship within a time limit, which the Uganda authorities conducted, particularly disclaiming those with incomplete papers or dual citizenship, reduced the numbers of Asian citizens considerably from earlier estimates. Thereby also arose special difficulties for those who thus found themselves 'stateless'. It has already been noted that those who acquired Uganda citizenship otherwise than automatically by birth were required to renounce any other citizenship held; however, UK citizenship was not lost by such a renunciation if in fact it was not followed by the acquisition of another citizenship within six months—in such circumstances the citizen was deemed by English law never to have renounced his UK citizenship.[37] Even where the other citizenship (within the Commonwealth) was acquired, special provision had been made for the person who had renounced his UK citizenship subsequently to reacquire it by registration but this was automatic only where the former citizen could show a 'qualifying connection' with the UK (or a colony or protectorate existing at the time of application) in that he, his father, or grandfather had been born there.[38] (In the absence of such a qualifying connection there is a discretion in the Secretary of State to register such a person as a citizen.) This provision, enacted after the independence of Kenya, was regarded as the fulfilment of a promise made to settlers and others of British descent in that country—presenting an opportunity, perhaps even an encouragement, for them to opt for local citizenship conditionally, as it were, with the prospect of opting back to UK citizenship again later. Since its enactment the racially limited nature of this measure has been criticized[39] and it is certainly notable in retrospect that in none of the parliamentary debates that attended its enactment was this discriminatory aspect mentioned;[40] suffice it to record that it was of little or no avail to the majority of those Ugandans who found that their new citizenship was ill-founded and thus became 'stateless'—in any event they would probably have been 'British protected persons', and not UK citizens, before opting for Uganda citizenship, and for this reason outside the scope of that Act.

Apparently in an attempt to restrict the impact of the expulsions to the trading sectors, where the arguments against foreign exploitation could be most readily deployed and where the exodus might be less damaging, the Uganda Minister for Internal Affairs was given power to exempt from expulsion persons otherwise affected by reinstating their entry permits 'in his absolute discretion'.[41] On the same day that the original Decree was published the Minister did in fact formally exempt government employees and 'professionals', including teachers, lawyers, doctors, chemists, architects, accountants, engineers, etc.[42] These exemptions accord with that interpretation of the policy which lays emphasis on its economic aspects but it is notable that exemption was also extended to 'managers or owners of banks and insurance companies; owners of and professionals and technicians engaged in plant, animal, agricultural and forestry production, processing and marketing of these products, and school owners'. Also exempted were employees of cooperatives, of the East African Community, and of international organizations. In fact many non-citizen Asians within these categories must have chosen to leave Uganda—although early in 1973 there were still 450 British Asians working in Uganda[43]—and ultimately it may well be their departure rather than that of the trading community which will have the greater impact on the country.

Was the expulsion Decree strictly legal? Although somewhat academic, the question has been posed elsewhere. Chapter III of the Constitution of the Republic of Uganda 1967, which protects fundamental individual rights and freedoms, has not been suspended or revoked by the military government but the provision which prohibits discriminatory laws expressly does not apply to a law which makes provision 'with respect to persons who are not citizens of Uganda'. A similar provision qualifies the guarantee of freedom of movement and residence and immunity from expulsion; this would, however, have been relevant if an attempt had been made (as it was not) to implement the policy announced by the Uganda government of dispersing the remaining Asian citizens to farms in rural areas. (No doubt that announcement had its effect in encouraging some citizens to leave the country 'voluntarily'.) Quite apart from the fact that the military government has assumed authority to override parts of the constitution, it appears that the expulsion Decree would in fact have been lawful within the terms of the constitution itself. There will, no doubt, be much discussion of its legality in terms of international law, an issue beyond the scope of this chapter.[44]

THE ADMINISTRATION OF THE PROPERTY OF EXPELLED ASIANS

In view of the swiftness with which President Amin's government acted, and the emphasis on the expulsion of Asian residents, it is perhaps not surprising that the legal implications of the affair with regard to the property and business interests of the Asians were at first neglected. There was no question of invoking the long-existing provisions in the laws of Uganda for the compulsory acquisition of property:[45] those provisions were designed for individual acts of acquisition involving possibly lengthy processes of enquiry and valuation, in each case leading to the payment of compensation (the right to which is constitutionally guaranteed). How were the abandoned properties to be administered? What legal rights in such assets could strictly be transferred to those to whom they were 'allocated'? What obligations—for rent, compensation, existing debts, etc.—could be imposed upon such allottees? Were expelled Asians to be allowed to deal with their property in Uganda from overseas, whether or not through agents? How were the individual rights of expelled Asians to be identified and recorded? Successive Decrees show a piecemeal, improvised approach to these and other vexed problems, an approach which becomes cumulative as the government's legal draftsmen respond—often retrospectively—to policy decisions and actions; but the time factor can have allowed them little opportunity for careful examination of such legal complexities, while the novelty of the operation meant that they were deprived of the lawyers' usual standby, precedents of comparable legislation from other jurisdictions. The basic elements in the legal scheme which has emerged include an early requirement that departing Asians first declare their assets and then the ultimate vesting of these assets in the government—although this step was not taken until more than a year after the exodus. Evidently it was only then discovered that there was no alternative practicable means for the exercise of adequate control over the allocated properties and businesses.

The first relevant provision was made by legislation of 4 October 1972 which prohibited 'departing Asians' from transferring or mortgaging immovable property, bus companies, or farms to any person and from issuing new shares in companies, appointing new directors, or changing salaries or terms of service of staff.[46] This 'standstill' Decree was thus designed to prevent both open and clandestine transfers and other means of frustrating the purposes of the government. The Decree postulated a complex and, in the circumstances, surely impractical, scheme of extensive paperwork to regularize the position. Every departing Asian was required to declare his assets and liabilities on official forms to the minister, enclosing copies of accounts for the last two years, lists of contracts, etc., and nominating an 'agent to sell his property or business', although the immediately following provisions of the same Decree expressly forbade the agent to do just that. The agent was required to ensure that the property or business 'is properly looked after until it is transferred by sale to a Uganda citizen' (an unintentionally pregnant piece of drafting). Unless the government or a state corporation applied to buy the property, the minister was to advertise it for sale, and if more than one application was received an advertising committee appointed by the minister was to consider them. Valuers would determine the price to be paid. If the appropriate documents were not submitted to the minister by the departing Asian —and this must have been not uncommon—the property could not be sold but would vest in the government; the difficulties which faced departing Asians may be surmised from the fact that this Decree, although first published on 6 October 1972 (just over a month before the final departure date), was deemed to have come into force on 4 August 1972.

The original Decree forbade the agent to sell the property, but an amending Decree shortly followed which permitted him to sell (or himself to acquire) the property with the approval of a newly established Abandoned Property Custodian Board, consisting of five ministers.[47] Property which vested in the government (e.g. for absence of proper documentation) was now vested in this Board. Furthermore, if property was abandoned by a departing Asian (a term now amplified to include a Ugandan citizen who had left) or 'left in such a way that no adequate arrangement has been made for its proper and efficient management', the Board could vest such property in itself by order. Four instruments were subsequently made under which 63 companies and properties (including manufacturing, trading, hotel, and other companies, and 20 saw mills) were vested in the Board (the majority of these—49 of them—were not so vested until August 1973).[48] The Board was given power to determine all claims arising against the property or business of a departing Asian; no creditor could exercise any right conferred on him by any other law—for example, in a court of law—but could only file his claim with the Board. However, an appeal lies to the High Court against the decision of a tribunal which has itself heard an appeal against the decision of valuers appointed by the Board to determine the amount of compensation payable to the former owner.

Early in 1973 provision was made to control the payment of rent by the new occupiers 'of premises belonging to the departed Asians'.[49] It was made clear that any property vested in the government passed to it for the same estate, interest, and rights as were held by the Asian owner; the government was expressly empowered to lease, sub-lease, or let the property or deal with it as it sees fit, rent being finally determined by the minister and payable to him (even if the new tenant went into occupation under an arrangement with the former owner). Significantly, it was provided that the government itself would pay the rent for any allottee who was a public officer or a member of the armed forces, police, or prison services. All rents paid were to be collected in the Special Rentals Fund which would then be used to pay compensation to the former owners, as well as for repairs, rates, etc.

Legislative rationalization of evolving policies has now resulted in two consolidating Decrees of late 1973 which together provide a convoluted legal scheme. The Acquired Asian Businesses (Rights and Obligations Ascertainment) Decree[50] defines the rights transferred to a person to whom a departed Asian's business has been allocated: such rights do not include ownership of the premises or of existing debts due to the business. The obligations imposed upon the allottee are threefold: to pay 'the value of the business' within a prescribed time; to avoid 'any business malpractice' or specified offence; to perform and observe all relevant requirements 'including any business-like practice specified'. The value of the business (which does not include any allowance for goodwill) is to be fixed by the Abandoned Property Custodian Board, established by the Decree of 1972, to which it is then payable; however, on the same day the Assets of Departed Asians Decree was enacted which repealed that Decree and renamed and re-established that Board, indicating a puzzling degree of discontinuity between contemporaneous legislation.

The allottee, or 'purchaser' as he is termed, will receive full ownership of the business, with a Certificate of Vesting, only when he has completed payment for it—such payment may be by instalments with interest as determined by the minister. Until completion of payment the purchaser cannot 'add any new line of business' or transfer the business without the Board's approval. A Business Promotion Committee (representatives of six ministries, the chief factory inspector, three representatives of the security forces, and 'a Uganda citizen of proven ability in business administration') was set up 'to review all allocated businesses periodically so as to ascertain how far the purchasers are running them as efficiently as should be and to offer such advice or give such directions to the purchasers as the Committee shall deem necessary. . .' The Committee can receive and investigate complaints from the public about allocated businesses, and there are business inspectors appointed by the minister to assist it. The Decree specifies business malpractices—failing to pay an instalment due, rates, or taxes, to keep proper books of account, to insure the premises and stock-in-trade, to keep plant, machinery, and vehicles in good order, to maintain reserves of raw material or spare parts, in the distributive trade to sell goods 'without any discrimination whatsoever', or 'to keep the business running commercially'—but these apply only to purchasers who have not yet received their certificates of vesting; the penalty for breach of these rules may be cancellation of the allocation. The minister can also cancel allocations on public policy grounds. Every purchaser must, upon allocation, nominate two persons—at least one of whom is a member of his family—to succeed him in the business upon his death, insanity, or retirement.

The Assets of Departed Asians Decree[51] reconstituted the Abandoned Property Custodian Board as the Departed Asians' Property Custodian Board (now consisting of the Ministers for Commerce and Industry, Finance and Land with the Attorney-General and two Presidential nominees) to 'take over and manage' all the assets vested in the government under the Decree, including assets declared by departing Asians and assets 'left behind by any Asian who failed to prove his citizenship at the time and in the manner specified by the Government' (which were vested in the government by the Decree) and other assets of departed Asians vested in the government by ministerial order. Liabilities 'attaching to' these assets also passed to the Board but these can be varied or disclaimed by the Board 'if it is in the public interest so to do' where it considers the liability 'to be of unreasonable disadvantage to the public interest'. The Board is responsible for allocating assets to Uganda citizens and for compensation payable to the departed Asians; such compensation is to be based 'upon the excess of the value of the assets transferred over the amount of any liabilities attaching to the said assets, and shall be payable over such period as the Minister shall determine, having regard to the period within which the said assets may generate sufficient income to offset the amount of compensation payable'. From any decision of the Board on this matter, appeal lies (within thirty days) to the Minister and from his decision (within thirty days) to the High Court. The Board must also pay compensation to any Uganda citizen who had a share, as partner or shareholder, in any business which the Board has allocated; moreover, if property has been allocated which was owned by a Uganda citizen of Asian origin who has confirmed his citizenship as prescribed, it must be restored to him or, if restoration is not possible, compensation must be paid by the Board. This compensation to citizens takes precedence over compensation to others. The Special Rentals Fund, into which rent for allocated premises is paid, is renamed the Departed Asians Special Fund. Banks holding accounts for departed Asians had to report them to the Board; all moneys in such accounts were transferred to the Departed Asians' Account Common Pool Fund controlled by the Board, the purposes of the Fund being stated as: 'to provide an effective means of overseeing the accounts of the departed Asians; to enable payments to be made to approved claimants out of the account of any departed Asian'. Money in either Fund may be invested by the Board in trustee securities. The Decree establishes a Tribunal, the members of which are appointed by the Minister but include a Chief Magistrate of five years' experience as chairman and four to six members including a qualified accountant and a person with proven ability in business administration or banking, with exclusive jurisdiction to hear and determine at first instance any claims against a departed Asian for recovery of any debt. Appeal from the Tribunal's decision lies to the High Court. The Board itself can be sued for such a debt (before the Tribunal) and can itself sue (in the ordinary courts) for any debt owed to a departed Asian; it is not liable for any debt beyond the amount of assets vested in it in respect of the Asian concerned.

The complexity of the legal machinery which has thus been set up to unravel the network of Asian business relationships in Uganda no doubt betokens a serious intent on the part of the Uganda government to pursue as far as possible an orderly conduct of its 'economic war'— and particularly, of course, to achieve an efficient performance by Uganda citizens in the running of the businesses, etc. which they have acquired. Whether, in the circumstances of the hasty expulsion, the improvised reactions, the lack of preparation, the legal imponderables, and the human problems occasioned by the policies, the legal machinery can be effective may be doubted. Further amendments to the scheme can be expected. But the Uganda government has constantly affirmed its intention to pay compensation to the former owners, and the legal provisions could certainly make that possible. As to the commercial viability of the businesses 'under new management', time alone will tell the full story but a visit early in 1974 afforded impressionistic evidence that in Kampala at least many of the former Asian businesses of varying sizes and specializations were operating apparently effectively.[52]

CONCLUSION

As a result of the expulsion 28,608 persons arrived in the UK and were assisted by the Uganda Resettlement Board which had been set up on 23 August 1972 to aid UK passport holders and their dependants ordinarily resident in Uganda on the date of President Amin's first announcement of the expulsion.[53] The majority of these were 'British protected persons' rather than UK citizens proper (the published statistics do not distinguish between these categories). The net balance of increase in the UK passport holders from East Africa was thus 39,371 in 1972 (in 1971 it had been 15,853) made up of 13,033 men, 10,805 women and 15,533 children.[54]

The racial aspect of Uganda's policy—significant as this aspect is—must be seen in the context of Africa in the early 1970s: the Uganda government's policy was not fundamentally different from, and indeed was in many ways less far-reaching than, policies which had been adopted by several other governments of varying complexion. The trend towards 'purifying the nation' of alien—and, as part of the apologetic, allegedly exploitative—elements was demonstrated, for example, by the expulsion of aliens from Ghana by Dr Busia's civilian government. They were African aliens and so attracted less international interest, but the policy affected allegedly half a million citizens of Upper Volta and probably more Nigerian Yorubas alone than there were formerly British Asians in Uganda, as well as many others.[55] In other countries—e.g. Sierra Leone, Zaire—expulsions have resulted from the exclusion of aliens from specified types of commercial enterprises, rather than by simple expulsion. These policies were in part the reactions of modern nation states, themselves the creation of colonialism, against the policies of freedom of movement within former regional-colonial boundaries which that same colonialism had facilitated. 'Whatever the sins of colonialism the colonial regimes made possible large-scale migrations for economic reasons. . .When independence came many newly independent states found that they were playing host to large immigrant communities, African and other, who sometimes appeared to dominate certain sectors of the economy.'[56]

The expulsion policies were thus the responses of governments anxious to demonstrate to their own citizens that the satisfaction of their rising expectations was not to be unduly deferred while foreigners apparently prospered at their expense. The celebrated 'Indigenisation Decree' in Nigeria[57] is a more measured response to the same basic dilemma. President Amin's action, so severely condemned in Europe and other parts of the world, was thus little criticized, and was even applauded, in Africa itself (with the notable exceptions of the strictures voiced by Presidents Nyerere and Kaunda). An extreme reaction was that of President Sekou Touré of Guinea, formerly an opponent of the Uganda military government, who was reportedly converted by the events of 1972 to become a supporter of it.[58] In post-colonial situations the racial factor in national policy formulation cannot easily be ignored —a principle applicable to the UK itself (which is also in such a situation from the opposite end): the forceful opposition which was stirred in certain sections of public opinion in the UK to the admission of the 'Ugandan Asians' (so miscalled, even by official spokesmen and government ministers) surely itself mirrored the racialist attitudes which the very same sections of opinion detected and condemned in Uganda?

NOTES

I. WAS THE EXPULSION INEVITABLE?

1. D. Humphry and M. Ward, *Passports and Politics* (Harmondsworth, 1974) pp.12–13.

2. The best guide to this subject at present is Nizar Motani, 'The growth of an African civil service in Uganda 1912–1940' (unpublished PhD thesis, University of London, 1972).

3. F. Furedi, 'The development of anti-Asian opinion among Africans in Nakuru District, Kenya', *African Affairs*, lxxiii (1974), pp.347–58.

4. The fullest account is D. P. Ghai, 'The Bugandan Trade Boycott: A Study in Tribal, Political and Economic Development', in R. I. Rotberg and A. A. Mazrui (eds.), *Protest and Power in Black Africa* (New York, 1970), pp.755–70.

5. For a differing view see J. D. Parson, 'Africanising Trade in Uganda: The Final Solution', *Africa Today*, xx (1973), pp.59–72.

6. Apa Pant, untitled reminiscences in mimeo, Indian High Commission, London, 4 October 1972.

7. See, for example, D. A. Low, *Buganda in Modern History* (London, 1971), passim, and M. Twaddle, 'Ganda receptivity to change', *Journal of African History*, xv (1974), pp.303–15.

8. I am indebted to Dr Richard Rathbone for discussion on this point.

9. Hilda Kuper, ' "Strangers" in plural societies: Asians in South Africa and Uganda', in L. Kuper and M. G. Smith (eds.), *Pluralism in Africa* (Berkeley, 1969), pp.267–8.

10. See M. Twaddle, 'The Amin coup', *Journal of Commonwealth Political Studies*, x (1972), pp.99–112.

11. Some further implications of this are outlined in my article, 'Order and disorder in Uganda', *The World Today*, xxix (1973), pp.449–54.

12. A. M. H. Sheriff, 'Indians in East Africa', *Tanzania Notes and Records*, lxxii (1973), pp.75–80.

13. H. S. Morris, *The Indians in Uganda* (London, 1968).

14. P. Marris, 'Ambiguity and Commitment', *Mawazo*, iii (1971), pp.17–25.

15. *Speech by His Excellency the President of Uganda to the Asian Conference held on 8th December 1971 at the Uganda International Conference Centre*; reproduced as an appendix to J. O'Brien, *Brown Britons, The Crisis of the Ugandan Asians* (London, Runnymede Trust, 1972), p.27.

16. *Memorandum of the Asian leaders. . .in response to His Excellency's speech dated 8th December 1971*, reproduced in O'Brien, op. cit.

17. Y. Tandon, *Problems of a Displaced Minority* (London, Minority Rights Group, 1973), p.13.

18. See M. V. Pylee, *Constitutional Government in India* (2nd edition, London, 1965), pp.176–84. I am indebted to Professor W. H. Morris-Jones for this reference.

19. Prem Bhatia, *Indian Ordeal in Africa* (Delhi, 1973), p. 132. Bhatia was then Indian High Commissioner in Kenya.

NOTES

211

2. INDIANS ABROAD: EMIGRATION, RESTRICTION, AND REJECTION

1. A full-scale bibliography would be out of place here but there are three useful pamphlets: D. P. Ghai and Y. P. Ghai, *The Asian Minorities of East and Central Africa* (London, Minority Rights Group, 1971) (this is also included in B. Whitaker (ed.), *The Fourth World. Victims of Group Oppression* (London, 1972)); Mariyam Harris, *The 'D' Valued Passport* (London, Christian Action, 1971); D. Tilbe, *The Ugandan Asian Crisis* (London, British Council of Churches, 1972).

2. Cmd 1922, *Indians in Kenya: Memorandum* (1923).

3. See B. Pachai, *The South African Indian Question, 1860–1971* (Cape Town, 1971), for an account compiled from published materials.

4. In 1911 whites formed 21 per cent of total South African population; by 1960 they were only 19 per cent. Whereas Coloureds and Indians together equalled only 53 per cent of the white total in 1911, by 1960 their combined numbers equalled 65 per cent of the whites. By 2000, if present trends continue, there will be more Coloureds and Indians than whites in South Africa. Starting with a low growth rate, the Indians are now a steadily growing group in South Africa.

3. THE ISMAILIS IN UGANDA

1. For the period before 1958 the most important study is H. S. Morris, 'Immigrant Indian Communities in East Africa' (PhD thesis, University of London, 1963), which depends on fieldwork undertaken between 1952 and 1955. In a modified form it was published as *The Indians in Uganda* (London, 1968) and this, because of its selective emphasis upon Ismailis, remains the most useful published survey of Ismaili social structure.

The present study benefited enormously from numerous informal discussions with members of the Ismaili community made possible by two years' teaching at the Aga Khan Secondary School, Kampala, 1970–2. Since then interviews with a cross-section of Ismaili refugees in this country have added a further dimension and, besides perusal of such secondary works as exist on Ismailis, the Uganda press has been scanned for the period between 1958 and 1972 with particular attention being paid to the English-language *Uganda Argus* for the decolonizing era (1958–1964) and the time between Amin's initial seizure of power and the expulsion. Given such sources as well as the contemporary character of the subject under discussion, this essay is necessarily provisional.

2. Figures for late 1972 estimated by a senior Ismaili Association official in Uganda: Tanzania 30,000; Kenya 15,000; Uganda (pre-expulsion) 14,000.

3. In this century the community has been led by Aga Khan III (1885–1957) and since 1957 by his grandson Karim, Aga Khan IV.

4. Quoted from correspondence with a sixth-form Ismaili student.

5. Coverage of this subject is to be found in C. Dobbin, *Urban Leadership in Western India. Politics and Communities in Bombay City 1840–1885* (Oxford, 1972).

6. Ibid., p.119.

7. This was the doctrine by which Shias were permitted to disguise their true identity in circumstances of persecution.

8. Report of C. P. Rigby (1860), referred to in C. S. Nicholls, *The Swahili Coast* (London, 1971), p.290.

9. Quoted in J. S. Mangat, *The History of the Asians in East Africa, 1886–1945* (Oxford, 1969), p.52.

10. Morris, op. cit., p.11.

11. H. M. Amiji, 'The Asian Communities', in J. Kritzeck and W. Lewis (eds.), *Islam in Africa* (New York, 1969), p.148.

12. W. Frischauer, *The Aga Khans* (London, 1970), p.158.

13. Amiji, op. cit., p.155.

14. In 1953 31 out of 100 Indian schools in Uganda belonged to the Ismailis. Morris, op. cit., p.151.

15. J. S. Trimingham, *Islam in East Africa* (Oxford, 1964), p.106.

16. J. N. D. Anderson, 'The Ismaili Khojas of East Africa: A New Constitution and Personal Law for the Community', *Journal of Middle Eastern Studies*, i (1964), p.23.

17. Amiji, op. cit., p.149.

18. Anderson, op. cit., p.26.

19. Anderson, op. cit., p.24.

20. See note 4.

21. Amiji, op. cit., p.151.

22. 'Upper class' is a term commonly used to describe the most prominent of all races who mixed freely at cocktail party level before independence. 'Class' is used in conversation by Ismailis in reference to distinctions in wealth within their community.

23. Quoted from conversation with a prominent Kampala businessman and store owner.

24. J. Verjee, Administrator of Ismaili Education Department for Uganda, in a speech at the opening of the new Secondary School, claimed that there had been African children in Ismaili schools for eight years: *Uganda Argus*, 25 June 1959. Yet it was in February 1958 that the admission of the first five Africans to the Government Indian Secondary School in Kampala was hailed as 'the beginning of the government's policy of inter-racial education', *Uganda Argus*, 14 February 1958, which suggests that the Ismailis set an example here not only to other Asians but to the colonial government.

25. *Uganda Argus*, 2 March 1960. Two days later it was reported that, on hearing that seven local Ismaili families would still be homeless after the completion of this project, seven anonymous members of the community offered them interest-free loans so that homes might be built in sufficient numbers.

26. *Uganda Argus*, 25 March 1963.

27. Frischauer, op. cit., p.247.

28. D. P. Ghai and Y. P. Ghai, *The Asian Minorities of East and Central Africa* (London, 1971), p.5.

29. Y. Tandon, 'A Political Survey', in D. P. Ghai and Y. P. Ghai (eds.), *Portrait of a Minority* (revised edition, Nairobi, 1970), p.93.

30. This appears from Sir Andrew Cohen's memoirs, *British Policy in Changing Africa* (London, 1959), to have been deliberate. Cohen maintained that 'constitutional advance is not a puppet show' and, 'since timetables for political advance do not work', he preferred 'moving step by step'.

31. Thus R. J. Mehta, President of the Central Council of Indian Associations, in a statement endorsed by the Central Council of Muslim Associations, was reported to be awaiting explicit Asian programmes from African political party leaders, *Uganda Argus*, 27 October 1959.

32. Uganda, *Colonial Report* (1959), p.6.

33. The *Uganda Argus* reported the murder of a shopkeeper, S. S. Patel, at Ntwetwe (24 February 1960) and associated it with the boycott.

34. *Uganda Argus*, 9 March 1960.

35. See e.g. D. Apter, *The Political Kingdom in Uganda* (Princeton, 1961),

wherein anti-Asian sentiment is seen to be linked, in Buganda, with intra-Bugandan politics—'a common charge was that the chiefs were government agents, therefore disloyal to the Baganda, and that they were all bribed by Asians', p.246.

36. See D. A. Low, *Buganda in Modern History* (London, 1971), pp.155, 126. A later instance of controversy surrounding a Ugandan Asian minister came in 1958 when Ugandan students in London protested at the presence of Sir Amar Maini, then Minister of Corporations and Regional Communications, as representative of the Uganda government at the opening of Uganda House, London.

37. H. Ingrams, *Uganda* (London, 1960), p.3.

38. Stressed by Y. Tandon in *Problems of a Displaced Minority* (London, Minority Rights Group, 1973).

39. Rumours of these were published in the *Uganda Argus* during 1960.

40. The UPC and DP were considering non-African candidates in 1960 (*Uganda Argus*, 24 November 1960) and did indeed appoint many to urban constituencies for the 1961 elections. A pattern developed of Asian candidates from the two main parties competing for certain constituencies, e.g. in 1961 Asian candidates won two out of three Kampala seats, plus Mbale and Jinja South. Ministerial appointments followed. Although the total Asian population in 1959 was, at 69,000, a small fraction of Uganda's total population of 6½ million, their concentration in urban areas had important electoral implications. (See H. W. West, *Land Policy in Buganda* (London, 1972) for legal distinctions between rural and urban land ownership for non-Africans.) In Kampala, for example, there were 19,500 Asians out of a total of 46,714, while there were a further 9,085 (out of 29,741) in Jinja, and 4,739 (out of 13,569) in Mbale. (Figures from the 1959 census as published in the Uganda *Colonial Report* (1959), pp.16, 17.) However, D. Parkin in his study of the 1962 Kampala Municipal elections, *Neighbours and Nationals in an African City Ward* (London, 1969), showed that even in the predominantly African ward of Kampala, Kampala East, three out of the ten candidates were Asians.

41. There is also the idea developed in, e.g., E. Hopkins, 'Racial Minorities in British East Africa', in S. Diamond and F. Burke (eds.), *The Transformation of East Africa* (Syracuse NY, 1966), of a 'deflection of hostility' from Europeans to the more vulnerable Asians.

42. These first took place, to a limited extent, in 1958.

43. See for example Ingrams, op. cit.

44. Letters to the *Uganda Argus* argued that it would be suicide, in the absence of guarantees and in the light of the boycott, to demand anything less than separate representation.

45. See below, p.41.

46. Thus a 'religious' balance was maintained among the six representatives on the Legislative Council up to the period of decolonization. See, e.g., Uganda *Colonial Report* (1958), pp.144–6.

47. This is described in G. Bennett and C. Rosberg, *The Kenyatta Election* (London, 1961). Also note Bennett's remark in 'The Development of Political Organisations in Kenya', *Political Studies*, v (1957), pp.113–30, that 'the Asians in Kenya have demonstrated the failure of the common roll system which would appear to demand a measure of homogeneity not possessed by them'.

48. Tandon, *Problems of a Displaced Minority*.

49. *Uganda Argus*, 14 April 1959, 2 September 1959, etc.

50. *Uganda Argus*, 17 October 1959, 9 September 1960 and 27 October 1959 respectively.

51. Their radicalism won them access to the PAFMECA Conference in September 1959.

52. H. Kuper, ' "Strangers" in Plural Societies: Asians in South Africa and Uganda', in L. Kuper and M. G. Smith (eds.), *Pluralism in Africa* (Berkeley, 1969), p.268.

53. Low, op. cit., p.173.

54. Morris, op. cit., p.175.

55. *Uganda Argus*, 16 April 1960. After independence the CCIA held a series of mass meetings in urban centres to persuade Asians to apply for citizenship.

56. Quoted in *Uganda Argus*, 12 July 1958, from a speech in Kampala given by the Aga Khan shortly after his installation.

57. *Uganda Argus*, 18 September 1959.

58. *Uganda Argus*, 12 July 1958, op. cit.

59. Ugandan Government *Annual Report* (1964), p.221.

60. *Uganda Argus*, 24 March 1961, interview with the Aga Khan.

61. *Uganda Argus*, 17 October 1959.

62. *Uganda Argus*, 24 October 1960.

63. Each party claimed that it had been the first to open up to non-Africans and to make commitments to them. While the UPC posed as the only truly national party, the DP reminded Asians that it alone had not associated itself with the 1959 boycott.

64. The Ugandan African Civil Service Association complained that at the end of 1960, for example, there were still 2,023 expatriates in the Ugandan Service. *Uganda Agus*, 20 December 1960.

65. Memoirs of Aga Khan III, *World Enough and Time* (London, 1954), p.190.

66. Ibid.

67. Cf. A. Gupta, 'The Asians in East Africa', *International Studies*, x (1969), p.273; Ghai and Ghai (eds.), op. cit., p.37; and Tandon, *Problems of a Displaced Minority*, respectively.

68. Quoted in *Uganda Argus*, 12 July 1958.

69. Gupta gives a figure of 98 per cent, op. cit., p.273.

70. To have been born, and one parent to have been born, in Uganda.

71. Frischauer, op. cit., p.247.

72. Tandon, *Problems of a Displaced Minority*.

73. *Uganda Argus*, 25 July 1964.

74. This charge in the Kenyan situation was well documented and examined in D. Rothchild, 'Kenya's Minorities and the African Crisis over Citizenship', *Race*, ix (1968), pp.421-37.

75. *Uganda Argus*, 13 September 1960.

76. Y. P. Ghai, 'The Future Prospects', in Ghai and Ghai (eds.), op. cit., p.217.

77. Frischauer, op. cit., p.247.

78. *Uganda Argus* editorial, 22 February 1972.

79. The Society did not set itself political goals; the Aga Khan said in 1955: 'I appeal to the Moslems of all sections to look upon this society as a pan-Islamic brotherhood, working especially for the uplift of African Moslems and the encouragement of mission efforts for the expansion of Islam to the African population' (quoted in Trimingham, op. cit., p.172).

80. N. Q. King, *Christian and Moslem in Africa* (New York, 1971), p.3.

81. M. Lowenkopf, 'Uganda', in J. Kritzeck and W. Lewis (eds.), op. cit., p.225.

82. *Uganda Argus*, 1 September 1959.

83. 'The Political Relevance of Islam in East Africa', *International Affairs*, xlii (1966), pp.35-44.

84. Tandon, *Problems of a Displaced Minority*.
85. J. S. Furnivall, quoted in Morris, op. cit., pp.161, 167.
86. Kuper, op. cit., p.251.
87. Morris, op. cit., p.172.
88. T. Mboya, *Freedom and After* (London, 1963).
89. Ghai and Ghai (eds.), op. cit., p.36.
90. Tandon, *Problems of a Displaced Minority*.
91. Anderson, op. cit., p.35.
92. This was a 'middle-class' Ismaili family where Ismaili girl married Ithnasheri boy but retained her religion, Ismaili girl married Bohra boy but retained her religion, and Ismaili boy married Hindu girl, who became an Ismaili. Such examples of limited intermarriage could be multiplied.
93. Kuper uses this term to describe the Asians as a category of mobile, uncommitted immigrants with different conventions, ambivalent relations with their hosts, and, in the East African case, segregated but privileged.
94. Quoted in Frischauer, op. cit., p.24.
95. That is an eighth of *net* income.
96. A. Bharati, 'A Social Survey', in Ghai and Ghai (eds.), op. cit., p.55.
97. See note 23.
98. Story recounted in Frischauer, op. cit., p.96.
99. Y. P. Ghai, op. cit., p.17.
100. Quoted in Trimingham, op. cit., p.107.
101. Anderson in Kritzeck and Lewis, op. cit., p.37.
102. Anderson, op. cit., p.21.
103. *Uganda Argus*, 12 July 1959.
104. *Uganda Argus*, 6 October 1959.
105. An illuminating interview with A. Samji (see note 115) was published in the *Sunday Telegraph*, 5 August 1973. Mr Samji 'politely declined' to say what assets he had outside Uganda but the interview was accompanied by a photograph of his two sons sitting on his Rolls Royce in Knightsbridge. Samji was a member of the Supreme Council.
106. See D. Tilbe, *East African Asians* (London, Race Relations Committee of the Society of Friends, 1970).
107. e.g., *Uganda Argus*, 21 March 1963.
108. Only citizens could apply but discrimination was practised on racial grounds over, for example, choice of courses.
109. Gupta, op. cit., p.285.
110. This was the celebrated 'Move to the Left' in *The Common Man's Charter* (Entebbe, 1970).
111. Note the almost immediate recognition of the Amin government by Great Britain.
112. These were the two biggest industrialists in the country (both non-Ismaili).
113. *Uganda Argus*, 22 February 1972.
114. See note 2.
115. A. Samji, leader of the Ismaili community, chaired the committee of leading Asians which tried to negotiate with Amin. 'He supposed this was the reason why Amin imprisoned him for three days before he was expelled.' *Sunday Telegraph*, op. cit.
116. See note 4.
117. Tandon, *Problems of a Displaced Minority*.
118. J. O'Brien, 'General Amin and the Uganda Asians', *Round Table*, 249 (1973), pp.98, 99.

4. THE GOAN COMMUNITY IN KAMPALA

1. Republic of Uganda, *Statistical Abstract 1968*.
2. A. Bharati, 'A Social Survey', in D. P. Ghai and Y. P. Ghai (eds.), *Portrait of a Minority: Asians in East Africa* (Oxford, 1970).
3. J. S. Kuper, 'The Goan Community in Kampala, Uganda' (unpublished PhD thesis, University of London, 1973).
4. Sir Charles Eliot, *The East African Protectorate* (London, 1905), p.34.
5. J. S. Mangat, *The History of the Asians in East Africa, 1886–1945* (Oxford, 1969), p.27.
6. Mangat, op. cit., p.75.
7. Mangat, op. cit., p.74.
8. R. Desai, 'On Joking Relationships among Asians in East Africa', unpublished paper (cyclostyled), presented at Puberty and Joking Conference, Makerere University, December 1966.
9. Ibid.
10. *Goan Voice* (Nairobi), 22 December 1956.
11. *Goan Voice*, 30 December 1961.
12. H. S. Morris, *The Indians in Uganda* (London, 1968).
13. *Goan Voice*, 23 March 1957.
14. Morris, op. cit., p.43.
15. Morris, op. cit., p.108.

5. THE HINDUS OF BAKULI

1. The material for this chapter is derived from a study of dispute settlement I carried out in 1967 and 1968. I thank Professor Raymond Apthorpe and Professor Burton Benedict for their valuable comments on earlier drafts. I also express my sincere gratitude to the Joint Board of Makerere College (now Makerere University) for its financial support.
2. The terms Indians and Asians are used in East Africa to refer to immigrants who originate from India and Pakistan.
3. L. W. Hollingsworth, *The Asians of East Africa* (London, 1960).
4. G. Delf, *The Asians in East Africa* (London, 1963).
5. D. P. Ghai and Y. P. Ghai (eds.), *Portrait of a Minority* (Oxford, 1970).
6. H. S. Morris, *The Indians in Uganda* (London, 1968).
7. B. M. Schwartz (ed.), *Caste in Overseas Indian Communities* (San Francisco, 1967).
8. J. S. Mangat, *A History of the Asians in East Africa* (Oxford, 1969).
9. Ibid., pp.142–3.
10. Morris, op. cit., pp.27–44.
11. Ibid., pp.30, 34.
12. M. N. Srinivas, *Religion and Society among the Coorgs of South India* (Bombay, 1952), p.31.
13. *Sri Sanatan Dharma Mandal*, Gujerati booklet published at the inauguration of the Hindu Temple, Kampala, nd, p.13.
14. In their studies of Indians in Uganda and East Africa, Morris and Bharati use the term *jāti*. Even though this standard Sanskrit/Hindi term is understood in Gujerati, it is the term *nāt-jāt* that Gujerati-speakers use consistently. Interchangeably used, both *nāt* and *jāt* signify the endogamous character of an Indian group. In Sanskrit *jāti* (rendered *jāt* in Gujerati) means birth or origin while *gnyati*

(rendered *nāt*) refers to near blood relation (see A. A. Macdonell, *Practical Sanskrit Dictionary* (1929), pp. 100–3).

15. D. Pocock, ' "Difference" in East Africa: a study of caste and religion in modern Indian society', *Southwestern Journal of Anthropology*, xiii (1957), pp.289–300.

16. As implied here, in general the rules of caste pollution do not govern the relationship between Indians and Africans. In small trading posts in Uganda, however, I have occasionally seen orthodox Hindu merchants asking their African customers to stand away from their shops if the latter were carrying meat or fish with them. In the mid-sixties, at a Uganda sugar factory in Lugazi, an Indian supervisor beat up an African worker for drinking water from his pot and thus making it 'unclean'. This was clearly a case of a pollution rule becoming relevant in a specific situation. The event led to protests by African workers who demanded the Indian should be deported. The event was well reported in the local press and alluded to in A. K. Inguita's article 'Caste in India, in Africa. What is ritual pollution?', *Transition*, xxiii (1965), pp.15–18.

17. I thank Professor Burton Benedict for drawing my attention to similarities between *atak* and *gotra*. J. H. Hutton defines *gotra* as an exogamous unit of individuals theoretically descended from a single ancestor. Such exogamous units are described by such different terms as *illam, kul, mul, phaid, pal, pangat, bani, nukh, kuri, khel,* etc. Despite this striking congruence between *gotra* and *atak*, I found no Lohana informants or others using these coterminously.

18. A. Bharati, 'A Social Survey', in Ghai and Ghai, op. cit., p.288.

19. Bharati, 'Ideology and content among the Indians in East Africa', in Schwartz, op. cit., p.308.

20. Bharati in Ghai and Ghai, op. cit., pp.31, 15, 16; in Schwartz, op. cit., p.304.

21. Bharati in Ghai and Ghai, op. cit., p.17.

22. Morris, 'Caste among the Indians of Uganda', in Schwartz, op. cit., p.270.

23. Morris, *Indians in Uganda*, p.91.

24. Cf. A. Beteille, *Caste, Class and Power* (Berkeley, 1965), p.45.

25. E. Leach, 'Class, Caste and Slavery: the taxonomic problem', in A. de Reuck and Julie Knight (eds.), *Caste and Race: Comparative Approaches* (Boston, 1967), p.10.

26. Morris and Bharati in Schwartz, op. cit., pp.270 and 284 respectively.

6. BLACK ATTITUDES TO THE BROWN AND WHITE COLONIZERS OF EAST AFRICA

1. I am grateful to colleagues in the Department of Political Science and Public Administration, Makerere University, Kampala, for their stimulating and critical comments.

2. It is traditional nowadays to refer to the immigrants to East Africa from India and Pakistan as 'Asians'. Before the partition both groups were referred to as 'Indians'.

3. 'A number of published as well as unpublished works deal directly with Asian community in East Africa, but none can be defined as definitive.' See J. S. Mangat, *The History of the Asians in East Africa* (Oxford, 1969).

4. Lord Lugard, *The Dual Mandate*, cited in Grace Ibingira, *The Forging of an African Nation* (Kampala, 1973), p.19.

5. N. Sithole, *African Nationalism* (Oxford, 1959), pp.146–7.

6. Ibid.

7. Ibid. Emphasis added.

218 NOTES

8. Frantz Fanon's treatment in *Black Skin, White Masks* of this problem is yet to be superseded.

9. *Dobozi lya Buganda* (Voice of Buganda) undated draft editorial, in J. F. Scotton, 'The Early Ugandan Press: From Protest to Nationalism', paper presented at the thirteenth Annual Meeting of the African Studies Association, Boston, 21–4 October 1970, p.8.

10. See Dent Ocaya-Lakidi and Ali A. Mazrui, 'Secular Skills and Sacred Values in Uganda Schools: Problems of Technical and Moral Acculturation', paper presented at a Conference on Conflict and Harmony Between Traditional and Western Education in Africa at the School of Oriental and African Studies, University of London, March 1973.

11. Johnston to Jackson, 24 January 1900; cited in T. Watson, 'History of Christian Missionary Society High Schools in Uganda 1900–1925; The Education of a Protestant Elite' (unpublished PhD thesis, Makerere University).

12. Mangat, op. cit., p.23.

13. Ibid., pp.24–5.

14. Ibid., p.22.

15. See, for example, the views of the Young Baganda Association, *Uganda Herald*, 29 July 1921.

16. Ibid., 15 July 1921.

17. Watson, op. cit.,

18. *Uganda Herald*, 22 July 1921.

19. Ibid., 29 July 1921.

20. Y. Tandon, 'A Political Survey', in D. P. Ghai and Y. P. Ghai (eds.), *Portrait of a Minority: Asians in East Africa* (Oxford, 1970).

21. Ibingira, op. cit., p.68. Emphasis added.

22. See Ali A. Mazrui, 'The Lumpen Proletariat and the Lumpen Militariat: African Soldiers as a New Political Class' (unpublished seminar paper, Department of Political Science and Public Administration, Makerere University, 18 August 1972).

23. *Uganda Herald*, 19 August 1921.

24. Ibid., 13 January 1937.

25. Ibid., 21 June 1939.

26. Department of Political Science and Public Administration, Makerere University, paper (mimeo 1973).

27. *Uganda Argus*, 19 August 1972.

28. Y. Tandon, *The New Position of the Asians in East Africa* (London, Minority Rights Group, 1973).

29. Mangat, op. cit., p.32.

30. Tandon, *New Position*.

31. *Rise of Our East African Empire*, cited in Mangat, p.30.

32. C. Ehrlich, 'The Uganda Economy 1903–1945', in V. Harlow and E. Chilver eds.), *History of East Africa*, volume II (Oxford, 1965), p.396.

33. Ibid., p.402.

34. Ibid., p.410.

35. Ibid., p.425.

36. C. C. Wrigley, 'Kenya: The Pattern of Economic Life 1902–1945', in Harlow and Chilver, op. cit., p.236.

37. H. S. Morris, *The Indians in Uganda* (London, 1968), p.11.

38. Ehrlich, op. cit., p.441.

39. Ibid., p.467.

40. Cmd 947, *East African Royal Commission Report* (1956), pp.70–1.

41. J. Parson, 'The Africanisation of Trade in Uganda: Background To and Perspectives on Government Policy', Department of Political Science and Public Administration, Makerere University (mimeo, 1970).
42. Ghai and Ghai, op. cit., p.6.
43. *Uganda Argus*, 25 August 1972.
44. Ghai and Ghai, op. cit., p.104.
45. Ibid.
46. Tandon, 'A Political Survey', p.76.
47. Ibingira, op. cit., p. 30.
48. P. Nazareth, *In a Brown Mantle* (Nairobi, 1972).
49. *Uganda Argus*, 6 October 1972.

7. THE UGANDAN CIVIL SERVICE AND THE ASIAN PROBLEM 1894–1972

1. H. S. Morris, *The Indians in Uganda* (London, 1968), ch. x; D. A. Low, *Buganda in Modern History* (London, 1971), pp.154–8; D. P. Ghai and Y. P. Ghai (eds.), *Portrait of a Minority* (Oxford, 1970), pp.6–7, ch. IV; D. E. Apter, *The Political Kingdom in Uganda* (Princeton, 1967), pp.181–3, 195ff.
2. Other contributors to this book have explored this issue. Also see N. Motani, 'The Asians in East Africa', Minorities Seminar paper, May 1969, School of Oriental and African Studies, University of London.
3. See N. Motani, 'The Growth of an African Civil Service in Uganda, 1912–1940' (unpublished PhD thesis, University of London, 1972). There is a microfilm of this thesis in Makerere University Library. This chapter is based on this dissertation; primary sources are more fully cited there.
4. E.g., see H. A. C. Cairns, *Prelude to Imperialism* (London, 1965), p.246.
5. Foreign Office Confidential Print: FO 403/228, no 168, Berkeley to Salisbury, 28 August 1896.
6. British eyes were almost always focused on Buganda in such matters because, among other things, all medical, industrial, and general educational developments began in Buganda.
7. 'Indians' and 'Asians' are used interchangeably and they embrace all the communities of Indo-Pakistani origin.
8. Uganda National Archives (UNA), SMP 2351, min. 1, G. Lyall to CS, 15 January 1912.
9. E.g., see, UNA, SMP 2437, *Report* enclosed in min. 22, PMG to CS, Uganda, 13 May 1921.
10. UNA, SMP 3597, min. 52, Native Clerks and Interpreters to Governor, ufs. CS, 20 March 1918.
11. Colonial Office (CO) 536/99, *Report*, enc. in Carter to S of S, 15 January 1920. Makerere College was not started until 1921–2 and the two-year clerical course was not introduced until 1929, only to be discontinued in 1935.
12. 'Educated', in this chapter, means those men with the elementary literacy and vocational training available in Uganda at that time.
13. *Uganda Herald*, 16 April 1920, p.17.
14. Ibid., 5 August 1921, p.10.
15. UNA, SMP 6371, min. 22, 38 African employees to CS, 7 January 1922.
16. *Uganda Herald*, 24 November 1922, p.10.
17. Colonial Office Confidential Print (COCP), CO 879/121, Gov. to S of S, 9 May 1923.
18. UNA, SMP 6257, min. 46, S. Katiko to CS, 8 June 1925.
19. Legco, summary, 31 October 1929, pp. 3–4. Also see, R. C. Pratt in V.

Harlow and E. Chilver (eds.), *History of East Africa*, vol. ii (Oxford, 1965), pp. 514–15.

20. *Uganda Herald*, 20 May 1936, p.17.
21. CO 536/40035, Gov. to S of S, Confidential, 24 June 1935.
22. *Uganda Herald*, 24 January 1934, p. 18; ibid., 5 September 1934, p.19.
23. Legco summary, 9 November 1936, pp.6–7.
24. Uganda Education Dept., *Report*, 1938, pp.6, 23.
25. Ibid., p.23.
26. CO 536/201, Gov. to S of S, Confidential, 14 August 1939.
27. *Regulations for the LCS and other Local Employees* (Entebbe, 1940).
28. Asiatic CS Ass. file no 52/1, memo. presented to the Lidbury Commission, 14 April 1953.
29. Interviews: A. L. Kagobya, P. Semakula, K. D. Gupta, and J. E. de Souza, Kampala, 1970.
30. Teso District Archives, XSTF, MP no 58/2, min. 35, Secretary LCSB to DC, Soroti, 6 September 1946; Buganda MP no 386, min. 33, Paulo Kawesa (African Financial Assistant) to Resident, Buganda, 9 January 1945; C. J. Bryant, 'Some Problems of Public Administration in Uganda' (unpublished PhD thesis, University of London, 1963), pp.176–81.
31. *Uganda Herald*, 28 February 1945, p.6.
32. *Report of the Commission on the Civil Services of Kenya, Tanganyika, Uganda, and Zanzibar*, 1948, col. 223, pp.23–8.
33. Interviews: A. L. Kagobya, P. Semakula, K. D. Gupta, and J. E. de Souza, Kampala, 1970.
34. A. F. M. Evans, 'The Africanization of the Civil Service in Uganda: A Problem in Decolonisation', unpublished MA thesis, Manchester University, 1964, pp.100–9.
35. Ibid., pp.73–95; See also *Uganda Herald*, 1950–4, passim, esp. 6 December 1951, p.4, speech of the President, Caledonian Society of Uganda, and Governor's reply thereto.
36. Evans, op. cit., pp.78–86; D. A. Gugin, 'Africanization of the Uganda Public Service' (unpublished PhD thesis, University of Wisconsin, 1967), pp.72–76ff.
37. See *Uganda Argus*, 1955–9, letters to the Editor.
38. E.g., Bryant, op. cit., pp.67–8.
39. Also see Gugin, op. cit., pp.184–93.
40. Ibid.
41. E.g., R. Clark, *Aid in Uganda* (London, 1966), pp.66–7.
42. President Amin's address to the Asian Conference, 8 December 1971. This speech also appears as Appendix 1 in J. O'Brien, *Brown Britons* (London, Runnymede Trust, 1972).
43. *Uganda Argus*, 21 April 1970, pp.1–3.
44. Abolition of overtime payments, car loans, acting, duty, and disturbance allowances, increment during the probation period, biannual instead of annual salary increments, etc.
45. See p.107 above.
46. Motani, thesis, op. cit., pp.302–15.
47. Besides the UCS, it now embraced urban authorities, parastatal bodies, district administrations, and so on. See *Uganda Argus*, 21 April 1970.
48. E.g., Amin's speech to the Asian Conference, cited in note 42.
49. See p.111 below.
50. *The People*, 21 March 1970, p.8.

51. Amin's speech, op. cit., p.29.
52. E.g., see B. L. Jacobs, 'The State of the Uganda Civil Service Two Years After Independence', EAISR Conference paper, 1965; *The People*, 21 April 1970, editorial.
53. Jacobs, op. cit., pp.5–12.
54. *The People*, 21 March 1970, p.9, 14 February 1970, p.9, 12 February 1970, p.5.
55. Ibid., 30 January 1970.

9. INDIA AND THE ASIANS IN EAST AFRICA

1. For a detailed discussion see D. Rothchild, 'Kenya's Minorities and the African Crisis over Citizenship', *Race* (London), ix (1968), pp.421–37.
2. After the partition of the Indian sub-continent, some Muslims have switched their loyalty to Pakistan. The Bohras, who have their religious head in Bombay, however, continue their religious and familial contacts with India. The Khoja Ismailis, who, as followers of the Aga Khan, have a chain of hospitals, schools, and religious centres in East Africa, seem to have outgrown their ancestral ties with either India or Pakistan. See Chapter 3.
3. Quoted in N. V. Raj Kumar, *Indians Outside India* (New Delhi, 1951), p. 3.
4. For a comprehensive account see R. G. Gregory, *India and East Africa: A History of Race Relations Within the British Empire 1890–1939* (London, 1971), chs. VIII, IX.
5. This view was upheld by the Hindu conservative elements among the Indian nationalists. At present parties like the Jana Sangh and Hindu Mahasabha advocate that India's overseas population must be protected by India.
6. *Indian National Congress Resolutions on Foreign Policy, 1947–66* (New Delhi, 1966), p.21.
7. Ibid.
8. See F. Dodson and Lilian Dodson, *The Indian Minority in Zambia, Rhodesia and Malawi* (New Haven, 1968), pp.320–33.
9. See Chanan Singh, 'The Problem of Citizenship', in A. Gupta (ed.), *Indians Abroad: Asia and Africa* (New Delhi, 1971), pp.175–90.
10. Government of India, *Report of the Ministry of External Affairs 1953–54* (New Delhi, 1954), p.19.
11. Quoted in V. McKay, *Africa in World Politics* (New York, 1963), p.175.
12. As the problem was posed in a symposium: 'The Indians in Africa are either Indians on a temporary sojourn abroad or for all intents and purposes they are Africans—which is what the phrase "complete identification with Africans" should mean.' *Seminar* (New Delhi), June 1960, p.14.
13. See also Singh, op. cit.
14. A former Indian High Commissioner to Nairobi relates how this was made clear to him 'in plain language', by a member of the Kenyan administration as early as 1966: 'We don't want the Asian *Dukawala*', he said, 'for we can do without him.' P. Bhatia, *Indian Ordeal in Africa* (New Delhi, 1973), p.43.
15. In a public statement Kenya's Vice-President, Daniel Arap Moi, elucidated this theme further. 'Some Asians', he said, 'take Africans into business as figureheads. . .This type of people have got to learn to respect the people of Kenya. . . Otherwise they can pack up and go.' *Daily Nation* (Nairobi), 13 October 1967.
16. That some sort of informal relations were growing between the rich Asians and a section of the African elite was suspected by many. As a correspondent wrote: 'a definite business alliance has been formed between the immigrant

communities and an ever growing local bourgeoisie'. He further noted that this
was done at the expense of the majority at the bottom, 'whether black or brown'.
See Iconoclast, 'That Asian Exodus: Who's Responsible?', *East Africa Journal*
(Nairobi), April 1968, pp.5–8.

17. It is true that India had asked the Asians to take British passports on the
ground that this would help them to achieve a status similar to that of the Africans.
But with independence new citizenship laws were framed by the African governments. It was to make the Asians realize this change that India advised them to take
African citizenship.

18. B. K. Pandya, 'Indian Attitude', *Seminar*, op. cit., pp.22–5.

19. Quoted in Bhatia, op. cit., p.73.

20. *Hindustan Times* (New Delhi), 8 March 1963.

21. The statement was criticized by Dr Milton Obote, then Prime Minister of
Uganda. K. P. Shah, a leading member of KANU in Kenya, thought that the East
African Indians did not have a bright future unless they declared 'and put into
practice their undivided loyalty to their country of adoption. It is morally wrong
to try to get best of both worlds.' *Hindustan Times*, 3 February 1963.

22. *AICC Economic Review* (New Delhi), October 1966, p.36.

23. For further details see A. Gupta, 'The Asians in East Africa: Problems and
Prospects', *International Studies* (New Delhi) (January 1969), pp.270–302.

24. J. O'Brien, *Brown Britons: The Crisis of the Ugandan Asians* (London,
Runnymede Trust, 1972), p.18.

25. At a meeting of the Congress Parliamentary Party, Mrs Indira Gandhi
warned that if attempts were made to send back British Asians to India, her
government would take 'adequate counter-measures'. *Times of India* (Bombay),
24 February 1968.

26. *Times of India*, 26 March 1968.

27. The High Commissioner related the incident in his book six years later:
'My opposition made no difference. I was informed that the move was based on
a political decision and that it had already been announced as a government
commitment. In the event I had no alternative but to prepare myself to make the
best of a bad job.' Bhatia, op. cit., p.130.

28. *Times of India*, 26 March 1968.

29. Ibid.

30. Ibid.

31. Prem Bhatia to the writer in an interview in Nairobi, 8 June 1968.

32. The widow of one of the Madhvani brothers in Jinja. Having learnt of
Amin's intentions, she fled to the UK in early 1972.

33. *Africa Diary* (New Delhi), 23–9 September 1972, p.6157.

34. Ibid.

10. ECONOMIC ASPECTS OF THE EXPULSION OF ASIANS

1. I am grateful for the helpful comments of Vincent Cable, Norman Clark,
Irving Gershenberg, Garth Glentworth, Fred Nixson, Jack Parson, Emil Rado, and
Michael Safier on the first draft of this chapter. In addition most useful discussions
with the editor and Sir Amar Maini were much appreciated.

2. J. O'Brien, *Brown Britons* (London, Runnymede Trust, 1972), p.28.

3. Some of these are discussed in the text below. Note 84 relates to a number of
relevant references, but in addition Government and Bank of Uganda reports
expand on the economy as a whole. See for example Republic of Uganda,
Background to the Budget 1970–71 (Entebbe, 1970); Republic of Uganda, *The Third*

Five Year Development Plan 1971–76 (Entebbe, 1973), ch. 2. Bank of Uganda, *Quarterly Bulletin* and *Annual Report*.

4. Republic of Uganda, *Statistical Abstract* 1971 (Entebbe, 1972) Table B4, p.13.

5. For discussion of this point see p.171ff.

6. This discussion is necessarily selective, but for fuller coverage see for example M. A. Tribe in *Mawazo*, iii (1971), H. Elliot, M. Hall, and F. Nixson in *Uganda Economic Journal*, i (1971) and *Financial Times* supplement, 24 January 1972.

7. The unit of currency used in this chapter is the Uganda shilling. Prior to UK devaluation in 1967 U.Shs 20.00 = £1.00 sterling; after devaluation of 1967 the rate of exchange was approximately Shs 17.00 = £1.00; after the December 1971 realignment the East African currencies were tied to the US dollar and rates of exchange moved accordingly.

8. Of which Shs 100 million was on account of the local incorporation of foreign commercial banks (see note 80).

9. Bank of Uganda, *Quarterly Bulletin*, iii (1971), p.27, and *Annual Report 1969–1970*, p.33.

10. Republic of Uganda, *Budget Speech* 1971 (Entebbe, 1971).

11. H. Elliot, 'The Uganda Budget 1971–72', *Uganda Economic Journal*, i (1971), p.25.

12. Bank of Uganda, *Quarterly Bulletin*, op. cit., p.19.

13. Ibid., p.23.

14. Bank of Uganda, *Annual Report* 1970–1, Table 25, p.90.

15. Elliot, op. cit., p.10. Under-recording of imports would appear in the 'errors and omissions', while over-invoicing of imports would raise the 'value' of imports on merchandise account.

16. Bank of Uganda, *Quarterly Bulletin*, iii (1970), Table 18, p.73.

17. Republic of Uganda, *The Common Man's Charter* (with appendices) (Entebbe, 1970).

18. Elliot, op. cit., and M. Hall, 'The Balance of Payments of Uganda 1966–71', *Uganda Economic Journal*, i (1971).

19. IBRD, *The Economic Development of Uganda* (Entebbe, 1961), p.24.

20. Bank of England, *Quarterly Bulletin*, xii (September 1972), pp.310–11.

21. See Y. Tandon, *Problems of a Displaced Minority* (London, 1973), pp.17–18.

22. Republic of Uganda, *Background to the Budget 1970–71*, op. cit., pp.17, 21, 77.

23. D. P. Ghai and Y. P. Ghai (eds.), *Portrait of a Minority* (Oxford, 1970), pp.86–7. D. P. Ghai, 'The Buganda Trade Boycott: A Study in Tribal, Political and Economic Nationalism', in R. Rotberg and A. Mazrui (eds.), *Protest and Power in Black Africa* (New York, 1970), p.769.

24. O'Brien, op. cit., pp.28–9. See also Ocaya-Lakidi in this volume.

25. Ghai and Ghai, op. cit., pp.124–6.

26. J. Parson, 'The Africanization of Trade in Uganda: Background and Perspectives on Government Policy', Department of Political Science, Makerere University (mimeo 1971).

27. J. Parson, 'Africanizing Trade in Uganda: The Final Solution', *Africa Today*, xx (1973), p.65.

28. See other chapters in this volume.

29. Parson, 'Africanization of Trade', pp.15–16.

30. Parson, 'Africanization of Trade', p.66.

31. Uganda Government, *Report of the Board of Enquiry into a Claim for a Rise in Salaries of E Scale Public Officers* (Entebbe, 1966), paras 19–25.

32. This consisted of a relatively inflexible agricultural system so that supplies of *matoke* were coming from gradually further and further from Kampala with

differential rent probably going to traders rather than to farmers. The lack of agricultural research in food crop production in the colonial period must be at least partly to blame for this.

33. The fact that rents were always excluded from the indices is clearly an important shortcoming but I will not pursue the point here. Elliot, op. cit., p.18. M. A. Tribe, 'The Housing Market in Kampala', Department of Economics, Makerere University (mimeo, 1971).

34. Republic of Uganda, *Statistical Abstract* 1970 (Entebbe, 1971), Table UO3.

35. 'The Economics of Kenyanization', *East Africa Journal*, v (1968), pp.21–31.

36. Bank of Uganda, *Quarterly Bulletin*, iii (1971), p. 19.

37. J. O'Brien, 'General Amin and the Uganda Asians', *The Round Table*, 249 (1973), pp.91–104.

38. I have used the term 'Asian community' here in the full knowledge that such a homogeneous community never existed. As a convenient shorthand it has merit but conceals important heterogeneities. For a fuller discussion see not only the chapters by Rohit Barot, Jessica Kuper and Gardner Thompson in this book but, for example, A. Bharati, 'A Social Survey', in Ghai and Ghai, op. cit.

39. Ghai and Ghai, op. cit., p.102.

40. Republic of Uganda, *Enumeration of Employees 1969* (Entebbe, 1971), p.1.

41. Republic of Uganda, *Enumeration of Employees 1966* (Entebbe, 1967), Appendix XVII, and *Census of Distribution 1966* (Entebbe, 1967), p.6.

42. Republic of Uganda, *Quarterly Economic and Statistical Bulletin, June 1971* (Entebbe, 1971), special supplement, Table 1.

43. *Statistical Abstract* 1970, op. cit., Table UF6. *Background to the Budget* 1970–1, op. cit., Tables 1.1, 5.2.

44. For a good discussion of income distribution see Ghai and Ghai, op. cit., pp.107–10.

45. A. Southall and P. Gutkind, *Townsmen in the Making* (East African Institute of Social Research, Kampala, 1957), pp.26–7.

46. Uganda Protectorate, 'Asian Overcrowding in Kampala', mimeo 1950, in Makerere Institute of Social Research Library. Uganda Government, *Minimum Wages Advisory Board Report 1964* (Entebbe, 1965), para 13.

47. Quick reference to the *Trades and Commerce 1970 Directory* (Kampala, 1970) gives an indication of the situation but no directly comparable data. *Trade and Industry in Uganda* (Kampala, 1971) is a similar publication.

48. Perhaps the closest argument of this type would be that of McLelland in relation to his notion of 'n' achievement. Some elements of this appear in Marris and Somerset's work, but in considerably more sophisticated form. P. Marris and A. Somerset, *African Businessmen* (Nairobi, 1971). D. McLelland, *The Achieving Society* (Princeton, 1961).

49. O'Brien, *Brown Britons*, p.25.

50. Parson, 'Africanization of Trade', p.3, and 'Africanizing Trade in Uganda', pp.59–72.

51. P. Kilby, *Industrialization in an Open Economy* (Cambridge, 1969), chs. 3 and 4.

52. F. Nixson, 'Industrial Location in East Africa' (unpublished PhD thesis, University of Leeds, 1970); *Economic Integration and Industrial Location. An East African Case Study* (London, 1973).

53. Ghai and Ghai, op. cit., p.102. 'Natural protection' refers to a situation where local production may be carried out at a lower unit cost, at current exchange rates, than for similar imported items. Transport costs, perishability etc., are

important factors leading to natural protection. This may be contrasted with protection of markets through tariffs, subsidies, import quotas etc.

54. I have used the term 'economic surplus' here largely in Paul Baran's sense in ch. 2 of *The Political Economy of Growth* (New York, 1957). It is not synonymous with the term 'profit', which is probably less clear depending on whether it is used in an economic or accounting sense, is net or gross of depreciation, company taxes etc. In the discussion which follows I have referred to 'profits' in relation to individual industries and 'surplus' in relation to the economy as a whole. Any contradictions which appear to arise from this do not interfere with the discussion.

55. W. Elkan, 'A Half Century of Cotton Marketing in Uganda', *Indian Economic Journal*, xxxviii (1958), pp.365–74.

56. C. Ehrlich, 'The Uganda Economy 1903–1945', in V. Harlow and E. Chilver (eds.), *History of East Africa*, volume II (Oxford, 1965), p.442.

57. Elkan, op. cit., Republic of Uganda, *Report of the Committee of Inquiry into the Affairs of all Cooperative Unions in Uganda* (Entebbe, 1968), ch. IX; Ghai and Ghai, op. cit., pp.6–7, 118; Ehrlich, op. cit., p.468; E. A. Brett, *Colonialism and Underdevelopment in East Africa* (London, 1973), ch. 8.

58. Republic of Uganda, *Report of the Committee of Inquiry into the Affairs of all Cooperative Unions in Uganda*, pp.106–7.

59. Ibid., p.126.

60. Ibid., pp.279, 107.

61. Ibid., p.110.

62. Ibid., p.111.

63. Y. Tandon, 'A Political Survey', in Ghai and Ghai, op. cit., p.87.

64. Ehrlich, op. cit., p.433.

65. M. Merhav, *Technological Dependence, Monopoly and Growth* (Oxford, 1969). This refers to the diversification of industrial investment internally and internationally in response to the limited size of the domestic market.

66. An *import* parity price of this type would take the London landed price and *add* transport costs from London to Uganda (in fact half-way between Kakira and Lugazi the two main sugar estates). An *export* parity price would take the landed London price and *deduct* transport costs. The difference between the two is therefore twice the transport costs.

67. IBRD, op. cit., pp.139–40.

68. Republic of Uganda, *Statistical Abstract 1968* (Entebbe, 1969), Tables UF10, UF11.

69. C. R. Frank, *The Sugar Industry in East Africa* (Nairobi, nd but 1966), Table II.7, p.20.

70. Ibid., p.26.

71. International Sugar Council, *World Sugar Economy*, volume I (1963), p.275.

72. J. R. M. Rooke et al., 'A New Sugar Project in the Uganda Protectorate', Report to Booker Brothers McConnell and Company Limited (mimeo), Appendix F.

73. IBRD, op. cit., p.99, Table 9.

74. See for example P. C. W. Gutkind, *The Royal Capital of Buganda* (The Hague, 1963), ch. v.

75. See for example A. Martin, *The Marketing of Minor Crops in Uganda* (London, 1963), p.17.

76. E. M. S. Kate, 'The Relevance and Implications of Land Tenure to Urban Development in Uganda' in J. Oboh Ochola (ed.), *Land Law Reform in East Africa* (Kampala, 1969).

77. The issue of rent control has a history dating back to the Rent Restriction

Ordinance of 1943. Successive references to the issue were made both in published works and in local debate without any specific actions being taken from the time of derestriction to the present. See the Okae Commission and the review committee report of 1956. Uganda Government, *Report of the Commission of Inquiry into the Structure and Level of Rents in the City of Kampala, Municipalities and Towns of Uganda* (Entebbe, 1964), para 7.

78. Ibid., para 14. Republic of Uganda, *Report of the Committee on Africanization of Commerce and Industry in Uganda* (Entebbe, 1968), paras 1.7, 1.8.

79. Tribe, op. cit.

80. D. L. Cohen and M. A. Tribe, 'Suppliers' Credits in Ghana and Uganda', *Journal of Modern African Studies*, x (1972), pp.525–42.

81. M. A. Tribe, 'Uganda's Construction Industry', *African Development* (1971).

82. Some work in Tanzania relating to practices of depreciating equipment over single projects, and to other business practices regularly used in the construction industry, is relevant here. M. A. Bienefeld, *The Construction Industry in Tanzania* (University of Dar es Salaam, ERB Paper 70.22), p.C.29.

83. J. Wells, 'Huku na Huko', *East Africa Journal*, v (1968), p.10.

84. I am thinking here of pieces such as those by O'Brien, Parson (which did not set out to discuss this aspect), and M. F. Lofchie, 'The Uganda Coup: Class Action by the Military', *Journal of Modern African Studies*, x (1972), pp. 19–37, and comments by J. Chick and I. Gershenberg in volume x, no 4 of the same journal.

85. M. Hall, 'Mechanisation in East African Agriculture', in G. Helleiner (ed.), *Agricultural Planning in East Africa* (Nairobi, 1968), pp.81–116.

86. Republic of Uganda, *Third Five Year Development Plan*, p.253.

87. B. van Arkadie, 'Dependency in Kenya', in C. Allen and K. King (eds.), *Developmental Trends in Kenya*, Centre of African Studies, University of Edinburgh (mimeo, 1972).

88. M. A. Tribe, 'Some Aspects of Urban Housing Development in Kenya', in Allen and King, op. cit.

89. See for example *The Guardian*, 26 August 1972.

90. Budget Speech 1973 in *Voice of Uganda*, 15 June 1973.

91. Ibid.

92. In a recently published article James Tobin uses relatively standard neo-classical production theory in an interesting attempt to assess the effects of an expulsion of the type discussed in this chapter. ('Notes on the Economic Theory of Expulsion and Expropriation', *Journal of Development Economics*, i (1974).) My concern in this chapter has been to illustrate the importance of wealth accumulation, skill distribution, and other structural processes in helping to understand both the circumstances leading up to the expulsion and its effects. Readers are referred to Professor Tobin's article to observe the similarity of the conclusions where the subject matter of the discussion overlaps with this chapter.

93. This discussion is not intended to be an extended commentary on recent political developments in Uganda. Lofchie's over-simplification has been adequately rebutted by Chick and Gershenberg. Further discussion of the last developments of the Obote government and of the Amin period may be found in Lofchie, op. cit.; Chick, op. cit.; Gershenberg, op. cit. and 'Slouching Towards Socialism: Obote's Uganda', *African Studies Review*, xv (1972), pp.79–95; M. Twaddle, 'The Amin Coup', *Journal of Commonwealth Political Studies*, x (1972), pp.99–112; D. Cohen and J. Parson, 'The Uganda Peoples Congress Branch and Constituency Elections of 1970', *Journal of Commonwealth Political Studies*, xi

(1973), pp.46–66; G. Glentworth and I. Hancock, 'Change and Continuity in Modern Uganda Politics', *African Affairs*, lxxii (1973), pp.237–55. Here I am merely concerned to establish some of the background to the expulsion.

94. *Daily Nation*, 22 November 1971. *Uganda Argus*, 2 December 1971.

95. *The Guardian*, 30 November 1972, 12 January 1973, 26 February 1973.

96. C. Leys, 'The Limits of African Capitalism: The Formation of the Monopolistic Petty-Bourgeoisie in Kenya', in Allen and King, op. cit.

97. *East African Standard*, 5 May 1971.

II. THE NUBIANS: THEIR PERCEIVED STRATIFICATION SYSTEM
AND ITS RELATION TO THE ASIAN ISSUE

1. I am grateful for comments made when I presented this paper at a seminar on African Urban Politics at the Institute of Commonwealth Studies, University of London, in May 1973. Little of the material in this chapter will be new to Ugandans, as can be seen from Amin's own speech, mentioned in note 12.

2. Information on the origins and history of the Nubians in Uganda is to be found in the following works: S. W. Baker, *The Albert Nyanza* (London, 1866, republished 1962), *The Nile Tributaries of Abyssinia* (London, 1871), *Ismailia* (London, 1874); J. Bruce, *Travels to Observe the Sources of the Nile 1768–73* (Edinburgh, 1790); E. A. W. Budge, *The Egyptian Sudan* (London, 1907), especially volume II; J. L. Burkhardt, *Travels in Nubia* (London, 1819); O. G. S. Crawford *The Fung Kingdom of Sennaar* (Gloucester, 1951), 'Dongola', *Encyclopaedia Britannica* (1936); R. W. Felkin, 'Notes on the Moru Tribe', Address to the Royal Society, Edinburgh, 1883; Pasha R. Gessi, *Seven Years in the Soudan* (London, 1892); F. K. Girling, 'The Acholi of Uganda' (unpublished PhD thesis, Oxford University, 1952); J. M. Gray, 'Acholi History 1860–1901', *Uganda Journal* (1951 and 1952), 'The Diaries of Emin Pasha', ibid. (1961 to 1968); Lord Hailey, *Native Administration in British African Territories*, Part I (London, 1950); H. Johnston, *The Ugandan Protectorate* (London, 1902); H. A. MacMichael, *A History of the Arabs in the Sudan* (Cambridge, 1922), especially volume I; H. Moyse-Bartlett, *The King's African Rifles (1890–1945)* (Aldershot, 1956); M. Perham and M. Bull (eds.), *The Diaries of Lord Lugard: East Africa 1889–1892* (London, 1959); J. R. P. Postlethwaite, *I Look Back* (London, 1947); Schweinfurth, Felkin, et al. (eds.), *The Khedive Ismail and Slavery in the Sudan* (Cairo, 1938); H. M. Stanley, *In Darkest Africa (or the Quest, Rescue and Retreat of Emin)* (London, 1890); H. B. Thomas and R. Scott, *Uganda* (Oxford, 1949); J. S. Trimingham, *Islam in the Sudan* (Oxford, 1949), *Islam in East Africa* (Oxford, 1964). Most of the later data draw heavily on published sources, such as government *Reports* and, more recently, *Uganda Argus* (later taken over fully by the government and styled *The Voice of Uganda*), the official daily English-language newspaper of the government.

3. Johnston, op. cit., pp.237–8.

4. Postlethwaite, op. cit., remembers as DC disarming the Acholi with the old 'A' Company of the 4th KAR. 'From that time dated my great affection and respect for that very gallant regiment and, in particular, for the 4th Battalion and the old Nubis, of which in those days it was largely composed. It is the fashion, nowadays [1947], to look upon the Nubi as a relic of the past, of no modern value and chiefly to be remembered by the so-called Nubi Mutiny—to which, incidentally, in my opinion the men were driven by the ill-conceived and unjust treatment accorded them. A further statement is often made that there are no real

Nubis now, only riff-raff who have cut their faces and call themselves Nubis. This seems to me to ignore the fact that the term Nubi never referred to a tribe, but was given to the Nilotic mercenaries who came from the North with Emin and others, and that qualification to be called a Nubi rested in having been brought up in Nubi traditions and under military discipline. Many such still exist in the various Mulkis, as the civilian settlements of ex-soldiers are called, but unfortunately are not duly conscripted on reaching manhood. Few present-day officers or officials seem to realise that it has always been definitely against the Nubi code to enlist voluntarily, and that if a man did so, he was looked upon with suspicion. The Nubi expected to be seized by force, and enrolled; then, having signed on, he felt that he enjoyed a new prestige as a fighting man, and owed unwavering loyalty to the regiment of which he was now a member.

'Be that as it may, I do feel, as all those who knew them in the past must feel, that we have a very real obligation to these natives who have followed and fought under our flag, and who are now strangers in a strange land; and that obligation, I claim also, extends in some degree to their children, even if we now no longer require their services as military material. Fortunately, during the week of disarmament, I knew Nilotic Arabic sufficiently well to deal with the native officers and men—in fact, better than their own officers, who had only recently arrived from home.

'I have endeavoured to pay my tribute to a fine body of men, but I would hasten to dissociate myself from the idea prevalent at that time that they were in character otherwise than many other Africans; or, as it was put to me once by one of their (British) officers, "just like white men under their black exteriors".'

5. Johnston, op. cit., p.106.

6. Ibid., p.294.

7. Ernest Haddon, who was an administrator in the north at the beginning of this century in such places as Gondokoro in what is now Southern Sudan, remembers how the ideal of Nubian families at that time was for the eldest son to join the army, the second to become an Islamic specialist, while the third entered into trade.

8. Both quotations are from the *General Report on the Uganda Protectorate* for the year ending 31 March 1903.

9. Ibid., for the year ending 31 March 1904.

10. Ibid., for year 1912–13.

11. D. R. Pain, 'The Chameleon' (unpublished paper, 1973).

12. Much of what I have said has been paralleled by Amin himself in a speech he made at his childhood home of Bombo on 21 April 1973, after a football match between the Bombo Nubian Sports Club and the Kibera Nubian Sports Club from Nairobi (Kibera is the area of the Nubian community in Nairobi, situated between former Asian and European areas). This was fully reported by the official government organs of Radio Uganda and the *Voice of Uganda* in its headline news item. Amin told those who had been wondering what tribe is called Nubians that 'Nubians are a unique tribe consisting of all tribes in Africa', especially East Africa. He pointed out that 'Nubians speak all languages in East Africa and in Uganda there are Nubians who are Baganda, Basoga, Banyoro, Acholi, Langi, Batoro, and Kakwa. In Kenya there are also Kikuyu, Kamba and Luo Nubians.' He went on to say that 'everybody in Africa is free to become a member of the Nubian tribe', and to talk of tribalism as the stumbling-block of Africa today. He 'appealed to Nubian elders to see to it that the spirit of co-operation and unity for which the Nubians are renowned is followed by future generations. Nubians of the past were very friendly with all the people they lived with and

that was why the late Kabaka Chwa and Kabaka Mutesa used to visit the Nubians and give them land'. The editorial of the same issue, headed 'This Unique Tribe', is also interesting. 'Nubians were described as a unique tribe in East Africa by the President over the weekend. The venue, ironically, was a football game between a Ugandan Nubian sports club and another Nubian sports club from Kenya, but then life itself is full of irony. However, the important point that the President made is that you will find Nubians all over East Africa and that they have not remained aloof but have been completely assimilated. And that attitude of theirs is what all people in Uganda should adopt. Tribalism is a scourge of new nations and a people will realise this and deal with it easily and seriously enough to build a strong nation. Uganda kicked out non-Ugandan Asians recently because they were a haughty inward-working close group cut off from the rest of us except where getting money is concerned. With this alien separatist group gone, the more welcome will be the fusion of the People of Uganda into a strong nation. If Nubians can be Baganda, Basoga, Acholi or Langi why can't all the tribes of Uganda learn from them and belong to the only tribe we should all be proud to belong to—the tribe of Ugandans.' *Voice of Uganda*, 23 April 1973.

13. Girling, op. cit., p. 342.
14. EASCO, *Report of the Africanisation Committee*, 1963, para 36.
15. Government of Uganda, Sessional Paper no 7, 1962: Government Statement on 'Report of the Commissioners for Africanisation', para 5.
16. Some years after 'suitable citizenship legislation had been enacted', the Minister of Internal Affairs was able to state, in reply to a question in the National Assembly on 26 April 1967 in relation to Uganda Citizenship, that '(a) 14,450 persons of Asian origin have been registered as Uganda Citizens and (b) 10,527 Asians have applied but have not yet been granted Uganda Citizenship'.
17. *Report of the Committee on Africanisation of Commerce and Industry in Uganda* (Entebbe, 1968), para 6.1.
18. *The Constitution of the Republic of Uganda*, 8 September 1967.
19. Y. Tandon in D. P. Ghai and Y. P. Ghai (eds.), *Portrait of a Minority* (Oxford, 1965), p.85.
20. The Minister of Culture and Community Development, in answer to questions in parliament on 20 April 1967 concerning Rwandan refugees, stated that, of nearly 70,000 Rwandan refugees in Uganda, none had acquired Uganda citizenship and that 'International Law is that refugees remain alien refugees. No matter how long they stay in the country, they remain refugees.'
21. *Communication from the Chair of the National Assembly on 20th April, 1970* (Entebbe, 1970).
22. The wedding in July 1973 of the daughter of one of the handful of Uganda citizen Asians remaining in the country to a Nubian army officer was the occasion for a propaganda exercise by Amin.
23. Uganda *Statistical Abstracts* for 1961 and 1971.
24. From above, Amin was also in need of a fief system of rewards to satisfy soldiers and to give to men whose loyalty might be in doubt as well as to those whose loyalty was proven, and also to some whose support he hoped to win thereby. In affirming his faith in a system of competitive capitalism Amin often says how he wants to see more African millionaires.

12. SOME LEGAL ASPECTS OF THE EXPULSION

1. Population figures quoted here are based upon the census taken on 18–19 August 1969, as printed in the *Statistical Abstract 1971* (Entebbe).

2. *Third Five-Year Development Plan 1971/2–1975/6* (Entebbe), p.70 and Table V-2.

3. Hence the term 'UK Passport-holders' was officially used to describe the persons for whom the UK accepted responsibility. The majority of the Asians expelled from Uganda were likely to have been protected persons rather than UK citizens. The precise implications of protected status are imponderable and certainly anomalous: their rights have been described as minimal (Y. P. Ghai in D. P. Ghai and Y. P. Ghai (eds.), *Portrait of a Minority* (Nairobi, 1970), p.197—the best general account of the Asian communities of East Africa). See also K. Polack in *Modern Law Review*, xxvi (1963), pp.138–55.

4. *Uganda 1964* (Entebbe, 1965), p.21.

5. Uganda Citizenship Act 1962, Cap. 58. For the independence Constitution, see SI 1962 no 2175 and for a fuller discussion, H. F. Morris and J. S. Read, *Uganda, The Development of its Laws and Constitution* (London, 1966), pp.177–82

6. Nos 25 and 33 of 1967.

7. 11 and 12 Geo. 6, c. 56.

8. C. 21.

9. *R v Home Secretary, ex parte Bhurosah* [1967] 3 All ER 831, CA; [1968] QB 266.

10. C. 9.

11. Hansard, House of Commons, vol. 759, cols. 1241–368, 1421–542, 1543–69, 1696–714.

12. Hansard, House of Lords, vol. 289, cols. 903–1217.

13. UN General Assembly, 27 September 1972.

14. *R v An Immigration Officer at Heathrow Airport, ex parte Thakrar* [1974] 1 All ER 415. *Thakrar v Secretary of State* [1974] 2 All ER 261, CA.

15. I. A. Macdonald, *The New Immigration Law* (London, 1972), pp. 117–18.

16. The failure has been ascribed to the then Prime Minister's acceptance of official advice to procrastinate: D. Humphry and M. Ward, *Passports and Politics* (Harmondsworth, 1974), p.20.

17. Official figures of UK passport holders from East Africa and India refused admission to UK were: 1970—817; 1971—26; 1972—392 (Cmnd 4951 and Cmnd 5285, *Control of Immigration Statistics 1971* and *1972*, Table 1).

18. C. 77. For a commentary and analysis see Macdonald, op. cit., note 15.

19. *Immigration Rules*, House of Commons Paper, HC 1972–73 no 79, para 27.

20. This point is emphasized by Macdonald, op. cit., p. 4.

21. Cmnd 4610, *Control after Entry*, rule 19.

22. HC 1972–3 no 81, para 52.

23. HC 1972–3 no 79, para 38.

24. See reply of Under-Secretary of State at the Home Office in the House of Commons, Hansard, vol. 847, col. 440, 6 December 1972.

25. They were excluded from the definition of the term 'National' for purposes of the Treaties of Accession: see Cmnd 4862, 1, p.118.

26. Hansard, House of Commons, vol. 849, col. 655, 25 January 1973.

27. *The Times*, 29 January 1973.

28. No 14 of 1969.

29. SI 1969 no 196.

30. SI 1969 no 170.

31. Memorandum published with the Bill; the Act is no. 19 of 1969.

32. No 57 of 1963.

33. Hansard, House of Commons, vol. 818, col. 380–5, 26 May 1971.

34. Cmnd 4951, Table 1.

35. Immigration (Cancellation of Entry Permits and Certificates of Residence) Decree 1972, Decree 17.
36. Immigration (etc.) (Amendment) Decree 1972, Decree 30.
37. British Nationality Act 1964, c. 22, s. 2.
38. Ibid., s. 1.
39. Humphry and Ward, op. cit., note 16, pp. 14–15.
40. Hansard, House of Commons, vol. 688, col. 1291–6; Hansard, House of Lords, vol. 256, col. 14–26, 31–4.
41. Decree 17, s. 2.
42. Immigration (Entry Permits and Certificates of Residence) Reinstatement Order 1972, SI 1972 no 124.
43. Hansard, House of Commons, vol. 849, col. 916, 29 January 1973.
44. See, for example, V. R. Krishna Iyer, 'Mass Expulsion as Violation of Human Rights', *Indian Journal of International Law*, xiii (1973), pp. 169–75.
45. Land Acquisition Act, no 14 of 1965; etc.
46. Declaration of Assets (Non-Citizen Asians) Decree 1972, Decree 27.
47. Decree 29.
48. SI 1972 nos 169, 174; SI 1973 nos 101, 102.
49. Rent (Premises of Departed Asians) (Special Provisions) Decree 1973, Decree 5.
50. Decree 26 of 1973.
51. Decree 27 of 1973.
52. Recent official returns indicate some measure of economic recovery from the downturn at the end of 1972 and early 1973: motor spirit consumption climbed to a new peak in the second quarter of 1973, when industrial production had also risen (beer, spirits, and cigarettes reaching new peak levels and cement recovering to 42,886 tonnes from a figure of 12,415 in the last quarter of 1972). *Quarterly Economic and Statistical Bulletin*, September 1973 (Entebbe).
53. For the Interim (May 1973) and Final (April 1974) Reports of the Board see Cmnd 5296 and Cmnd 5594 respectively.
54. Cmnd 5285, Table 1.
55. *West Africa*, 19 February 1973, p. 227.
56. Ibid., 25 August 1972, p.1109.
57. Nigerian Enterprises Promotion Decree, no 4 of 1972; the main provisions came into effect from 31 March 1974.
58. *The Times*, 23 December 1972.

INDEX

Abdalla-Anyuru, 111

Acholi, 182

ACS, African Civil Service (1930), 103

African attitudes towards Asians, 81–97

africanization, of trade, 4, 6, 148–9; Royal Commission report on (1955), 92–3; of civil service, 100–11; and India, 133; and Nubians, 186; and 'Ugandanization', 186–9

Aga Khans, 6, 19, 33, 66, 149, 211, 214; see also Ismailis and *firman*

agitation, illegitimate by Asians under colonial rule, 121; by Africans undertaken over cotton and coffee, 116; for return of Kabaka, 121; against Asians in 1945 and 1949, 114; but otherwise intermittently, 5, 8

agriculture, 110, 112, 141, 140–76

'America of the Hindu', East Africa not, 1–3, 15–29

Amery, L., 22

Amiji, H. M., 36, 212

Amin, President, topples Obote and welcomed by Asians in Uganda, 8; conducts census of Asians, 50, 200; summons Asian conference, 12, 46–750, 109, 140, 210, 220–1; on Nubians, 228–9; on marriage, 96, 189–90; 1, 101–2, 137

Amin, Prince, 44

Anderson, J. N. D., 212, 215

Ankole, 182

Apter, D. E., 212–3, 219

Arain, Shafiq, 59–61

Arkadie, B van, 226

army, Ugandan, 10, 88–9, 120, 182

artisans, 2, 49, 54, 101, 152–7, 165, 181–2

Arua, 181

Arusha Declaration, 175

assimilation, see 'integration'

atak, exogamous unit, 79

Bajpai, Sir Girji Shankar, 21

Baganda, in civil service, 99ff; marriage with Nubians, 182; in Bakuli neighbourhood, 73; see also Mutesa II, boycott, Baganda, and Young Baganda Association

Bakaluba, E., 102

Bakuli, neighbourhood of Kampala, 12, 70–80

Baker, Sir S. W., 227

Bampade, J., 100

Bamuta, Y., 100, 102

Bandaranaike, Mrs, 26

'Banyan', 85

Baran, P., 225

Barot, Rohit, 6, 11, 70–80, 224

'bargaining', Asian, 93

Bengal relief fund, disputes over, 119

Bennett, G., 213

Beteille, A., 217

BGNEA, British Government Native Employers Association, 102

Bhagat, Bali Ram, 13, 135–6

Bharati, 70, 77–9, 80, 215–17, 224

Bhatia, Prem, 13, 210, 221–2

Bienefeld, M. A., 226

Blundell, Michael, 25

Bohras, 113, 221

Bombay, 55

Rothchild, D., 214, 221

St Francis Xavier Society of Taylors, 63
St Vincent de Paul Society (for poor Goans), 65–6
Samji, A., 215
Sapru, Tej Bahadur, 28
Sastri, Lal Bahadur, 26
Sastri, Srinivasa, 16, 18
SC, School Certificate, 104, 120, 191
Schwartz, B. M., 216
Schweinfurth, 227
Scott, R., 227
Scotton, J. F., 218
Sekanyolya, 101
Sekou Touké, 209
Sempa, Amos, 122
Sentongo, Z. K., 101
Serumaga, Petero, 102
Shah, K. P., 222
shamba, vegetable and fruit garden, 110
Sheriff, A. M. H., 11, 210
Shukry, M. E., 227
Sierra Leone, 208
Sikhs, 53, 73, 189
Singh, C., 221
Sithole, N., 83–4, 217
Smuts, 17, 18
Somerset, A., 224
Southall, A. W., 224
South Africa, 17–28
Southern Rhodesia, 18
Speke, J. H., 85
squatters, African views of Asians in Kenya, 3
Srinivas, M. N., 74, 216
Stanley, H. M., 227
statistics, non-existent, 2; of Asians in Uganda, 15, 32, 53, 140–1, 193
stratification, colonial, 1–2, 81–3, 98–99, 158; among Asians, 36–7, 53–69, 70–4, 113, 114, 156; and Nubians, 189–90, in Natal, 27
stereotypes, of Asians, 3–4; among Asians, 125ff

sugar, 161–3
Swahilis, see Nubians

tan, body, 13
taqiyya, doctrine of, 32, 211
Tandon, Yash, 46, 87, 90, 95, 188, 210–29 passim
TANU, Ismailis in, 44
Tanzania, 50, 175, 191
taylors, Goans, 63ff
textiles, 116
Thomas, H. B., 227
Thompson, Gardner, 4, 7, 30–52, 224
Tilbe, D., 211, 215
Tinker, Hugh, 3, 15–29, 112
Tobin, J., 226
Topan, Tarya, 32
Toronto, Goans there, 58, 68–9
tourism, 116
TPS, Tourist Promotion Services, 44; see also IPS
Trade commissioner, Indian proposal for, 20
Trade Licensing Act (1969), 8, 50, 120, 148, 185, 199–200
Trade Ordinance (1938), 93
traders, African in Kenya, 3; in Uganda, 4
transport business, 116
Tribe, Michael, 8–9, 140–76, 223, 224, 226
Trimingham, J. S., 212, 227
Twaddle, Michael, 1–14, 210, 226

UAG, Uganda Action Group, 7, 40–1, 117, 161
UACSA, Uganda African Civil Servants Association, 214
UCS, Uganda Civil Service, 98–111, 116
UDC, Uganda Development Commission (1920), 101; Uganda Development Corporation, 44, 161
Udoiji report, 186
'Ugandanization', see africanization
Uganda Railway, 2, 91
UN, United Nations, 28